Career Construction Theory

Life Portraits of Attachment, Adaptability, and Identity

Mark L. Savickas

To Bob:
Friend, Colleague, and Collaborator.
Mark

Career Construction Theory:
Life Portraits of Attachment, Adaptability, and Identity

Copyright © 2019 by Mark L. Savickas

All rights reserved. No part of this book may be reproduced or transmitted in any form or by any means without written permission from the author.

ISBN: 978-1-7341178-0-6 (paperback)
ISBN: 978-1-7341178-1-3 (hardcover)

Printed in USA by 48HrBooks (www.48HrBooks.com)

DEDICATION

This book is dedicated to Professor Alan P. Bell (1932 – 2002) who inspired the study and taught me how to use his method of life portraiture in it. An astute clinician and celebrated teacher, Dr. Bell was emeritus Professor of Counseling and Educational Psychology at Indiana University where he also had served for 12 years as a senior research psychologist and vice-president at the Alfred C. Kinsey Institute for Sex Research. In 1981, he published the groundbreaking Kinsey Institute study suggesting that same-sex sexual orientation is a predisposition with a biological basis, and not influenced by traumatic experiences during childhood. A thousand interviews lasting as long as five hours led him to this conclusion and, in due course, prompted him to develop the technique of life portraiture based on in-depth, quasi-clinical interviews that allow researchers to see not only the trees but also their roots.

I first learned of Professor Bell's (1969, 1970) work by reading his doctoral dissertation and ensuing publications on the importance of role models in vocational development. His research strongly influenced my thinking about career construction. I came to believe that choosing a role model is an individual's first career decision.

Years later I met Professor Bell who then tutored me in his method of life portraiture and how to apply it to the four biographies in the present book. Professor Bell's portrayal of lives as works of art influenced my adopting the phrase "life design" to denote career construction dialogues in which counselors help clients to construct their own life portrait. I remain grateful to Professor Bell for important advice and feedback on drafts of chapters that described the early years in the participants' life portraits.

Finally, I admire and respect the four men who bravely shared their career stories. For decades their biographies have served as my learning laboratory. They taught me about turning passive suffering into active mastery, introduced me to the fundamental role of attachment schemas, showed me how to use projective techniques in career construction counseling, and so much more. And of course, I am forever thankful for the love and support of my wife, Mary Ann Savickas, who offered insights and encouragement during the decades in which I wrote and repeatedly revised this book.

Mark L. Savickas

TABLE OF CONTENTS

Introduction 1

Chapter One: Career Construction Theory 3

Chapter Two: Career Construction Case Study Methods 45

Chapter Three: The Drive of a Pathmaker 59

Chapter Four: The Obligations of a Guardian 103

Chapter Five: The Adventures of a Searcher 155

Chapter Six: The Disquiet of a Drifter 199

Chapter Seven: A Collective Perspective on the Case Studies . 247

References 269

Appendix A 285

Appendix B 291

Glossary of Key Terms 295

INTRODUCTION

Career Construction Theory explains the interpretive and interpersonal processes through which individuals organize their behavioral dispositions, impose direction on their vocational behavior, and make meaning of their vocational development. The purpose of this book is to present an updated exposition of the theory and demonstrate its application in a longitudinal study of four men's careers. I use the case studies for expository and didactic purposes; not to validate, but to illustrate, explain, and demonstrate theorems in Career Construction Theory.

The first chapter presents a definitive explication of the theory. In addition to stating the theory in terms of three premises and forty-five propositions, the first chapter explains the theory's fundamental meta-theory. The remainder of the book reports the results of a multiple-case study concentrated on how four men constructed their careers from the ninth grade through retirement. In the second chapter I expound the rationale for the study along with its methods and materials.

Each of the next four chapters presents a case study that examines a participant's self-making and career constructing from the perspective of Career Construction Theory. The report of the four case studies each begins with a "life portrait" that recounts a character sketch of a participant, drawing upon his own statements for illustration whenever appropriate. Following each life portrait, the second half of the chapter considers a participant's career construction from the perspectives of his experience as a self-organizing social actor, self-regulating motivated agent, and self-conceiving autobiographical actor (cf., McAdams, 2013).

As you read the case studies from the perspective of Career Construction Theory, recognize how a participant used his (a) *attachment schema* to organize and maintain a perso*nality disposition*; (b) *self-regulation schema* to guide an *adaptability strategy* for setting and pursuing goals; and *reflexive schema* to conceive a *vocational identity* and compose a career story.

In the first case study, Robert's secure attachment schema and extroverted, norm-accepting orientation to relationships and rules disposed him to focus on needs for development and self-realization. He used a hybrid motivational schema focused both promotion and prevention goals to regulate a strategy for integrative adapting that in due course shaped an autonomous reflexive schema (cf., Archer, 2012) and a vocational identity strategy as a Pathmaker (cf., Josselson, 2017). In the second case study, William's anxious-ambivalent attachment schema and introverted, norm-accepting orientation to relationships and rules disposed him to focus on needs for security and safety. He used a prevention-focused motivational schema to regulate a strategy for adjustive defending that in due course shaped a communicative reflexive schema and a vocational identity strategy as a Guardian. In the third case study, Paul's dismissive-avoidant attachment schema and extroverted, norm-doubting orientation to relationships and rules disposed him to focus on advancement and adventure. He used a promotion-focused motivational schema to regulate a strategy for adjustive defending that in due course shaped a meta- reflexive schema and a vocational identity strategy as a Searcher. And in the fourth case study, Fred's fearful-disorganized attachment schema and introverted, norm-accepting orientation to relationships and rules disposed him to remain disengaged and dispirited. His lack of motivational focus produced difficulties in self-regulation and adaptability that in due course shaped a fragmented reflexive schema and a diffused vocational identity as a Drifter.

In the final chapter, I take a collective perspective on the four cases to revisit the concepts and theorems in Career Construction Theory. I considered the collection of four case studies as a group to further understand the career trajectory that each participant represented and to refine construal of career constructing processes and constructed patterns. A list of references appears after the final chapter, followed by Appendix A that summarizes the premises and propositions in Career Construction Theory and Appendix B that describes the psychometric inventories and tests used in the study. The book concludes with a glossary of key terms.

CHAPTER ONE
Career Construction Theory

The theory of career construction explains the interpretive and interpersonal processes through which individuals organize themselves, impose direction on their vocational behavior, and make meaning of their careers. According to the theory, individuals construct careers by adapting to social life. As agents acting in and on the world, they manage their motivation and position themselves as social actors in work roles that match their occupational characteristics and implement their vocational self-concepts. Responding to changes occasioned by vocational development tasks, occupational transitions, and work troubles, individuals reflexively shape and repeatedly elaborate a career story about their work lives, that is, a narrative with an occupational plot describing what happened and a career theme explaining why it happened. With each transition, individuals elaborate and revise the story as they reposition themselves in a new work role.

Career Construction Theory (CCT; Savickas, 2002, 2013) presents a connected set of terms and statements that constitute a way of thinking and talking about careers in the 21st century. CCT systematizes, in a formal and functional manner, knowledge about how individuals make themselves and build their careers in cultural and social contexts. To do so, CCT conceptualizes work lives using a social constructionist epistemology, acknowledging that a theory is as much about the researcher as it is about the topic. The social constructionist lens of self-as-process warrants a definition of career as a carrier of personal meaning that defines and structures significant events in a work life, not as a path through an organization. From this perspective, *career becomes a story that individuals tell about their working lives*, rather than life-time employment climbing an organizational ladder. This socially-constituted understanding of self and career serves as the epistemic position that locates CCT's meta-theory among other career theories.

Career Construction Meta-Theory

CCT incorporates existing knowledge about careers and their development using the inductive method (Locke, 2007). The theory serves as an interpretive repertoire that organizes an inter-related set of terms and coherent ideas about the topic of career. As an "empirical integration" (Underwood, 1957, p. 290) of existing knowledge, CCT requires an explicit theoretic scheme to narrow delineation of the domain, identify relevant findings, and notice unforeseen relationships. To achieve this coherence, CCT situates, evaluates, and interprets research and reflection about vocational behavior and its development within an explicit meta-theory that explains the architecture of CCT itself, hence the prefix "meta-" as a theory about a theory. The CCT meta-theoretical matrix represents a selection of special cases rather than a general meta-theoretical model. The meta-theory provides a grounding foundation and overarching framework that both sustain and constrain the theory.

CCT's meta-theory addresses two basic questions that the theory must answer about the phenomenon of career construction: What are the concepts used to understand the phenomenon? and How do the concepts function and change? CCT's conceptual model identifies the content that constitutes career construction while its process model explains the mental operations that organize, operate, and maintain career constructing. Both the conceptual and process models concentrate on the self as a psychological construct. From an epistemic stance of constructionism, the meta-theory regards the self as a fundamental concept in the behavioral and social sciences (Leary & Tangney, 2003). CCT defines the self not as an entity but as a mental process that enables people to take themselves as an object of attention and think consciously about their characteristics, motives, and experiences as the "I" observes the "Me" (James, 1892; Taylor, 1989). The self's mental processes evolve in activity as the "knower" internalizes "known" elements of the external world including cultural symbols, language, and practices. Through social conduct the mental processes produce the content operating in the psychological self, that is, material that was originally in society (Vygotsky, 1978).

The bedrock tenet of CCT's meta-theory professes that adaptation is the master motive in the social lives of individuals. Adaptation typically moves toward the general goals of overcoming adversity and increasing mastery (Angyal, 1965). Mastery is not an immediate goal like finishing a book but rather a life goal toward which individuals continually strive yet never fully complete. The actual content of particular motives in career adaptation is determined by individuals' need for mastery and the requirements of the context that embeds them. Of course not every goal arises from the need for mastery or the press of the context, some goals are based on physiological requirements or are pursued for their own sake.

To situate, articulate, and integrate the processes and products that foster adaptation, CCT's meta-theory uses two existing meta-theoretical frameworks, basing its process model on Ford's (1987) Living Systems Framework and basing its conceptual model on Bakan's (1966) two fundamental modes of social perception and adaptation. The CCT meta-theory inter-relates these two models using McAdam's (1995) overarching framework of psychological selves.

Meta-Theoretical Process Model

The meta-theory process model adopts Donald Ford's Living Systems Framework (LSF) to explain how the CCT's career constructing processes form, function, and change. The meta-theory of the LSF has been applied previously to articulate several psychological theories (Ford & Ford, 1987), including theories that concentrate on development (D. H. Ford & Lerner, 1992), motivation (M.E. Ford, 1992), vocational behavior (Vondracek, Ford, & Porfeli, 2014), and career guidance (Vondracek & Ford, 2019a; Vondracek, Porfeli, & Ford, 2019). The LSF manifest in CCT's meta-theory's process model concentrates on career constructing, that is, the mental processes that guide, produce, and make sense of people's vocational patterns and pathways. In comprehending how individuals construct their characteristics, motives, and experiences, CCT highlights the information-processing functions of self-organizing, self-regulating, and self-conceiving. These three self-making, autopoietic processes enable individuals to deal with career uncertainties and challenges as they attempt to turn problems into opportunities. When faced with new situations, the impetus to adapt activates these self-constructing processes of organizing, regulating, and conceiving to elaborate and revise existing vocational patterns, occupational plans, and career themes.

Self-organizing encompasses the mental processes by which individuals selectively become aware of, differentiate, and inter-relate their knowledge, competencies, beliefs, and experiences to form schematic and strategic repertoires of similar content in similar contexts (Vondracek, & Ford, 2019b). These self-organized repertoires of perceptions, dispositions, and behaviors provide the basis for self-consistency, that is, the temporal continuity in an individual's vocational personality characteristics and the cross-situational regularity in activities. Self-organizing includes the processes of self-awareness and self-evaluation. Self-awareness enables an individual to observe and recognize oneself as distinct from the environment and from other individuals. When they focus attention on themselves, individuals consciously construct their own characteristics, feelings, motives, and desires as well as form self-concepts. The resulting self-percepltions represent a subjectively constructed truth that may be factual or fictional. Self-evaluating enables individuals to compare their personal characteristics to internal ideals and their behavior to external standards. In addition to forming self-concepts, the processes of self-organizing are instrumental in producing the prototypical repertoires that characterize Holland's (1997) vocational personality types or what Ford calls generalized Behavior Episode Activity Patterns (Ford, 1987).

Self-regulating means control of self by the self. It encompasses the processes of self-direction in establishing goals, self-management in guiding one's own behavior, and self-monitoring in assessing progress. As self-regulation develops, individuals become increasingly capable of taking primary responsibility for choosing, planning, implementing, and assessing their own experiences. However, "capable" does not mean they necessarily become increasingly self-determining and inner-directed. They may still let family members and other people set their goals and regulate their actions. In any case, self-regulating processes produce decision-making strategies as well as the content of values, interests, and goals with which individuals identify pathways, make plans, implement strategies, and assess outcomes.

Self-conceiving means composing symbolic representations for making sense of oneself, social roles, and the world. It encompasses *self*-representation to examine internal thoughts and feelings and self-coherence to consider what they mean. Self-representation provides symbolic meaning to give form and substance to perceptions, ideas, and emotions. Self-coherence integrates these thoughts and feeling to make one's experiences and ambitions more understandable. Self-conceiving can compose autobiographical identity narratives. These identity narratives or stories about self in particular social roles make meaning and produce insight into life purpose and career themes.

The maturation and arborization of neurons in cortical thickening and thinning are functionally important in improving the capacity for self-constructing processes (Fandakova, Selmeczy, Leckey, Grimm, Wendelken, & Ghetti, 2017). These predictable neurological processes together with life experiences support cognitive development and increasing sophistication in thought.

Meta-Theoretical Content Model

The Career Construction Meta-Theory treats functional patterns of content produced by self-constructing processes separately from the processes themselves. Over time and through repeated use in a particular domain, the mental processes of organizing, regulating, and conceiving form relatively self-sustaining cognitive structures for categorizing information and judging situations. These schemas are formed as individuals recognize commonalities among successive experiences and organize them as a mental structure (Bartlett, 1932; Kelly, 1955). The cognitive schemas then become habitual modes of mental processing that serve as generalized conceptual patterns with which to simplify and interpret complex information. Individuals elaborate and revise their schemas over time based on performance feedback. As a way of thinking about a current situation that resembles prior experiences, individuals use a relevant schema or prior interpretation to focus attention, shape perception, absorb new information, and make judgements. The more important the previous experiences are to a person, the more accessible the schema will be for an analogous current situation. For example, a schema for father may be readily accessible implicit theory for dealing with authority figures later in life.

In addition to judging social situations, the interpretations from psychological cognitive schema lead individuals to construct psychosocial performance strategies for conducting themselves in particular contexts and specific roles. Thus schemas provide a basis for the cross-situational and temporal consistency that represents an individual's personality, motivation, and identity. With time and experience, individuals do elaborate and revise their self-constructed performance strategies based on feedback and what needs to be accomplished. CCT considers the performance strategies to be psychosocial in that they combine psychological (thought) and social (behavior) aspects that direct functioning in society. In CCT, the three major psychosocial strategies for social functions are dispositions, adaptability, and identity -- each of which will be described later in this chapter.

The conceptual model in CCT meta-theory postulates that the content of cognitive schemas and performance strategies both are produced by the interaction between two basic ways of judging and adapting to the social world (cf., Blatt & Levy, 2003). The meta-concepts of agency and communion denote the "two fundamental modalities in the existence of living forms" (Bakan, 1966, pp. 114-115) as they interact with their contexts. The meta-concept of agency refers to getting ahead of other people (Hogan, 1983) as manifest through motives such as autonomy, achievement, power, and dominance. Passivity is the opposite pole of agency. The meta-concept of communion refers to getting along with other people (Hogan, 1983) as manifest in motives such as affiliation, cooperation, nurturance, and succorance. Alienation is the opposite pole of communion. The fundamental adaptive modalities of agency to stand out from others and communion to fit in with others are not in opposition; one can value both, neither, or one but not the other. Accordingly, the meta-theoretical conceptual matrix crosses the coordinates of agency and communion in two-dimensional space. Figure 1 depicts the resulting four quadrants in the conceptual matrix. One quadrant represents agency and communion while the diagonal quadrant represents passivity and communion. The two ambivalent quadrants represent either agency with alienation or passivity with communion.

Figure 1. Meta-Theoretical Conceptual Matrix of Agency and Communion

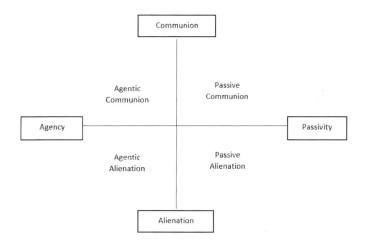

This meta-theoretical conceptual framework provides a heuristic template for recognizing later developing cognitive schemas and performance strategies employed by psychological selves, each of which is assumed to emerge from the foundational matrix of agentic individuation and communal integration. The specific schemas and strategies serve as "templates of possibility," a term coined by Josselson (2017, p. 22) to denote master narratives with which psychologists may understand a life in progress. The CCT schema and strategy templates are each adapted from pre-existing models and well-established mid-range theories with limited scope that explain a set of phenomena rather than from a grand theory that addresses all phenomena (Locke, 2007). As templates of possibility, the CCT schemas and strategies draw attention to and aid analysis of career construction processes and content.

Selfhood Framework for Meta-Theoretical Models

The process and content models in the CCT meta-theory are interrelated and coordinated using McAdam's (2013) overarching framework of three different psychological selves. Applying this broad framework systematizes the self-constructing processes and constructed patterns in relation to a psychological self as (a) a social actor who displays distinguishing characteristics while performing work roles, (b) a motivated agent who draws out inner needs to impose direction on vocational behavior, and (c) an autobiographical author who makes sense of career stories by recognizing themes that clarify purpose and show continuity. In CCT, the three self-constructing processes of organizing, regulating, and conceiving each align *primarily* with the cognitive schemas and performance strategies that characterize one of the psychological selves. Around the age of 18 months, individuals begin to organize a psychological self as a *social actor* with intellectual abilities and personal characteristics, quickly recognized by other people in terms of a reputation. Here self-organizing takes the lead yet self-regulating and self-conceiving occur, although in less elaborate forms. By the end of childhood, self-regulating joins more closely with self-organizing as a social actor becomes a *motivated agent* who regulates educational-vocational goals and plans projects to achieve them. In comparison to personal characteristics that describe the social actor, motives explain the actor's behavior. During late adolescence and emerging adulthood, self-conceiving takes an equal place with self-organizing and self-regulating to produce and maintain an *autobiographical author* who composes a career story with increasing clarity, coherence, and continuity.

Within each of the three psychological selves in McAdam's (2013) framework, CCT conceptualizes vocational behavior with two "templates of possibility" formed from related yet different mid-range theories. Each of the three dimensions of actor, agent, and author is characterized by two templates, one facet of a dimension being a cognitive schema and the other facet of that dimension being a performance strategy. Initially, CCT views the career of the social actor through the template of four self-organizing *attachment schemas* (Bowlby, 1982). Then CCT understands the social actor's personality by relating the four attachment schemas to a model of four *dispositional strategies* (Gough, 1990). The term "disposition" refers to unique, individual characteristics within a person that produce, initiate, and guide consistent forms of social behavior (Allport, 1961). In CCT, disposition denotes a preparation, a state of readiness, or a tendency to act in a specified way. For the dimension of the self-regulating motivated agent, CCT uses four motivational schema of *regulatory focus* (Higgins, 1997) that shape the content of the social actor's motives such as needs, interests, and values as well as form performance strategies for adapting to developmental tasks, occupational transitions, and work troubles (Savickas, 2005). For the dimension of the self-conceiving autobiographical author, CCT links the four quadrants in the meta-theoretical matrix to four *reflexive schemas* for authoring career narratives (Archer, 2012) related to four strategies for performing a *vocational identity* (Marcia, 1980; Berzonsky, 1989; Josselson, 1996). Figure 2 depicts a summary of the self-constructing processes and self-constructed content in each dimension of the psychological self.

Figure 2. Self-Constructing Processes and Content

Self-Constructing *Process* Leader	Cognitive Schema *Content*	Performing Strategy *Content*
Self-Organizing Actor	Attachment	Disposition
Self-Regulating Agent	Motivational Focus	Adaptability
Self-Conceiving Author	Reflexivity	Identity

The foundational matrix specifies that the cognitive schema and performance strategy facets in each dimension of a psychological self as actor, agent, and author do not constitute competing nor alternative explanations, rather each one offers a complementary vantage point from which to view career construction processes, products, and patterns. Each of these three pairs of schemas and strategies for understanding vocational behavior and career construction emerges from the foundational matrix and arise as a natural consequence from its predecessor, which is thought to foreshadow what may come next in the course of a career, thus suggesting functional relationships among the dimensions of the psychological self. The stable structure and analytic power provided by this meta-theoretical matrix enables practitioners and researchers to grasp the sequential emergence, reciprocal interaction, and continuity of career construction schemas and strategies across the life course. Viewing careers through the templates of schemas and strategies inter-related by the motivational matrix of agency and communion enables a deeper and more complete understanding of the complexity and unity of individuals and their continuity across time.

Of course analyzing people's lives in terms of four possible pathways overly simplifies complicated biographies and minimizes individuality. The way that people act in situations and think about themselves in relation to the social world may change over the life course, especially in response to transformations in circumstances, contexts, and experiences. Individuals do not necessarily follow a particular trajectory in lockstep, there can be twists and turns as people migrate to a different path that alters the trajectory of their careers and journey through life. Rotation of the CCT templates of cognitive schemas and performing strategies results in viewing myriad career patterns produced by endless variations in life design. Although for a large portion of individuals, the kaleidoscopic template lenses need not be rotated from their original position in the foundational matrix. Thus the plan of this book is to present four case studies that each illustrate a participant's stable trajectory of career construction, without rotation of later conceptual templates. This stable framing of life histories enables readers to view each participant's trajectory as they move along one of four major pathways mapped by the foundational matrix of agentic individuation and communal integration.

In summary, the visual illustration in Figure 3 depicts the unifying architecture of CCT's explicit meta-theory. Practitioners and researchers may use the meta-theory to understand CCT as well as a tool with which to focus thinking and clarify complex problems.

Figure 3. Meta-Theoretical Architecture of Career Construction Theory

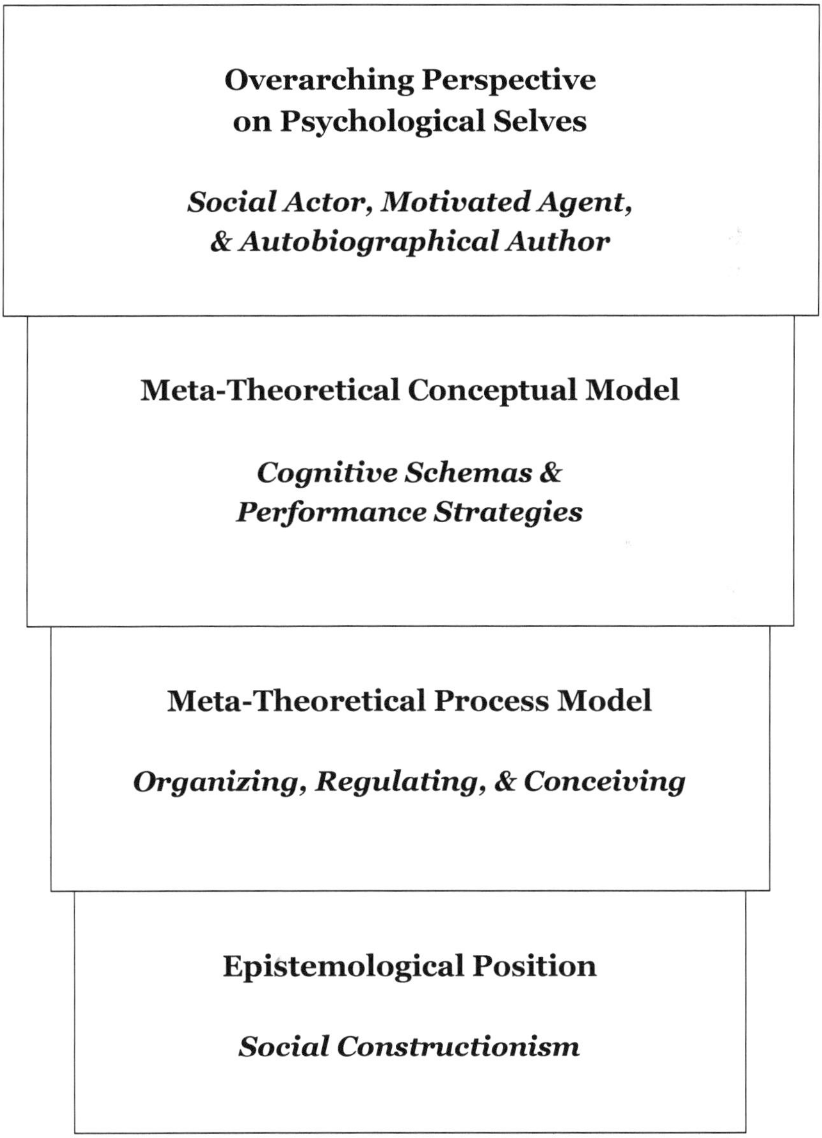

Overarching Perspective on Psychological Selves

Social Actor, Motivated Agent, & Autobiographical Author

Meta-Theoretical Conceptual Model

Cognitive Schemas & Performance Strategies

Meta-Theoretical Process Model

Organizing, Regulating, & Conceiving

Epistemological Position

Social Constructionism

Career Construction Theory Propositions

A theory is a credible set of analytic principles or statements about phenomena that are designed to guide observation, inform understanding, and provide explanation. In crafting CCT, I have conceptualized vocational behavior and its development by selecting descriptive propositions based on existing research, making CCT an integration of empirical conclusions not a prescriptive theory. The propositions in CCT are situated according to the three psychological selves in McAdam's (2013) overarching framework. In what follows, each premise is elaborated by CCT propositions [*each denoted by an italicized number*] that describe concise and systematic conclusions based on prior research and reflection. The 45 propositions themselves appear in Appendix B. The first group of propositions deals with how an individual as a social actor uses self-organizing processes to selectively make and maintain characteristics, capabilities, and interactions that eventually shape a career trajectory. This section is followed in turn by propositions dealing with how an individual as a motivated agent directs and controls educational-vocational behavior through self-regulating processes that shape perceptions, feelings, and actions in pursuit of goals. The third group of propositions deals with how an individual as an autobiographical author shapes an identity and composes a career story through self-conceiving processes. Each proposition is explicated in more or less detail and illustrated in four subsequent chapters that each present a case study to exemplify one of the four major trajectories presupposed by CCT.

The Self-Organizing Social Actor

Premise A: *Individuals co-construct a psychological self as a social actor within their families by organizing an attachment schema and dispositional strategy.*

A major concept in all career theories is that congruence, or the fit between a person and environment, influences adaptation to a context. The first situation into which individuals must position themselves is within their families. People are born into dialogues to which they learn to respond and contribute. Beginning in the second year of life, individuals organize and elaborate a psychological self as an actor in the family drama. A sense of self emerges through the process of self-organizing in which an infant begins to shape herself or himself in relation to others in the home. Families teach us who we are. In the words of a former client, "Home is where I became me." CCT considers both how individuals learn to fit into their families as a social actor and how families prepare children to perform life roles, including the work role. Through primary socialization processes -- such as gendering, relationship patterns, and family values -- parents prepare their children for social roles, launch them on life course trajectories, and guide their initial movement in the world. As children move into society, they carry forward these strategies for living that profoundly influence the paths they make in their careers. In due course, the social roles proffered by society and its institutions structure the context and sequence of events that individuals enact and experience during their lives. The opportunities to perform work roles that individuals perceive are co-constructed by social forces in the family and conditioned by societal institutions in the community as well as the momentum propelled by earlier choices and actions [Proposition 1].

Individuals learn to perform as social actors in the family drama by introjecting parental influences and coordinating their emotions and intentions with their parents, who serve as *guiding lines* for moving in the social world [Proposition 2]. How individuals attach to their parents, and how their parents bond with them in providing nurturance and security, co-constructs the social actor and influences career construction. CCT views how the self-organizing actor develops an attachment schema and dispositional strategy through the meta-dimensional elements of agency and communion, this time as manifest in the two mid-range models of attachment schemas (Bowlby, 1982)) and personality dispositions (Gough, 1987).

Attachment Schema

To make their place in the family and develop personal characteristics, individuals use self-organizing processes to inhabit the cultural discourses and social categories available to them -- such as gender, race, ethnicity, class, and birth order. Through interaction with their parents, children co-construct a working model for understanding themselves, other people, and the world (Bowlby, 1982). In due course, these internal working models form an attachment schema, that is, a generally consistent organization of mental representations that serves as a prime way of thinking about the social world as well as a script for interpersonal interactions and need fulfillment in work roles [Proposition 3]. Throughout life, individuals use their attachment schemas as heuristic templates to guide interpersonal relationships, direct attention, interpret events, and generate expectations [Proposition 4].

Repeated use of an attachment schema forms psychological needs, some of which are fulfilled through work roles. In their jobs, individuals use attachment schema formed in the family as an interpretive system to direct need fulfillment as well as interpersonal interactions. Individuals' basic approach to attaching to parents produces a strategy for going forward in life, one that that significantly influences their career plans, patterns, and pathways. Accordingly, CCT proposes that individuals' family functioning anticipates their occupational functioning. As stated by MacGregor and Cochran (1988), "in working, a person re-stages a drama from one's family of origin" (p. 138). Thus, attachment schema shape how individuals view interactions with their coworkers and supervisors as well as influence perception of organizational culture.

Based on different underlying working models of the self and others built from relationships with their parents, people show different attachment schema. Ideally, children's secure attachment to their parents provides safety and support that helps them to deal with perceived danger and disruptive emotions. Unfortunately, some children experience insecure relationships with their caregivers. Bowlby (1982) delineated a model of four prototypical attachment schemas and associated relational strategies based on two forms of insecurity: *anxiety* over abandonment and *avoidance* of intimacy. These twin coordinates intersect to formulate attachment schemas that align well with the underlying conceptual coordinates of agency and communion.

The four distinct attachment schemas in the template are described as secure-autonomous, anxious-ambivalent, dismissive-avoidant, and fearful-disorganized. Low anxiety coupled with low avoidance characterizes a *secure-autonomous* attachment schema from which individuals view themselves and others as positive, leading to ease and comfort with both intimacy and autonomy. High anxiety coupled with low avoidance characterizes an *anxious-ambivalent* attachment schema from which individuals view themselves as negative and other people as positive leading to a preoccupation with an intimacy marked by low autonomy. High avoidance coupled with low anxiety characterizes a *dismissive-avoidant* attachment schema from which individuals view themselves as positive and other people as negative leading to a counter-dependency that prizes autonomy and resists closeness and intimacy. High avoidance coupled with high anxiety characterizes a *fearful-disorganized* attachment schema from which negative views of both self and other people cause a disorientation characterized by fear of and discomfort in social interactions. Individuals can be described, from an individual differences perspective, as operating primarily from one of the attachment schemas; yet they may form different attachment relationships with particular individuals. And of course not all individuals fit neatly into one quadrant because individuals can operate from a range of positions within a quadrant or across quadrants.

Dispositional Strategy

Following from their attachment schema, individuals form dispositional strategies for performing social roles, including the work role [*Proposition 5*]. They also develop trait reputations as other people recognize their performance strategies or usual way of relating to other people and cultural norms. CCT views the self as an actor in social contexts through Gough's (1987) template of personality dispositions, that is, an individual's general tendencies in social behavior. Gough's template of possibilities aligns well with the underlying conceptual coordinates of agency and communion (e.g., Trapnell & Paulhus, 2011). Gough's (1987) framework of personality dispositions uses two dimensions of higher-order personality structure to broadly classify individuals' as displaying one of four dispositions. In Gough's cuboid typology of personality, the two basic modes of functioning involve relating to other people and responding to normative regulation. Hogan (1982) -- who worked with Gough at the Institute for Personality Assessment and Research at the University of California, Berkley -- used the terms sociability and conformity to denote these two basic dimensions in his socioanalytic theory of personality. Gough referred to the first vector as an interpersonal orientation toward relationships with other people (cf., agency). Its two poles are an extroverted external focus on action versus an introverted internal focus on inner life. Gough referred to the second vector as an orientation to social adjustment (cf., communion). Its two poles are norm-favoring acceptance of social rules versus norm-questioning doubt about social rules. Using these two dimensions of higher-order personality structure, individuals may be broadly classified into one of four types, with each type displaying distinct dispositional characteristics (Domino & Domino, 2006; Gough, 1987, 1990).

Gough referred to an extroverted, norm-accepting disposition as an Alpha orientation to relationships and rules. Individuals who display this tendency combine an extroverted orientation to other people and action with a norm-accepting orientation toward social standards and conventional values. Individuals with an Alpha disposition and lifestyle may see themselves as ambitious, active, productive, and socially poised. Other people tend to see them as dominant, enterprising, confident, talkative, intrepid, and encouraging. On the job, Alphas at their best may be leaders; at their worst they may be opportunistic and manipulative.

Gough referred to an introverted, norm-accepting disposition as a Beta orientation to relationships and rules. Individuals who display this tendency combine an introverted orientation to other people and interpersonal experience with a norm-accepting orientation toward social standards and conventional values. They resemble Alphas in respecting rules yet are more reserved and less active. Individuals with a Beta disposition typically nurture other people, and often put the needs of others before their own. Being so good at delaying gratification, they often live without adventure. They may see themselves as ethical, methodical, conscientious, dependable, modest, persevering, and responsible. Other people may see them as careful, reserved, inhibited, conforming, and submissive. On the job, Betas at their best may be conscientious and ethical; at their worst they may be rigidly conformist and live in denial of their own needs.

Gough referred to an extroverted, norm-questioning disposition as a Gamma orientation to relationships and rules. Individuals who display this tendency combine an extroverted orientation to other people and action while questioning rules, social norms, and conventional values. They may see themselves as innovative, forthright, versatile, and clever. Other people may see them as adventurous, impulsive, headstrong, non-conforming and quick to perceive flaws and absurdities in aspects of everyday life. On the job, Gammas at their best may be seen as creative in producing new ideas, products, or services; at their worst they may be seen as intolerant, disruptive, rebellious, and self-indulgent.

Gough referred to an introverted, norm-questioning disposition as a Delta orientation to relationships and rules. Individuals who display this tendency combine an introverted orientation to other people and action while questioning rules, social norms, and conventional values. They perceive things differently than other people, yet keep their thoughts and lack of personal meaning private. They may see themselves as shy, quiet, withdrawn, unnoticed, detached, and preoccupied. Other people may see them as timid, self-defeating, and passive. On the job, Deltas at their best may be imaginative and creative; at their worst they may be enmeshed in inner conflicts, alienated from other people, and prone to decompensation.

CCT views dispositional strategies as flowing from the fountainhead of attachment schemas: Alphas from the wellspring of secure-autonomous attachment schema, Betas from anxious-ambivalent attachment schemas, Gammas from dismissing-avoidant attachment schemas, and Deltas from a fearful-disorganized attachment schemas. Attachment schemas and dispositional strategies condition how individuals seek to meet their basic emotional, social, and career needs [*Proposition 6*]. Figure 4 depicts CCT's template of social actors, with each type constituted by pairing an attachment schema with a dispositional strategy, both of which link to the meta-theoretical conceptual matrix of agency and communion.

Figure 4. Patterns of Attachment Schemas and Personality Strategies

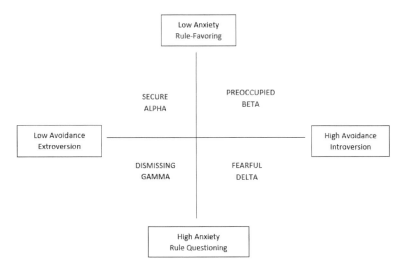

Role Models

As part of self-construction during early childhood, individuals begin to look to cultural discourses to identify role models who display characteristics and behaviors that would be useful in solving their own problems in growing up and for fulfilling their psychological needs [Proposition 7]. Individuals then model their self-construction and ways to regard themselves on these admired characteristics and behaviors. Identification as a core process of self-construction occurs when an individual imitates behaviors and incorporates characteristics of the models as a rather permanent part of the self [Proposition 8]. Choice of role models is the first career choice because imitating a model in fantasy and play, in due course, mobilizes interests and activities that through repetition and rehearsal develop vocational skills and preferences [Proposition 9]. In contrast to the parental authority of guiding lines, role models represent the wish to become and face the future. Guiding lines are *taken in* as introjected influences whereas role models are *taken on* as incorporated identifications. Whereas individuals introject guiding lines as a whole, they incorporate identity fragments from their various role models. Then beginning during late adolescence, individuals use self-conceiving processes to integrate these intact influences and partial identifications into a unified and cohesive psychosocial identity. Each individual leaves early childhood with an attachment schema for viewing interpersonal relationships, a dispositional strategy for performing social roles, and role models who display how to address unresolved issues and preoccupations [Proposition 10].

Social actors form core personal characteristics and interpersonal styles by repeatedly rehearsing their attachment schemas and dispositional strategies with parents and siblings and imitating role models. In research and practice, counselors may understand an individual as a social actor by inquiring about guiding lines and role models. An individual's guiding lines suggest the working model in their attachment schema. To learn about guiding lines, practitioners might ask individuals to report three words that best describe their mother and three more for their father. Individuals' role models suggest personal characteristics that they have taken on. To inquire about self-construction as a social actor, the simplest procedure is to ask individuals to identify three role models from early in life and then describe the personal characteristics of each exemplar. The descriptors may be organized by locating them on the dimensions of sociability and conformity (Hogan, 1983) or interpersonal orientation and social adjustment (Gough, 1987) as illustrated in Figure 5.

Figure 5. Mapping Personal Characteristics on Coordinates Charted by Hogan (1983) and Gough (1997)

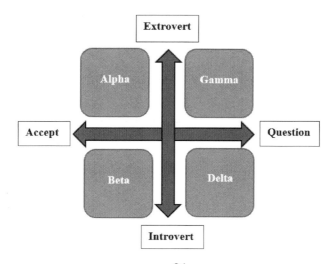

The Self-Regulating Motivated Agent

Premise B: *Late in childhood, individuals begin to function more often as motivated agents who direct their own lives toward congruent positions in society through self-regulation, that is, the processes by which individuals adapt their perceptions, feelings, and actions in the pursuit of a goal.*

The self as a social actor addresses questions such as "What is my character?" and "How should I conduct myself?" During middle childhood, individuals more fully elaborate their self-conceptions as they increase the use of a second dimension in the domain of the psychological selves to address new questions such as: "What is my relation to the world?" and "What shall I do next?" The self as an active agent in one's own life becomes responsible for positioning the individual as a social actor around the neighborhood, at school, and in society. The self-regulating agent's pursuit of goals, values, and interests in these contexts can be understood as efforts by a social actor to move purposefully from a present position to envisioned future positions [Proposition 11]. To move toward a currently desired position the agent must intentionally select and seek desired effects through a course of purposeful action (Tiedeman & Field, 1961). In assessing the suitability of possible positions, CCT concentrates on the three motivational constructs of needs, interests, and values [Proposition 12]. *Needs* consist of what individuals lack and believe they require to feel secure. Needs propel behavior, driving a person toward certain satisfactions. *Values* are desirable goals and objectives, residing in the environment, that satisfy needs. *Interests* denote a complex adaptive effort to use one's environment to satisfy needs and fulfill values (Savickas, 2014). While values represent objectives, interests concern the objects and activities through which objectives are attained (Super & Bohn, 1970). The symbolic representation of an interest is usually signified by the stimulus that evokes attention and action (e.g., "I like books").

With regard to forming and pursuing goals, the self as agent adopts a persistent, self-regulation schema that focuses motivation and shapes adaptation strategies [Proposition 13]. CCT views how the self as agent sets goals, make plans, and performs purposeful action again through the conceptual coordinates of agency and communion, this time as manifest in the two mid-range models of regulatory focus (Higgins, 1997) and career adaptation (Savickas, 2005).

Motivation Focus Schema

Motivational focus schema represent inclinations for attaining desired outcomes. Children learn to get along in the world by self-regulating their feelings and actions based on reward contingencies in the social regulation provided by parents (Higgins, 1998), especially in response to a child's needs for nurturance and security [Proposition 14]. Social regulation that emphasizes nurturance fosters in children a self-regulation schema focused on educational-vocational goals that promote accomplishment by aiming for achievement, reward, and advancement. In contrast, social regulation that emphasizes security fosters in children a self-regulation schema focused on educational-vocational goals that prevent problems by maintaining responsibility, security, and safety. The two foci differ because a promotion schema plays to win whereas a prevention schema plays not to lose. In simple terms, a promotion focus directs behavior toward what one wants to do and personal growth whereas a prevention focus directs behavior toward what one ought to do and away from failure and psychological harm. Because promotion and prevention foci form independent dimensions (Higgins, 1997; Johnson & Chang, 2008), a person's self-regulation schema may display high levels in one focus, both foci, or neither focus.

Of course, healthy parents foster in their children a self-regulation schema that balances promotion and prevention among their vocational goals; other parents foster in their children either a promotion or a prevention schema; and troubled parents raise children who have difficulty with self-regulation. Individuals with a secure-autonomous attachment schema and an Alpha disposition tend to combine high levels of focus on both promotion and prevention; individuals with an anxious-ambivalent attachment schema and Beta disposition tend to combine a low level of promotion focus with a high level of prevention focus; individuals with an dismissive-avoidant attachment schema and Gamma disposition tend to combine a high level of promotion focus with a low level of prevention focus; and individuals with a fearful-disorganized attachment schema and Delta disposition tend to show low levels of focus on both promotion and prevention resulting in amotivation and difficulty in self-regulation.

Career Adaptation Strategies

Self-regulation schemas, whether focused on promotion or prevention, direct how people adapt to the vocational developmental tasks, occupational transitions, and work troubles involved in choosing and pursuing their career goals [Proposition 15]. *Developmental tasks* denote a life-long series of social expectations about preparing for and participating in jobs. A concept often invoked when considering developmental tasks is *vocational maturity*, linguistically defined as an individual's degree of vocational development and operationally defined by comparing the developmental tasks being encountered to those expected based on chronological age [Proposition 16]. *Occupational transitions* are changes in jobs, employers, or occupational fields. *Work troubles* include difficulty, disturbance, or difficulty on the job and can escalate into *work traumas* when employment is destabilized by socioeconomic or personal events such as illness and injury, plant closings and company layoffs, or job redesign and automation. When individuals encounter one of these types of career changes, they must adapt. A need to adapt activates self-regulation, that is, the capacity to alter one's responses so as to change oneself or something in the situation in order to implement a plan or reach a goal [Proposition 17]. CCT includes a sequential model of self-regulated adaptation. The sequence highlights the personality characteristics of adaptive readiness, the psychosocial capabilities of adaptability resources, the behaviors of adapting responses, and the outcomes of adaptation results [Proposition 18].

Adaptive readiness. The self-regulation sequence of career adaptation begins with adaptive readiness that denotes a willingness and readiness to change when encountering the challenges of developmental tasks, occupational transitions, or work troubles. Adaptive readiness serves as a filter through which motivated agents interpret the environment. It denotes the proactive inclination to activate self-regulation processes and initiate action when previously learned attitudes and activities cannot readily address career change, challenge, nor uncertainty. These disruptive conditions usually induce tension, anxiety, and diffused behavior until a new solution emerges. As a global construct, career adaptivity involves a compound mixture of multiple specific personality characteristics and motivations, including proactivity, conscientiousness, and openness. Given adaptive readiness, to function effectively a person must also possess the resources necessary for producing the desired consequences or avoiding undesired consequences.

Adaptability resources. Prompted by adaptive readiness, self-regulation resources come into play during times of transition. CCT defines these *adaptability resources* as psychosocial capacities for solving unfamiliar, complex, and ill-defined problems presented by disruptive conditions. As a meta-competence, *career adaptability* includes four transactional capacities that help to assess goal trajectories in changing environments: concern, control, curiosity, and confidence. *Concern* denotes the extent to which an individual is oriented toward the future and inclined to anticipate and prepare for career moves. *Control* denotes the extent to which an individual assumes responsibility for building a career. *Curiosity* denotes the extent to which an individual tends to imagine possible selves, explore opportunities, and gather information. *Confidence* denotes the extent to which an individual has faith in her or his ability to make viable career decisions and solve problems in reaching occupational goals. Career confidence supports the persistent pursuit of aspirations and anticipation of success despite obstacles. Using these four psychosocial resources, an adaptable individual is conceptualized as (a) becoming concerned about the vocational future, (b) taking control of shaping one's vocational future, (c) displaying curiosity by exploring possible selves and future scenarios, and (d) showing the confidence to pursue one's aspirations.

The configuration and strength of adaptability resources developed by individuals shape their responses to career changes and challenges. For example, with well-developed resources of concern and curiosity but not control and confidence, individuals mainly just *look ahead* to prepare for projects chosen by others. In comparison, individuals with well-developed control and confidence but not concern and curiosity mainly begin to *look around* only when the time comes for a change. They have been heard to say, "I'm not going to worry about choosing an occupation until I am out of school" or "I'll think about it when I retire." Individuals with limited adaptability resources live in the present. With regard to the future, they neither look ahead nor look around, just look out to protect themselves.

Adapting responses. With or without adaptability resources, at some point individuals make transitions using *adapting responses* that, at their best, are shaped by the adaptability resources of concern, control, curiosity, and confidence as well as strong self-efficacy beliefs about their ability to execute the responses. The actual adapting responses themselves are specific behaviors that play a part in a general category of large actions meant to bridge transitions. For example, visiting an occupational information website is a small action that contributes to the larger action called exploring. In CCT, the four important adapting actions are anticipating, exploring, deciding, and problem solving. Individuals may adapt more effectively by *anticipating* or looking ahead to a new transition, *exploring* or looking around for new options and opportunities, *deciding* after looking at preferred options, and looking into and *solving* problems confronted in making a stable commitment to a new project for a certain time period. Performing specific behaviors that carry out the large actions of anticipating, exploring, deciding, and solving usually results in adaptation to changing circumstances and displeasing disruptions.

Adaptation results. Career adaptation results denote the outcomes of adapting responses, achieving at best a new equilibrium or fit between the individual and the environment. The Career Construction model of adaptation evaluates adapting results as either integrative, adjustive, or maladaptive (Shaffer, 1936; Haan, 1977). *Integrative coping*, which is oriented to reality, both solves a problem and reduces tension and anxiety, moving the individual to greater stability at a higher level of organization, possibly involving a transformative development. Sometimes individuals cannot fully respond to a baffling problem so instead they adjust by reducing negative emotions. *Adjustive defending*, which distorts reality, does not solve a problem but does reduce tension and anxiety. Very often adjustive responses persist because anxiety reduction reinforces them. Although negative emotions are temporarily dispelled, anxiety and tension eventually return because the problem itself was not resolved. Nevertheless, adjustive defending may produce small, incremental change. Adjustive responses are often shaped by concern and curiosity or by control and confidence but not by all four adaptability resources. The third category of responses is neither integrative nor adjustive. *Maladaptive fragmenting* neither solves a problem nor reduces tension and anxiety because it is guided by idiosyncratic thoughts and feelings that do not correspond to reality nor change the existing state of affairs. Chronic use of maladaptive responses may produce repeated mistakes, personal difficulties, social withdrawal, or unregulated emotional reactions such as fearfulness and demoralization.

As an example of adaptation results, consider possible outcomes of deciding responses. Integrative coping may result in the outcome of decidedness, adjustive defending may result in undecidedness, and maladaptive fragmenting may result in indecisiveness. As a second example, consider possible adaptation results from exploring. Integrative coping may result in strategic information about long-term goals and tactical means gathered from both internal and external sources. Adjustive defending may result in tactical information about smaller steps and shorter time-frames gathered mostly from internal sources with a few external sources being used. Maladaptive fragmenting may result in a lack of basic information and unrealistic opinions.

Figure 6 depicts CCT's template of motivated agents, with each type constituted by pairing a motivational schema with an adaptation strategy, both of which have emerged from the meta-theoretical matrix of agency and communion. In Figure 6, the quadrant labeled "Integrative" represents a balance of promotion wants and prevention oughts combined with well-developed concern about the future, control to delay gratification, curiosity about options, and confidence in implementing plans. When faced with career decisions, individuals with this pattern of motivation look ahead and look around to make fitting educational and vocational choices. The quadrant labeled

"Dysfunctional" represents amotivation with limited adaptability resources. Individuals who display amotivation live in the present, with little sense of a future. When faced with career decisions, they just look out not to get hurt, rather than look ahead and look around for possible choices. The quadrant labeled "Adjustive looking ahead" represents a prevention focus with the adaptability resources of concern and curiosity concentrated on in-depth exploration of a choice imposed by others, without looking around to identify a self-chosen alternative. The quadrant labeled "Adjustive looking around" represents a promotion focus with minimal looking ahead to the future. Individuals with this pattern of motivation wait for problems to arise and then look around for solutions. The conceptual pairing of concern with curiosity for looking ahead and control with confidence for looking around emerged empirically from person-centered research and score profiles on the *Career Adapt-Abilities Scale* (Savickas & Porfeli, 2012), not from a pre-existing theoretical rationale.

Figure 6. Patterns of Motivational Schemas and Adaptation Strategies

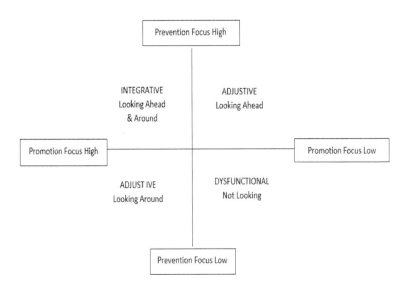

Work Roles

As agents directing their own lives through motivational schemas and adaptation strategies, individuals implement their self-concepts by constructing activity preferences or selecting work roles in which to pursue their career goals [Proposition 19]. Work-role preferences develop through the interaction of inherited aptitudes, physical make-up, opportunities to observe and play various roles, and evaluations of the extent to which the results of role playing meet with the approval of peers and supervisors [Proposition 20]. Role selection and entry involves a synthesis and compromise between individual and social factors. It evolves from role playing and learning from feedback, whether the role is played in fantasy, in a counseling interview, or in real-life activities such as hobbies, classes, clubs, part-time work, and entry-level jobs. The initial sites of social niche construction are hobbies and academic majors. For most people, an occupation eventually becomes a primary social niche and strategy for economic survival. Occupations provide a core role, although for some individuals this focus is peripheral, incidental, or even nonexistent. Then other life roles such as student, parent, homemaker, leisurite, and citizen may be at the core (Super, 1990) [Proposition 21].

Personal preferences for arranging these life roles and opportunities to enter occupations are deeply grounded in the social practices that engage individuals and locate them in unequal social positions. An individual's range of opportunities and possible choices can be constrained by hard-to-escape social biases and ideological systems. These boundaries and distortions may both precede and exceed an individual. Thus, an individual's capacity to choose freely is not complete; each person must deal with the unchosen conditions of her or his life. Some people push against constraints to achieve for themselves, and maybe others, the best possible choice and most vital life design. Other people may "grin and bear it" as they patiently wait for things to change in their favor. And still other people, may dramatically change the conditions of their lives by moving to a different context, whether it be a different city, state, or even country.

Because social actors differ in vocational characteristics and social opportunities, they enter different occupational environments, which Holland (1997) described as RIASEC environments [Proposition

22]. Each occupation requires a different pattern of vocational characteristics, with tolerances wide enough to allow a considerable variety of individuals in each occupation. People are qualified for a variety of occupations based on the match of their vocational abilities and interests to occupational requirements and rewards [Proposition 23]. Role selection and entry involves a synthesis and compromise between individual and social factors [Proposition 24]. Typically, *occupational success* depends on the extent to which an individual's abilities and actions meet the requirements of work roles [Proposition 25]. *Job satisfaction* depends on establishment in an occupation, a work situation, and a way of life in which one can play the type of roles that growth and exploratory experiences have led one to consider suitable for meeting needs, fulfilling values, and expressing interests [Proposition 26]. An individual's *career pattern* -- that is, the occupational level attained and the sequence, frequency, and duration of jobs -- is usually determined by the parents' socioeconomic level and the person's education, abilities, personality, self-concepts, and career adaptability in transaction with the opportunities presented by society [Proposition 27]. An objective career pattern is recorded in a resumé whereas a subjective career is a story that individuals tell about their work lives. The career story is composed by the self-conceiving autobiographical author.

The Self-Conceiving Autobiographical Author

Premise C: *Social actors who pursue goals can deliberate as an autobiographical author to conceive a vocational identity and compose a career story that imposes continuity and coherence on their actions over time.*

While children can perform self-conceiving processes, the self-organizing and self-regulating processes take the lead in their self-constructing. During late adolescence and emerging adulthood, self-conceiving comes to the fore to author a career story and authorize a vocational identity. To do so, the subjective "I" deliberates on the objective "Me" to author a career story about the self as a social actor and motivated agent [Proposition 28]. By arranging role model identifications and synthesizing experiences into a unified narrative, individuals compose a career story about their working lives, one that selectively appropriates and reconstructs past experiences into a story of the "Me" with coherence among self-definitions, consistency across situations, and stability over time. With the self-conceiving process of composing a career story, individuals declare a *vocational identity* that presents an argument justifying occupational choices by relating their private inner world to the public outer world [*Proposition* 29].

Career stories revolve around vocational identity as individuals explain how they developed, the way they currently conduct themselves as social actors, and where they have positioned themselves in society as motivated agents. A career story enables its author to engage in autobiographical reasoning to clarify beliefs and values, evaluate social positions, formulate goals and projects, and commit to relationships and roles that position the individual in society. This *career positioning*, whether in aspiration or actuality, locates a vocational identity in a particular occupation, that is, self-in-a-work-role [*Proposition* 30]. CCT views the self-conceiving autobiographical author through the meta-theoretical matrix of agency and communion, this time as manifest in reflexive schemas and vocational identity strategies.

Reflexive Schemas

When developmental tasks, occupational transitions, or work troubles obstruct routines and habitual behaviors, self-conceiving autobiographical authors deliberate about their career stories by thinking about who they are in relation to what they care about most and who they want to become in their social contexts. By way of the interchange between subjective personal dispositions and objective social positions, individuals analyze their conduct, shape life strategies, and guide action (Archer, 2012). CCT uses the term *biographicity* to denote the use of reflexive schemas to conceive vocational identities and compose career narratives in a "two-stage process" (Stedmon & Dallos, 2009, p. 5) of retrospective reflection and prospective reflexivity [*Proposition* 31].

Reflection involves a more receptive recognition of past experiences whereas reflexivity involves a more active conceptualization of the future. Reflection focuses attention on memories, experiences, and cognitions to bring the past into the present and heighten self-awareness. In comparison, reflexivity ponders over reflections and extends the present into the future. Thus, reflexivity is a second-order cognitive process, defined as an internal dialogue in which individuals use knowledge from first-order reflections to determine and design future projects. As explained by the German philosopher Odo Marquard (2001, p. 66), "the future needs the past." So too does the output of reflectivity need the prior input of reflection. In sum, the internal dialogues constituting biographicity enable individuals to (a) understand the self in relation to social contexts, (b) recognize patterns in autobiographical narratives, (c) determine and plan projects in light of objective social circumstances, and (d) guide action by conditioning responses to particular social situations. CCT views biographicity as a means by which individuals mediate the effect of social systems and cultural structures on their personal agency and courses of action, specifically in regard to the occupations that they seek, keep, or quit [*Proposition 32*].

Autobiographical authors differ in their reflexive schemas for deliberating about life design and career construction [*Proposition 33*]. CCT proposes that individuals' attachment and motivational schemas play a central role in structuring individuals' reflexive deliberations about vocational situations and career dissonance or disruption. Based on biographical interviews concerning life experiences and work histories, Archer (2012) conceptualized an individual differences typology of reflexive schemas that distinguishes four modes. CCT applies these possible modes to understand how individuals compose vocational identities and author career narratives. Each mode coincides with a different pattern of family socialization and parental guidance regarding how to set goals and commit to projects. Healthier families afford their children better opportunities for eventually taking control of their own lives. Archer (2012) denoted the four schemas for reflexive deliberation as autonomous, communicative, meta-, and fractured.

Autonomous reflexivity (cf., high agency and communion) involves self-contained internal dialogues that lead directly to action, without the need for validation by parents or other people. Archer (2012) used the term *independents* to describe individuals disposed to use autonomous reflexivity because they create their own paths following purposeful, self-contained, and instrumental deliberation. Individuals who routinely engage in autonomous reflexivity may display a secure attachment schema as they independently direct their own action without the need for validation by other individuals. They follow their parents' guiding lines only to the degree that parental dictates coincide with their own self-chosen paths. Independent individuals with autonomous reflexivity do not attempt to replicate their parents' projects nor their way of life. Instead, they set their own goals as "they think and act" (Archer, 2003, p. 7).

Communicative reflexivity (cf., low agency, high communion) involves internal dialogues that lead to action only after being completed and confirmed by parents or significant others. Archer (2012) used the term *identifiers* to describe individuals disposed to use communicative reflexivity because, without exploring alternatives, they commit to life projects chosen for them by their parents. Individuals who routinely engage in communicative reflexivity may display an anxious-ambivalent attachment schema. They seek to replicate the family's way of life and reproduce the status quo. Guided by family tradition, they set clear priorities yet their projects rarely exceed the confines of their family context. As part of communicative reflexivity, they turn to significant others in their immediate environment to talk things through and answer their questions. Focused on consensus, "they think and talk" (Archer, 2003, p. 7).

Meta-reflexivity (cf., high agency, low communion) involves internal dialogues in which individuals routinely question their own thoughts and critique their parents' way of life. Individuals who routinely engage in meta-reflexivity often criticize and disengage from parental values, which intensifies personal stress and social disorientation. Archer named this mode of reflexivity as "meta" to denote the self-monitoring or thinking about how one thinks. She characterized individuals disposed to use meta-reflexivity as *disengaged* because they find fault with their parents' life choices and so design for themselves very different ways of living. The term disengaged suggests that these individuals may have been physically detached from their parents at a young age or have mentally disassociated themselves from their parents' way of life. Cut loose from parental guiding lines, they cast about for their place in society by searching socio-cultural systems of beliefs as well as experimenting with different lifestyles. Preoccupied with their selves and single-mindedly pursuing their own interests, they frequently consider their jobs and relationships sorely wanting. In response to unrewarding contexts and relationships, they keep searching for new jobs and lifestyles. Focused on values, "they think and think" (Archer, 2003, p. 7).

Fractured reflexivity (cf., low agency and communion) Individuals who routinely engage in fractured reflexivity may feel rejected by parents and subsequently limit their own participation in interpersonal relationship and work roles. Archer (2012) used the term *rejecters* to describe individuals disposed to use fractured reflexivity because they renounce their family of origin. They distance themselves from their families believing that their parents caused their problems. Lacking parental modeling and guidance, they remain confused. Instead of designing their lives and guiding action, their internal deliberations intensify cognitive disorientation and cause emotional distress. They suffer intense anxiety as they just passively respond to circumstance beyond their control. Focused on daily survival, "they think and talk to themselves" (Archer, 2003, p .7).

Identity Strategies

Reflexive self-authorship produces identity, that is, a narrative about the self in a social role. Individuals have multiple identities, each one corresponding to a particular social role that they enact. For example, a vocational identity tells the story about an individual in a work role. Identity narratives unify an individual's experiences in a particular social role to build a coherent and credible framework for creating meaning and dealing with dislocation, disruption, or discord. An identity narrative heightens self-awareness of and provides a consistent orientation for role performance. In CCT, vocational identity organizes a psychosocial strategy for performing the work role. A vocational identity succeeds as a performance strategy to the degree that one is aware of it and other people validate it.

Viewing the distinct modes of reflexivity in terms of life strategies for dealing with career concerns leads directly to typologies of vocational identity formation and functioning. The four distinct reflexive schemas produce four different strategies for forming a vocational identity and dealing with career concerns [*Proposition* 34]. CCT views vocational identity strategies and career narratives through the templates of possibility delineated by identity statuses (Marcia, 1980), identity functioning (Josselson, 1996), and identity styles (Berzonsky, 1989). The foundational work of Erik Erikson (1968) on psychosocial identity was re-conceptualized by Marcia (1980) as a typology of four identity statuses formed by two axes of exploration and commitment. Marcia called the statuses achieved (cf., high agency and communion), foreclosed (cf., low agency, high communion), moratorium (cf., high agency, low communion), and diffused (cf., low agency and communion). Josselson (1996) renamed the four statuses to emphasize what individuals do rather than what they are. She called them Pathmakers, Guardians, Searchers, and Drifters. Berzonsky (1989) concentrated on the processes of identity formation rather than statuses. He explained that these four statuses result from three identity-shaping strategies by which people form, maintain, and revise their psychosocial identities: informational, normative, and avoidant.

Individuals *achieve* a vocational identity by making commitments to self-chosen goals after exploring alternatives. Securely attached individuals tend to use an *informational style* (Berzonsky, 1989) in which they actively gather and evaluate relevant information before committing to an occupational choice. This informational style of career construction typically includes planful attitudes toward the future, broad exploration of options, a rich fund of knowledge about preferred alternatives, and well-developed decision-making competencies. With a healthy separation from parents, individuals integrate identifications with role models into a cohesive and stable identity and then make suitable and viable choices to implement that vocational identity in occupational roles. Once individuals with an informational style select educational and vocational goals, they usually settle into a course of action, work persistently toward their goals, and use problem-focused coping to meet the challenges they encounter along the way. Josselson (1992) referred to identity achievers as *Pathmakers* because these individuals travel self-determined life courses.

Individuals living with *foreclosed* vocational identities commit to career goals chosen without a period of exploration that loosens ties to childhood certainties and convictions. Individuals with an anxious-ambivalent attachment schema tend to use a *normative style* (Berzonsky, 1989) in which they accept standards and prescriptions promulgated by significant others in making their choices. They often are highly anxious and engaged in a push-pull relationship with parents. Although they may struggle to differentiate themselves from caretakers, their ability to explore and report feelings of secure attachment is limited. This normative style for making occupational commitments springs from a preoccupation with meeting parental prescriptions and expectations in a way that preserve an existing identification as part of the family. Individuals who use a normative style often settle into a course of action without investigating occupational alternatives that may displease significant others. Rather than explore the self and situation in the process of forming commitments, they succumb to external pressures and protect themselves from external threats by adhering to the family's occupational specifications. The vocational identities that they form have coherence and continuity, but these features are produced by outside forces that shape and stabilize their commitments to circumscribed occupational preferences.

A normative style in and of itself is not problematic; it can lead to interdependent identity defined by relationships with others rather than by individual attributes. Individuals who display interdependent identities have been described as society-minded (Kegan, 1994) and norm-favoring (Gough, 1990). Josselson (1996) referred to them as *Guardians* because they prioritize connection to others and preserve what was. Problems arise when individuals adopt a normative style in responding to powerful others who forcefully constrain occupational options. Excessive family pressure to follow a preordained career path may cause an individual to inhibit exploration and forgo performance of choice behaviors, thereby delaying or impairing the individual's own adaptive efforts. Thus, the distinguishing feature that makes a normative style produce identity foreclosure appears to be the quality of relationships with parents. A normative style combined with healthy family relations may reflect an interdependent pattern of career construction, one in which an individual freely chooses the collective good of the family as the criterion for career choice. In contrast, a normative style combined with an inability to resolve relationship problems with parents typically leads to dependent decision making, foreclosed vocational identity, and constrained career construction.

Individuals living in *moratorium* avoid commitments and demand freedom to keep exploring. Individuals with a dismissive-avoidant attachment schema tend to use an *avoidant style* (Berzonsky, 1989) by which circumstances and situations dictate their choices. In an effort to ignore problems and choices for as long as possible, they adopt an avoidant style involving delay, procrastination, and indecision. Individuals who use the avoidant style prefer emotionally-focused coping and generally lack role models. When the situation does not make the choice for them, they resort to emotionally-focused coping. The avoidant style springs from negative perceptions of parents. Josselson (1996) referred to individuals who live in a moratorium as *Searchers* because that is what they are doing.

Individuals with *diffused* identities neither explore nor commit to any identity-defining vocational values or roles. With a fearful-disorganized attachment schema, individuals do little to process self-environment organization and may stay aschematic with regard to identity functioning. They remain unreflexive and show little capacity for self-definition and commitment to values, goals, or relationships. With no set ideological commitments nor occupational direction, their work histories are generally unstable, disjointed, and externally controlled. Berzonsky (1989) did not assign them a unique identity style, suggesting that they also use the avoidant style of identity formation. Being disoriented and disorganized, they may experience a painful sense of incoherence as well as feel a chronic sense of emptiness. According to Kernberg (1978), they may display superficiality, weak ego-strength, poor impulse control, and little tolerance for anxiety. Josselson (1996) referred to individuals with diffused identities as *Drifters* to emphasize that what they are doing is just getting bye as they take things as they come.

The reflexive schemas delineated by Archer (2013) have been linked to identity strategies in an analysis of career stories by Domecka and Mrozowicki (2013) who characterized four career patterns with distinct pairs of schemas and strategies. They reported that using an autonomous reflexive schema tends to shape an identity strategy of *integrating* to *build* a career; a communicative reflexive schema tends to shape an identity strategy of *embedding* to *anchor* a career; a meta-reflexive schema tends to shape an identity strategy of *constructing* to form a *patchwork* career; and finally, a fragmented reflexive schema tends to shape an identity strategy of *getting bye* in a *dead-end* job.

Figure 7 depicts CCT's template of autobiographical authors' career narratives, with each quadrant constituted by pairing a reflexive schema with a strategy for vocational identity formation and functioning, both of which have emerged from the meta-theoretical foundational matrix of agency and communion.

Figure 7. Patterns of Reflexive Modes and Identity Functioning in Career Story Genres

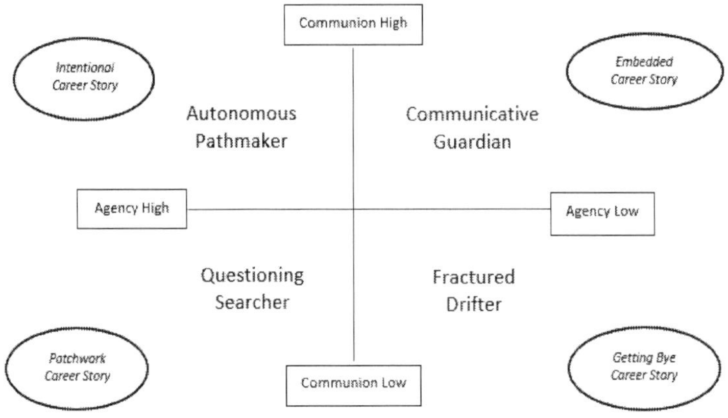

```
                        Communion High
    Intentional                                     Embedded
    Career Story                                    Career Story
                   Autonomous         Communicative
                   Pathmaker          Guardian
    Agency High ─────────────────────────────── Agency Low
                   Questioning        Fractured
                   Searcher           Drifter
    Patchwork                                       Getting Bye
    Career Story                                    Career Story
                        Communion Low
```

Authoring a Career Story

Late adolescence, individuals begin to make sense of their work lives by conceiving a vocational identity and composing a career story with an occupational plot and career theme [Proposition 35]. In its simplest form, a career story places the series of occupational positions held along a timeline [Proposition 36]. In this succinct form, the storyline as a sequence of what happened from start to finish may be recorded as a resumé. More elaborate career stories add an occupational plot to the storyline to form a meaningful whole that connects the positions and events by explaining cause and effect [Proposition 37]. In addition to an occupational plot that explains what happened, individuals may interpret why things happened by investing the explicit plot with meaning from an implicit life theme (Csikszentmihalyi & Beattie, 1979). A life theme refers to self-representations of needs, feelings, motives, and extended goal structures that a person is at first neither entirely aware nor able to fully communicate.

Thematic patterning of the occupational plot fully realizes a career story by adding a dominant motif or controlling idea meant to interpret why things happened, specify the means for meeting needs, highlight recurrent patterns of vocational behavior, and script future scenes [Proposition 38]. Considering the occupational plot in light of a theme typically identifies and interprets predictable patterns of events and experiences that seem to reoccur across the occupational plot, thereby increasing continuity and coherence in the occupational plot. Cumulating incidents and insights into an abstract theme also thickens the plot and amplifies larger meanings that may clarify choices to be made in advancing the story.

Researchers and practitioners interrogate stories for their themes using various approaches to literary criticism, including the mythic (Jungian), psychoanalytic (Freudian), structural (systemic), poststructural (deconstruction), Marxist (economic), and feminist (cultural). Each of these analytic structures for understanding stories and identifying themes contains preconceived expectations and principles of organization. CCT's structure for organizing an individual's biographical stories and recognizing career themes is called the *narrative paradigm*. "Narrative" denotes a story, and "paradigm" denotes a pattern. Hence the term "narrative paradigm" refers to CCT's perspective from which to apprehend thematic patterns in a career story.

The general pattern articulated by the structure of the narrative paradigm involves moving from passive to active [Proposition 39]. CCT suggests that researchers and practitioners formulate career themes by tracing how an individual uses work to move from passive suffering to active mastery, propelled by what Freud (1920) called the repetition compulsion. Development occurs and patterns emerge as people arrange their career stories around thematic problems that preoccupy them and solutions that occupy them. These themes typically originate in childhood and adolescence as unfinished situations, tensions, or conflicts that individuals endure and strive to master. The need to repeatedly master these issues and preoccupations at higher levels of stability influences career choices, work roles, and interactions with supervisors and coworkers.

CCT conceptualizes a person's career themes as an individual instance of the narrative paradigm. As an abstract principle, "turning passive suffering into active mastery" represents a latent motive within people-in-general, one that is always present in individual careers yet only visible when manifest in adapting to changing circumstances such as vocational development tasks, occupational transitions, and work troubles. Facing these novel situations, the drive for mastery readily emerges and may direct how to adapt to the role changes that prompt its manifestation by turning tension into intention and preoccupation into occupation. Each novel career situation provides yet another opportunity for individuals to address recurrent issues and tensions by using the work role to advance the story toward more completeness and greater wholeness. Individuals' career themes become more explicit through their repetition as experiences accumulate during adulthood.

Tracing current motives in contemporary contexts back to antecedent tensions and unfulfilled needs during childhood and adolescence usually realizes a life theme or through-line that provides the continuity and coherence required for vocational identity formation and functioning. Expounding a narrative theme for a career story preserves the past in the present by grounding the here-and-now in the there-and-then as well as expresses a vocational identity by elucidating how a person remains identical with self despite diverse experiences. In this way themes in the present are retrospective; it is the mastery motive that can be prospective in extending and elaborating a theme. CCT does not attribute causality to themes, rather themes represent attempts to unify past experiences with coherence and continuity. In this regard, CCT asserts that contemporary career motives are functionally autonomous from archaic causes (Allport, 1937). Because thematic continuity provide historical analyses rather than propel historic functions, practitioners and researchers must always remember that an individual's contemporary context is more significant in shaping current motives and their expression.

From a perspective of logical positivism rather than an epistemology of social constructionism, Holland (1966) conceptualized a career theme as "a complex cluster of personal attributes" (p. 10) resulting from resolving the multiple and inter-related experiences and influences of parents, school, friends, social class, community, hierarchy of prior choices, and chance (cf., Holland, 1966, p. 12). Holland's RIASEC model of vocational personality types states the essential theme of a career story in one word; for example, Realistic or Social. CCT proposes that each RIASEC theme can be elaborated with motifs that follow the narrative paradigm of actively mastering what has been passively suffered. For example, a fearful child may become a brave adult -- one need not be brave unless he or she has been frightened. Holland's RIASEC themes each encompass a set of mastery motifs (cf., McAdams, 2008), including for example from weakness to strength (Realistic), ignorance to knowledge (Investigative), persecution to freedom (Artistic), helplessness to helpfulness (Social), poor to rich (Enterprising); and chaos to order (Conventional). McAdams (2008) identified an important set of "redemptive" motif patterns in biographies that may intertwine with each of the career themes: the recovery motif from sickness to health; the developmental motif from immaturity to maturity; and the religious motif from immoral to moral. While themes in a career story can be typed as reflecting a general pattern described by Holland (1997) or McAdams (2008), people construct unique, complex themes in their career narratives.

Although vocational identities become increasingly stable and career stories become more coherent from late adolescence forward, providing some continuity in choice and adjustment, occupational plots and career themes do evolve and may change with time and experience as the situations in which people live and work change [*Prop-*

osition 40]. In responding to changes and challenges prompted by developmental tasks, occupational transitions, and work troubles, autobiographical authors re-conceptualize occupational plots and extend or amend career themes to redirect or revise their career stories in ways that reintegrate self, revitalize vocational identity, and rebuild work roles [*Proposition* 41]. An elaborated or revised story meant to direct transition to a new scene, episode, or chapter in a career is both *constructed by* the person and *constructive of* future behavior [*Proposition* 42]. Re-storied narratives empower individuals as motivated agents to make choices and adapt to changing career contexts and occupational situations [*Proposition* 43].

Fostering Career Construction by the Actor, Agent, and Author

As described in this chapter, CCT presents a set of principles that purport to explain and predict a number of interrelated phenomena concerning vocational behavior and its development. The theory is accompanied by a counseling discourse that concentrates on vocational behavior, occupational strivings, and career explanations relative to vocational development tasks, occupational transitions, and work troubles (Savickas, 2019). I use the term "counseling discourse" instead of "counseling theory" to indicate a focus on practice-based knowledge and observable outcomes not measurement, prediction, and experimentation. As a disciplinary discourse, Career Construction Counseling (CCC) provides language and definitions for speaking and writing about career practices, paradigms for thinking about client issues, and methods for encouraging clients to resolve their concerns.

CCC differs from the two main interventions of the 20th century, namely vocational guidance (Parsons, 1909) that matches social actors to occupational groups whom they resemble and career education (Super, 1954) that teaches motivated agents adaptability strategies and adapting responses for coping with developmental tasks and occupational transitions (Savickas, 2015a). In marked contrast to vocational guidance and career education, career construction dialogues focus on individual uniqueness to prompt autobiographical authors to reflexively transform career themes and extend their occupational plots by identifying fitting settings, possible scripts, and future scenarios [Proposition 44]. Thus, CCC aims to move clients beyond the reflection involved in guidance to a reflexivity that enables them to reconstruct their career stories and more intentionally use work roles to elaborate their life themes. CCC discourse proposes that vocational guidance and career education foster *retrospective reflection* within one's current perspective that can lead to small first-order change; whereas career construction dialogues foster *prospective reflexivity* from new perspectives that can lead to transformative second-order change (Fraser & Solovey, 2007) [Proposition 45]. A textbook (Savickas, 2019) and practice manual (Savickas, 2015b) provide more information about the CCC model, methods, and materials.

Conclusion

Career Construction Theory presents a connected set of terms and statements that constitute a way of thinking and talking about careers in the 21st century. Appendix A lists the three premises and 45 propositions that constitute the theory. They systematize, in a formal and functional manner, knowledge about how individuals make themselves and build their careers in cultural and social contexts. In particular, the theory explains the interpretive and interpersonal processes through which individuals organize themselves, impose direction on their vocational behavior, and make meaning of their careers. As agents acting in and on the world, individuals manage their motivation and position themselves as social actors in work roles that match their occupational characteristics and implement their vocational self-concepts. Responding to changes occasioned by vocational development tasks, occupational transitions, and work troubles, individuals reflexively revise their career stories as they reposition themselves in new work roles. Following this introduction to Career Construction Theory, the next chapter describes the methods and materials used in a multiple case study that examined and explicated the theory in the work lives of four men.

CHAPTER TWO
Career Construction Case Study Methods

The multiple case study research reported herein investigated the model of career construction, a theory of vocational behavior and development (Savickas, 2002, 2013). The case studies of four individuals illustrate how the processes and products of self-organizing attachment, self-regulating adaptability, and self-conceiving identity contribute to career construction. The cases also highlight the basic tenet in career construction theory, namely that the formation of interests and implementation of choices emerge through turning preoccupations to occupations, a transformation that enables individuals to actively master what they once passively suffered. Insight into this core principle of career construction was made possible by using a prospective research design that disclosed how preoccupations formed early in life led in adulthood to occupational choices and work adjustments. The life histories presented in this book clearly portray how the developmental trajectory from symptom to strength plays a large part in shaping lives and constructing careers.

In viewing the participants' lives from the perspective of Career Construction Theory, my goal was to use the case studies for expository and didactic purposes; not to validate, but to illustrate, explain, and demonstrate theorems in the Career Construction Theory. Furthermore, I hoped to infer new hypotheses from case studies if they introduced exceptions or discrepancies to some theorem that was otherwise well supported.

The Importance of Case Studies

While career theories comprehend vocational behavior using general concepts, no real understanding of careers is possible without knowledge of specific instances. If we assume that both the abstract and concrete are important in advancing the science of careers, then it follows that case studies, which get their validity from particulars, should be routinely used in vocational research. Unfortunately, most of the research in vocational psychology systematically evaluates the thoughts and behaviors of individuals with quantitative methods that artificially dismember the participants and result in studying variables not individuals. Quantitative methods conceptualize individuals as a constellation of distinct sociological and psychological characteristics that can be meaningfully related to a wide variety of vocational behaviors. Findings from such studies report correlation coefficients between two variables; for example self-efficacy and interests or adaptability and identity. Despite the generally low to moderate correlation coefficients between the variables, investigators are often satisfied with the results as long as the correlations are statistically significant. Researchers tend to avoid discussing the meaningfulness of the results and overlook the variance unaccounted for by the correlations.

Despite these delimitations, studies that quantify individual differences have been extremely useful in providing normative data about groups of individuals and for constructing inventories to measure how individuals compare to norm groups. Nevertheless, attention to the individual participants as unique composites of social and psychological characteristics, the sum of which cannot possibly account for individuals' particular responses to their environments, is forfeited in favor of an almost exclusive regard for the variables. It is this deficiency which prompted Henry Murray (1938) to insist that people be studied as living wholes.

The importance of studying individuals themselves rather than individual difference variables was first articulated by Stern (1911) in his classic book entitled *Methodological Foundations of Differential Psychology*. Stern distinguished between the *individual differences* focus on quantitative study of individuals' attributes and the *individuality* focus on the qualitative study of individuals themselves. For Stern (1911), quantitative studies result in knowledge of no one. As Lamiell (2003) later elaborated, individual difference variables are differences not persons. In comparison, qualitative methods applied in case studies concentrate on an individual as a whole, rather than on variables as parts. As a qualitative method, case studies represent an equally important approach to investigating careers and testing theories. When conducted with precision and rigor, case studies add an important complementary counterpart, not merely a supplemental addition, to studying the statistical significance of differences between group means. Systematic attention to the behavior and psychological life of individuals can illuminate the group differences that have been found or help to explain the lack of significant findings. Furthermore, case studies can often be far more fruitful than actuarial approaches in introducing modifications to a conceptual framework. In the case studies of career construction presented herein, I used narrative interviews to produce portraits of individuals studied as living wholes.

Life Portraits

Life portraiture is a qualitative methodological approach for composing a written narrative that describes, interprets, and analyzes a phenomena -- such as career -- based on systematic observations, interviews, and other data (Lawrence-Lightfoot & Hoffman Davis, 1997). The narrative portraits in the present book capture each participant's career experiences in a form that tells a credible and coherent story without imposing false consistency. In the life portraits, I sought to record the perspectives and experiences of the participants to document their lives and careers in social and cultural context. The portraits emerged from dialogues with the participants that negotiated the shape of the discourse. The interview transcripts were transformed into portraits that incorporated the two forms of narratives defined by Stalker (2009). The first-order or ontological narratives place the participants in the dominant position as they tell their life story. Being granted the privilege and responsibility of retelling the participants' stories, I have tried my best to respect their intentions in telling their stories. Accordingly, the portraits in the present book include many verbatim quotations that document how participants' voiced key life experiences. The second-order or epistemological narratives place researchers in a dominant position as they convey a story they wish to tell about a particular social order, in this case career. Following the advice of Eudora Welty (1998), I did not listen to a story, I listened for a story as formed by the particular constructs, relevant issues, and theoretical dimensions behind my questions. Combining ontological and epistemological narratives enabled me to compose rich and compelling portraits of career construction in a particular place and time.

Each of the four case studies in this volume begins with a "life portrait" that recounts a character sketch of the participant drawing upon his own statements for illustration whenever appropriate. The life portraits eschew diagnosis and interpretive analysis, instead they present, relatively completely and without comment, accounts of the participants' lives and careers. Separating a life portrait from its subsequent interpretive analysis and psychometric data allows readers and researchers to apply their preferred conceptual model for comprehending vocational behavior and work adjustment. I believe important things can be learned from each case, and as a collection they can lead to better understanding of any career theory. To this end, academics may demonstrate career theories for graduate students by using the life portraits as teaching cases, either through didactic lecturing or discovery learning.

While my first perspective in writing the life portraits was to present *intrinsically interesting* biographies, I had the second goal of viewing the cases from an *instrumental* perspective to generalize beyond the case itself. From this extrinsic perspective, I sought to illustrate and examine how well Career Construction Theory could comprehend individual careers. Each life portrait provided an empirical instance of career construction across the life course. Connecting the particulars of a case to Career Construction Theory concepts and theorems helped to understand something more general as I explored and interrogated the theory. Following the presentation of each life portrait, I present my analyses and interpretations of the portrait with accompanying psychometric data. Thus the second half of each chapter considers the participant's career constructing processes of self-organizing, self-regulating, and self-conceiving. Following McAdam's (2013) framework of selfhood, I then view career constructions in each participant's life portrait through the lenses of interpersonal relationships and personal dispositions as a social actor, regulatory focus and adaptability resources as a motivated agent, and reflexive deliberation and identity composition as an autobiographical author.

In the final chapter, I consider the collection of four instrumental case studies to further understand the types of careers that each participant represented and to broaden construal of career construction and vocational behavior. This *collective* perspective on the cases sought to extract themes from the cases and examine theorems in Career Construction Theory. Taken together, the intrinsic, instrumental, and collective perspectives on the cases (Stake, 1994) maximized the contributions of this project.

Methods

The Participants

Anticipating the great investment of time and energy needed to conduct the case studies required careful selection of the participants for inclusion in the study. Age, race, sex, and cultural context were held constant given the small number of participants that could be reasonably included. The participants selected were all White males in the ninth grade. On the one hand, this was an advantage in easing case comparisons of the theoretical constructs. On the other hand, it was a disadvantage in preventing a deeper exploration of how culture, gender, and race influence career construction.

Eight boys whose vocational development profiles indicated different concepts in career theory were studied. The participants varied systematically in how they were coping with the tasks of vocational development during the early career exploration stage. Two boys demonstrated mature attitudes and competencies, two boys expressed unrealistic expectations, two boys experienced indecision, and two boys showed indifference. It was thought that each pair of case studies selected for intensive study could eventually enact different trajectories of career construction and thus lead to better understanding of the theoretical constructs which they represented, and might even generate further hypotheses about that construct. In due course, I determined that four of the eight participants had biographies that best illuminated the four major life-course trajectories in Career Construction Theory. While the remaining four cases were intrinsically interesting and told unique life stories, only one case from each of the companion pairs of cases was needed to illustrate CCT. Presenting the four companion cases would have reinforced concepts and conclusions but at the price of lengthening the manuscript with duplication and redundancy.

Jointly the four cases in the present book cover the four major life-course trajectories in career construction. The order of presentations for the case studies followed the continuum of attachment styles from secure to disorganized (Ainsworth & Bowlby, 1991). The first case presented shows secure-autonomous attachment; the second case illustrates anxious-ambivalent attachment; the third case represents dismissive-avoidant attachment; and, the fourth case illustrates fearful-disorganized attachment. I engaged in a minimal amount of explicit case comparison as I introduced each case, relying on the implicit comparisons evoked by the continuum of presentation. I waited until the final chapter to make some observations and generalizations from a collective perspective on the multiple case studies (Stake, 1994).

Procedures

The interviews were conducted and four life portraits written from the standpoint of Career Construction Theory (Savickas, 2002, 2013), with the goal of using the case studies for expository and didactic purposes to illustrate, explain, and demonstrate concepts and theorems in that theory. Within this organizing framework, the goal was to have participants, as much as possible, speak for themselves in describing important moments and issues in their lives and careers. Toward this end, the interview topics were "narrativized" (Holloway & Jefferson, 2000) as questions to invite participants to tell detailed stories about processes, experiences, and interpersonal relationships related to their careers. For example, rather than asking "Who were important people to you at that time in your life?" the question became an invitation to "Tell me about the important people to you in your life at that time." Then transforming the interview data into life portraits I did not just edit their statements, I selected material from several hundred pages of typescripts to emphasize points of my own choosing. So readers should consider this caveat -- the approach in this study was neither wholly atheoretical nor grounded. If the interviews and write-ups were conducted by a researcher with a different theoretical inclination, there would certainly be systematic differences between how the information was selected, solicited, organized, interpreted, and reported.

Interview Time Periods

The choice of when to interview the participants is an example of a choice influenced by theory not the participants themselves. Using Super's (1957) model of career stages and developmental tasks as the general framework for the investigation functioned to highlight pivotal inflection points in the participants' vocational development. These predictable periods of transition guided selection of the ages at which the participants were interviewed. Thus the five career stages of growth, exploration, establishment, maintenance, and decline had their principal value in initially deciding when to interview participants as well as later organizing into plausible form the case material regarding vocational choice and work adjustment. This form enabled a clearer view of the dialectics of development, focusing especially on how predictable discontinuities in adaptation prompt new activities and produce novel results. The present study addressed the developmental tasks in each of Super's (1957) five career stages in more or less detail. Growth was represented only to the extent that it was viewed in retrospect by the participants and reported by their parents. Exploration, establishment, and management were documented in great detail. Deceleration, retirement planning, and retirement living were described to the degree that each individual had engaged in these tasks. At the completion of this project, some participants were just beginning to decelerate while others had been living in retirement for several years.

Data Collection

Each participant was first interviewed when he was in the ninth grade (ages 14-15). There were a total of four interviews covering, in turn, the topics of free-time activities, school experiences, family relationships, and career plans. Each interview lasted an hour. Due attention was paid to social determinants and cultural context including family expectations, school problems, relationships between parents, and interactions with mother, father, siblings, and peers. These determinants were highlighted because personal preoccupations are formed and maintained in the interpersonal matrix of the family and then elaborated in the broader social context of the neighborhood and school. While most of the questions inquired about contemporaneous events, several were directed at eliciting reports of growth stage experiences. This retrospective data was important in understanding childhood as an apprenticeship during which each participant formed a blueprint for his life. As a whole, the interview data provide an opportunity to consider the evolution of self, first as a social actor and then as a motivated agent.

Interviews with each boy's parents were conducted in their homes while the boys were ninth graders. The parents' backgrounds were also explored, and consideration was given to their influence on the lives of those who may at first glance appear so distant from them. The interviews of parents revealed the charactcristics and quality of those highly significant relationships. Parental contributions to the young person's self-image and his interpersonal style as an actor on the social stage were evident throughout the study.

In addition to the interviews, each participant completed a battery of aptitude tests, interest surveys, and personality inventories while he was in the ninth grade. The instruments in the assessment battery were selected both to measure parameters of the person which are not as well assessed in interview and to provide quantitative data to compare a participant's responses to those provided by various norm groups. The set of measures included the *Differential Aptitude Tests, Kuder Preference Record-Vocational Form CH, Nelson-Denny Reading Test, Otis Quick-Score Intelligence Test, Rotter Incomplete Sentence Blank* with the addition of 17 stems designed to obtain work-oriented responses, *Strong Vocational Interest Blank-Revised, Test of Mechanical Comprehension, Thematic Apperception Test*, and *Work Values Inventory*. Each of the psychometric and projective measures used in the study are described at the end of this book in Appendix B.

The participants were next interviewed intensively three years later when they were high school seniors (age 17-18). They again completed the *Rotter Incomplete Sentence Blank*, the *Thematic Apperception Test*, and the *Work Values Inventory*. Next, they were followed-up at age 21 when they answered questions about their careers. They were interviewed again at age 25, or seven years out of high school. They were contacted briefly every two years thereafter, and then interviewed extensively at age 35. Once again, they completed the *Rotter Incomplete Sentence Blank*, *Thematic Apperception Test*, and the *Work Values Inventory*.

At age 38, each participant was interviewed for about four hours. The semi-structured interview dealt with a wide range of experiences from childhood to adulthood in an attempt to determine what life had been like for them; relationships that had been important to them; goals that emerged over time; significant moments in life, and plans for the future. In addition to the interview, the participants completed the *Minnesota Multiphasic Personality Inventory*-2 and the *Dynamic Personality Inventory*. The participants were next surveyed when they were 50 years old, intensively interviewed for the last time at age 54, and contacted for a final time at age 59.

At the final interview, each man was reminded of what he had previously reported about himself. An attempt was to get caught up-to-date, usually over several hours and occasionally followed by a conversation with the man's spouse. The men were each asked to review the decisions they had made; describe the experiences that they believed had defined their lives; discuss what they had appreciated, regretted, and resented; identify the significant people in their lives; trace the course of their physical and mental health; delineate their daily routines; note any significant shifts in their attitudes or priorities; explain to what they look forward; discuss any special challenges or opportunities they anticipated; reveal their misgivings and fears about the future; consider what they would do differently if they had life to live over again; and share the advice they would give to others regarding how to live a life. In the end, the interview transcripts, scores on tests and inventories, responses to projective techniques, ratings on indices of career adaptability, and judgments made of vocational behaviors all provided the kind of information needed to fully describe a participant's style of functioning and for a complete elucidation of his career.

Composing Life Portraits

Throughout each interview, the participants were encouraged to tell their stories in their own way. Some sense of their being can be gleaned from how they composed their stories and arranged their telling. Thus, in writing a life portrait for each participant, I present abundant samples of the individual's own statements, highlighted with italics, so that a reader may consider the words that participants chose to create their character as well as the setting in which that character moved. After the first draft of a life portrait had been written, each participant reviewed the material to correct any erroneous impressions and revise the portrait to their satisfaction. Each participant was also asked to make any changes needed to assure himself that he would not be recognizable by others and that none of the information would be harmful to either himself or his family. The directions given by each participant for making deletions, corrections, and revisions were scrupulously executed. The participant then again gave permission to use the material. I did not change any of the psychometric data because it included no identifying information.

The identities of the participants have been and remain a secret. The portraits present life histories in which I have had to make changes to protect the identities of the participants. When needed to conceal a participant's identity, I made symbolically equivalent substitutes for aspects of a participant's identity and life circumstances. In their life portraits, the disguise is deep, penetrable only by the participants. The disguises would be defeated by explaining precisely how they were done. Without going into great and unreasonable detail, suffice it to state that I changed identifiable facts, yet I did not alter the basic anchoring elements nor the larger truths. The substance of the life portraits remains reliable and accurate. In short, objective facts revealing participants' identities may have been altered yet the life portraits convey narrative truth that remains faithful to a participant's life story. Any readers who believe they recognize one the participants will, I am certain, be mistaken.

In composing the life portraits, I remained sensitive to the ethical, legal, and moral lines between facts and fabrications (Sperry, Hartshorne, & Watts, 2010). There are no exaggerations nor falsifications for the sake of the story nor the theory. Nothing, even minor or unimportant, was made-up to enhance credibility nor trustworthiness. Of course, readers may question the veracity of the life portraits. In response to such concerns, Menkel-Meadow (2000) suggested that readers accept three assumptions. First, accept that the author composed the life portraits ethically and effectively. Second, assume that you can generate useful and generalizable ideas from the life portraits. And finally, believe that you can learn something more or something different from life portraits than from abstract theorems or empirical research. So what might be learned that is "more or different"? Well, reading a life portrait may confirm what you already know and heighten awareness about a general principle. Or, it might challenge some principle you hold dear, encouraging you to reinterpret it and broaden your perspective. A close reading could suggest inadequacies in a current theory and illuminate some abstract concepts with concrete instantiations. And finally, the case studies may suggest some new paths of inquiry. I invite you as reader to interrogate the stories for what you can learn from them about Career Construction Theory as well as your own favorite theory.

Analyses

Each case analysis includes the nomothetic measures of individual differences as well the ideographic assessments of individuality. After presenting each life portrait, I identify dispositional personality characteristics and then trace their expression in work roles and career construction. To aid identification of personality characteristics, I used objective inventories and projective techniques. To aid identification of career themes, I used ability tests, interest inventories, and value surveys. In the final chapter, I used each of the four cases to explore the basic premises of Career Construction Theory. In addition, I described how each of the four participants organized his life around a problem that preoccupied him and solutions that occupied him. I also considered the effectiveness of a technique for revealing career themes, namely drawing a career construction line from childhood memories through adolescent role models to adult occupations. In this way, I traced the trajectory of how each participant brought his inner world into relation with the outer world -- first in play, then through hobbies, and finally at work.

Conclusion

I remain deeply grateful to the four men who bravely and forthrightly shared their life stories for the advancement of career theory and practice. As the participants narrate their own stories, concentrate on how their perceptions of themselves and of others reveal conflicts and adjustments which were sometimes altered yet which more often persisted over time. The continuous process of choices, prompted by internal and external demands, together with their vocational consequences, will be reviewed. I will trace how fantasies become transformed into highly tentative aspirations and then into more realistic occupational goals. I will discuss how roles are tried out and then modified or rejected entirely as unsuitable for future functioning. The dialectic of activity and feedback, which ushers in new and ever-evolving forms of synthesis, will be examined. I will describe efforts which brought them success and satisfaction or failure and frustration, and how these experiences form the basis of new decisions and further effort. Examples related to the theoretical propositions will be identified and their interrelationships clarified. And finally, various aspects of an individual's own story will be further illuminated by test scores and their changes over time. In the end, I hope that these life portraits will illuminate how the self-constructing processes and contents of (a) social actors' self-organizing attachment schemas and dispositional strategies, (b) motivated agents' self-regulating motivational schemas and adaptation strategies, and (c) autobiographical authors' self-conceiving reflexivity schemas and identity strategies contribute to career construction as well as provide clear examples of how individuals may use work to actively solve problems in growing up and functioning effectively in adulthood.

Each of the following four chapters presents a case study that illustrates a participant's stable trajectory of career construction, without rotation of later conceptual templates. This stable framing of life histories enables readers to view each participant's trajectory as they move along one of four major pathways mapped by the foundational matrix of agentic individuation and communal integration. Figure 8 on the next page traces the four major trajectories of career construction schemas and strategies traversed by each of the participants as described in the following four chapters.

Figure 8. Four Major Trajectories of Career Construction Schemas and Strategies

Chapter 4 Robert's Trajectory	Chapter 5 William's Trajectory	Chapter 6 Paul's Trajectory	Chapter 7 Fred's Trajectory
Secure-Autonomous	Anxious-Ambivalent	Dismissive-Avoidant	Fearful-Disorganized
Alpha	Beta	Gamma	Delta
Promotion + Prevention	Prevention	Promotion	Amotivation
Integrative Coping	Adjustive Looking Ahead	Adjustive Looking Around	Maladaptive Fragmenting
Autonomous	Communicative	Meta-	Fractured
Pathmaker	Guardian	Searcher	Drifter

CHAPTER THREE
The Drive of a Pathmaker

Three interwoven processes for career construction are the social actor's attachment schema and dispositional personality strategies, the motivated agent's regulatory schema and adaptability strategy, and the autobiographical author's reflexive schema and identity strategy. As you read this chapter from the perspective of Career Construction Theory, recognize how Robert's *secure attachment schema* enabled him as a social actor to organize and maintain the strategies of an *extroverted, norm-accepting personality disposition*. As a motivated agent who blended *promotion* and *prevention schema* to set and pursue self-realization goals, he made vocational choices and work adjustments with *integrative adaptation strategies*. As an autobiographical author, Robert deliberated with *autonomous schema* to conceive a *Pathmaker's vocational identity* and compose a coherent career story. Now consider the details of how Robert Coyne's congruent career began with antecedents of family contentment and ended with consequent success, satisfaction, and stability.

PART I

A Life Portrait of Robert Coyne:
The Child is Father to the Man

Although Robert is a prosperous business executive, highly regarded by his peers in the community, his employees, and his many friends and acquaintances, this would be hard to tell by his demeanor. Now in his early 60s, there is nothing about him that smacks of pomposity, nothing about his clothes or his posture or those telltale little gestures that speak volumes about what we think our status entitles us to, nothing to suggest that he may set himself apart from others. Success wears well on him, and perhaps his ease with it accounts for his accomplishments. It also probably helps that his work is an extension of whom he is as a human being, entirely congruent with his deepest needs and interests, and that the time he devotes to it appears limitless. While a superficial view of the amount of time and energy he devotes to his profession might lead the casual observer to conclude that Robert is a workaholic, the essential ingredient of that syndrome is markedly absent. Here is no desperate man. We find in him not a hint of the insecurity that drives others who only apparently resemble him in their preoccupation with work. His successes have not come at the expense of others. His pride has not been gained through the humiliation of others. His sense of worth has not been derived from ruthless competition with those who would be his rivals. There are no inner demons to be projected onto and battled against in the work environment. At peace with himself, Robert has remained through the years largely peaceful with those with whom he does business, and at the end of the working day he can sleep the sleep of those who have meant no harm to anyone during their waking hours.

Family

Robert's vocational identity and career manifest his parent's values and teachings. His mother, Mary, did not remember her place of birth in Ireland, yet would never forget what it was like to live and work on soil not much different from the small plot of ground that had been worked by her immigrant parents, and their parents and grandparents before them. Farming, whether in Ireland or Ohio, involves the same backbreaking tasks, the same resignation to hardship without complaint, and the ability to be grateful for surviving another season. After finishing the seventh grade, better educated than either her mother or her father, Mary had to stay at home to help in the fields and in the house as well as augment her parents' meager income through housework for prosperous families. She made 25 cents an hour by working on her hands and knees to clean floors. As far as her parents were concerned, it was always *work and bring home the money*.

There was no time for frivolity; dances and even birthday parties were out of the question. Dates with boys were begrudged and supervised to a discouraging extent. Piano lessons were considered a useless luxury by a mother who never learned to do anything other than farm work, yet Mary defied this particular injunction by going to a girlfriend's home where she learned notes and various scales, and actually learned how to play the piano. Frustrated by her parents' harsh restrictions and keenly aware of a potential for something more and better than she had been allowed, Mary escaped these particular circumstances in the only way she could. At the age of 19, she married a man with an almost identical background.

Robert's father, Patrick, was the son of Irish immigrants whose farm could not provide the wherewithal for him to continue his schooling beyond the seventh grade. Patrick had wanted to be a railroad engineer, but his parents would not consent because they needed him on the farm. He remained working on the farm until, early in his marriage, he rented his own farm for a while and then, at Mary's urging, went to work in a machine shop. After fourteen years, during which his wife had to go back to doing housework to put the children through school, he heard about a better paying job in a furniture factory and decided to take it. He spent the rest of his working life as a furniture assembler, until the plant closed, putting 200 employees out of work. During his 14 years making furniture, Patrick never established a secure position nor stable routine. He was laid off repeatedly, for as long as six months at a time, when furniture sales slowed. Patrick worked swing shifts that kept him from spending as much time with the family as he would have liked. Although he earned enough income to allow Mary to work only part-time, she often disparaged furniture assembly as not a trade and the factory as a place where Patrick could not learn anything new. Nevertheless, he liked his work. Having little education and living in a community without much work for semi-skilled employees, Patrick had few options. During an interview, he frequently said he told his son that he would never get very far unless he had an education and that he shouldn't quit school the way he did. Although he was hardly able to help his son make sense of things at school or to help with schoolwork, Patrick maintained his influence. Years later his son recalled him as big and stern. Robert remembered that his father spoke with authority, and his word was the law as far as Robert was concerned. If he told Robert to do something, he did it.

It was Patrick who decided where the family would take their occasional automobile trips. He decided that Robert would attend parochial school, where the teaching nuns would demand no less of his son than he did himself. Always a hard worker, he expected the same of his son and would not permit him to waste time. Homework had to be done before anything else. Yet, he was more than a taskmaster. In his spare time, Patrick would work with his son cultivating the family garden. Although he was 45 years old when Robert was born, Patrick always took an interest in his son's hobbies. Beyond encouragement, he had little specific comment to offer about his son's academic activities or future educational plans, and could not afford to pay college tuition for Robert. Nevertheless, their warm relationship and the example of a man who tries his best against difficult odds made Robert's father a significant figure in his son's life, responsible in no small measure for what Robert would eventually become.

Perhaps even more influential was Robert's mother, 43 years old when he was born and already the mother of two grown children. Robert remembered her as a very hardworking person, always cleaning and baking. When she was not working at home where her vacuuming would lull him to sleep, she took her little boy with her to housecleaning jobs where, as he grew older, he would lend her a hand in whatever he could do. As a ninth-grader, Robert described his mother as just as good a person as you would want anybody to be. At age 35, he reported,

> She was a good mother. She loved me, was interested in me, took good care of me. In fact, if there were one word, I'd use to describe her it would be "caring." She cared about my feelings, about whether I was happy or not, whether or not I was enjoying school. She wanted me to get ahead, to have things she never had herself.

Unlike Patrick, Mary discussed Robert's educational and vocational plans with him, and even tried unsuccessfully to help him with his homework, all the while warning him not to become like his father or his older brother. She kept telling him to try to go as far as he possibly could. Their warm and very close relationship was accompanied by her example of a person whose kindness and sociability won many friends.

Whatever Mary's social skills and interests, they were probably made even more apparent to a son whose bashful father did not talk much and stayed home most of the time. She encouraged Robert to attend dances, participate in sports, and work part-time jobs. She was eager for him to experience a freedom she never enjoyed as well as to fulfill a potential she believed was untapped in herself. She acted as a buffer between him and his father, who had come to terms more easily with life's limitations and who was more anxious to preserve the little that had been meted out to him. While Robert's father kept making sure all the lights were turned off and the door to the refrigerator was closed, his mother was determined that her son have a set of encyclopedias, although she could hardly afford them.

One person in the family who could do more than wish Robert an education was his sister Julie. She had graduated from high school before Robert was born, and when he was four years old, she married a college graduate and moved away from the family. When Robert was in the seventh grade, Julie and her husband moved back in town, purchasing a house on the same block as her parents. During these years, Julie worked as a bookkeeper and cost analyst at a manufacturing firm. In the evenings, she helped Robert with his homework. She was familiar with all the subjects that he was taking and *would sit down with me a couple of hours to help me out.* She was very meticulous and never hurried. Robert thinks that she was in large part responsible for establishing his pattern of *trying to do a better than average job in anything I did.* He also came to share her interest in details and in *having everything be very exact.*

Robert's older brother played a different role, yet also an important one. Robert was only three years old when Gary quit high school to join the Army. Robert can still remember the day Gary left to go to the induction center. During the four years that he served in active duty, Gary maintained contact with his little brother through letters and pictures. Upon his return, Gary married and began work as a plumber and, when laid off, as a truck driver. Gary regularly visited the household although he was living elsewhere with his new wife. Robert felt that Gary cared about him and was especially interested in his sports activities. Robert's satisfaction with his older brother was supported further by other images of him at that time. As a child, Robert viewed Gary as *a hard worker who did not mess around if something had to be done. Furthermore, he stood on his own, nobody pushed him around.* Robert also viewed Gary as *fair*. Only later would Robert come to quite different opinions of an older brother who, *after killing so many soldiers in Viet Nam*, was never quite the same as the big brother he knew in early childhood.

Robert has fond memories of those early years. He remembers the very modest house in which they lived, the front room where his father would sit in his overstuffed chair and read the newspaper, the kitchen where his mother cooked and baked on an old stove, his parents' bedroom with a picture of Jesus surrounded by palms hanging on the wall, his own bedroom with its big box of toys as well as a statue of the Virgin Mary. He remembers feeling especially close to his parents. They would talk to him about current events and seldom, if ever, leave him alone. Having crackers and soup with his mother at noon is just one of many fond memories he has of that time, marred only by his sense that his parents both had to work too hard for too little in return. Later in life, he commented that *things were never handed to them.* They worked hard and got little for it. *They never had a heck of a lot.*

Career Growth

Robert easily made the transition from home to the parochial school. The rosary which he and his parents recited at home was the same. His teachers, striking in their black habits, demanded the same respect which his father had always required of him. He found ways of being helpful to the nuns as he had always been to his mother. He took charge of ordering the milk and collecting the money, making sure to account for everything. He helped decorate the classroom at Christmas time and for special events he made posters and set up chairs in the auditorium.

Robert earned excellent grades. Also, he thrived in the competitive atmosphere where if you did something outstanding you won a prize or had your name written on the bulletin board. Although his parents were occasionally displeased by a less than excellent grade and would ask if Robert's older sister could help him, they were happy with their son's performance. In addition to pleasing his parents with superior report cards, he enjoyed the respect of his classmates. He had many friends with whom he would play touch football after school or invite them home for supper. Later he earned their respect for his performance on the basketball court as well as on the baseball field. Sports were his way of being competitive. If he would be behind in the early innings, he would just try harder to come back.

Career Exploration

Robert entered high school well-prepared. The eight years he had spent in parochial school provided him with a host of successful experiences. Although his parents had been unable to help him with his homework, he believed that even this tended to make him more independent academically than he might otherwise have been. Besides, there was always his mother's interest in his school performance and, later, the help that his sister and brother-in-law were willing to give when he needed it. His name appeared regularly on the school honor roll, providing assurance that he could excel. Surrounded by friends who admired him as a person as well as for his athletic ability, Robert could look forward to further satisfactions in the contacts he would make and the activities he would pursue during his high school years. If Robert figured he had it made, no one acquainted with his circumstances at that time would question his conclusion.

Robert's high school years, however, turned out to be quite different from what he or others might have predicted. First, he found that, compared to parochial school, the public high school had a whole different atmosphere and classroom climate. It lacked strict discipline and the teachers were less watchful than the vigilant nuns. *Students could goof off if they wanted to do so*. Although Robert never played hooky and was no trouble to his teachers, he did spend less time on his schoolwork, becoming much more involved with sports and socializing. The result was only half-way decent grades, precluding any membership on the honor roll. His average marks barely kept him in the top third of his class. More than anything else he enjoyed playing baseball and basketball, having a nice time with his friends, and serving as the treasurer for his homeroom. Despite the fact that his extracurricular involvements cost him the grades to which he had always been accustomed, as a freshman he could still report good marks in algebra and in mechanical drawing. By his senior year he had continued to do well in science and mathematics. He looked forward to eventually attending an engineering school, where he would prepare himself for a career in electrical or civil engineering.

Although his parents were unable to save for their son's college education, a fact that somewhat dampened Robert's view of the future, he was reasonably confident that he could earn a scholarship on the strength of his grades and perhaps even his athletic ability. That confidence was short-lived, however. His relatively poor grades, the result of his gradual disengagement from academic pursuits during his high school years, did not qualify him to enter a university. The explanation for the change in Robert's circumstances during his high school years was no mystery to him. At age 40, he recalled:

> *My biggest problem was with my own home. My brother and his wife broke up, leaving my mother to take care of their three kids and his wife. She was too old to understand the kids even though she tried. She just couldn't cope. I'd help babysit from time to time, did a lot of the shopping for the household, and I'd often pick the kids up from school with the family car, but none of it did much good. With seven people in the house there was all kinds of noise and havoc. We were so crowded that we had to eat in shifts. The whole atmosphere changed. My parents were weighed down with problems they couldn't handle It changed the opinion I had of my brother. I just couldn't stand his "I don't care" attitude and the fact that he was going out with other women instead of helping out at home.*

With his family in an uproar, unable to study in these new surroundings, upset by his inability to improve a situation of someone else's making, worried about his parents and disillusioned by an older brother whom he had always respected, Robert dealt with the crisis by withdrawal. Because he could not cope with it, he got out of the house. During his senior year in high school, he hardly ever went home, preferring to stay with friends or at his sister's house.

The upheaval at home would have telling effect on his future. If things had been different, perhaps he would have tried less to lose himself in sports activities, although Robert attributed this more to his growing realization that his parents would not be in a position to help him pay for college regardless of his academic achievements. Perhaps his sister, if not burdened by helping their mother with the kids, would have had more time to attend to his academic work as she had done in the past. Perhaps the comfort he had always known in his parental relationships would have made it less necessary to become so deeply involved with a girlfriend that he put this relationship before all but his athletic pursuits. Perhaps even more disabling was the worrying he did about the plight of his parents, especially his mother, and the fact that there was so little he could do to remedy the situation. He just did not understand what was happening. He felt as if he should do something, but did not know what to do.

The climax of those painful years came much later, five years after Robert was out of high school. One Saturday morning, he was told that his mother, who by then suffered from depression, had died from a stroke. He deeply regretted not visiting her more during the previous year. His mother's death was followed first by his father's death and then by his brother's death. These experiences, all in the same year, made an indelible impression that devastated him. However, Robert characteristically could still find a redeeming feature to these tragedies just as he had with respect to his parents' inability to help him in school, which had made him realize that you have to be on your own. He had always been given to understand that nothing would be handed to him on a silver platter and that the challenge of his life would consist of overcoming inevitable obstacles and that success could be measured by the extent to which he had come from behind to be victorious.

After graduating from high school, he managed to enroll in a pre-engineering program at the local community college where, again, there was more freedom than he would have liked because the faculty never pushed him. He earned good grades during the first three semesters of the Associate Degree program but did not graduate. Sports had been a priority, and even more importantly, he fell in love. Instead of going to the late-afternoon calculus class, he and his future wife would often take a ride or have a picnic. Despite his lack of attendance at class, he took and passed the final examination in calculus, only to be informed that his attendance was too poor for a passing grade, without which he could not get his degree. He had wanted very much to continue with engineering as his uncle had done many years before, so this turn of events depressed him. He blamed no one but himself, feeling that he had disappointed his parents, sister, and brother-in-law. It was a real shock to them. What he did not share with them was the thought of how things might have been different had life at home remained undisturbed during his high school years and had his parents' high aspirations for him been backed by financial resources.

Career Establishment

Thinking that he might be able to save enough money to carry through with engineering school, Robert took a job as a payroll clerk in small company. He learned too late that, based on his high marks in mechanical drawing at the local community college, a prestigious company had offered him a job in mechanical drafting. Quite by accident he received the letter three weeks after it had been sent, and by the time he reported for work his position had been filled by someone else. Undaunted by this new disappointment, Robert remained at his post as a payroll clerk and applied elsewhere for drafting positions, to no avail. It was during this time that he became engaged to his future wife and decided that whatever money he could save from his low-paying job would go toward his future home not for further education. Except for his low salary, he was not displeased with life as a payroll clerk where his attention to detail, his need to make things definite, and his willingness to work harder than the job required, stood him in good stead. He was curious about all aspects of his department's operations, and within two years he was given additional responsibilities, more challenging work to do, and regular, albeit modest, pay increases. He and his fiancée saved enough money to get married, and Robert's part-time job as a night auditor at a local hotel more than made up for the money his wife no longer earned after being laid-off from her job at a department store. For almost two years Robert's life remained unchanged, as he felt stuck in a rut and just surviving.

Robert was dissatisfied with his pay and was further disenchanted by the knowledge that other employees, with higher status and much more seniority, were hardly earning more. He also saw few chances for advancement, believing that he could not get a promotion unless someone died. An auditor whom Robert knew described his work to him, suggesting that it ultimately provides opportunities for an individual to enter higher-level positions in the accounting world. With that encouragement, and that of his father-in-law, Robert began studying accounting. For the next seven years he worked during the day and completed his C.P.A. training at night. Two years after beginning his accounting studies, he secured a full-time position as an accounts manager, which paid considerably more money than he had been earning as a payroll clerk. At the age of 25, Robert reported that he was doing something substantial, learning something new each day, and completing challenging projects. He especially liked the security which his new job provided.

> *Security means a lot to me. Security is one of the most important things, because it gives you a chance to plan for your future. I like to plan ahead and know that tomorrow I have just so much.*

Over the years Robert worked as hard as any of his peers, if not harder, attributing his success not only to his long-held belief that real effort is invariably rewarded but also to the controller to whom he reported. As was the case at home where his father's word was law and in parochial school where infractions of any rule were always punished, Robert thrived under a demanding mentor who taught him the ropes. Under his tutelage Robert became the department's rising star. Stressing the importance of *having a goal and always looking ahead downfield*, Robert's work and the manner in which it was done impressed the various executives with whom he came in contact. The one thing he did not like about his demanding schedule of work and study was the fact that he was seldom home, and with the birth of his son, his absences became increasingly intolerable. Although he had become an assistant controller, supervising many employees, he began to think in terms of an accounting position which would allow him an opportunity to enlarge the scope of his interests and activities which went far beyond the manipulation of financial figures. He looked for a new position with an opportunity to grow. Not surprisingly he was offered a number of jobs even before he completed his training as a C.P.A. yet Robert bid his time until the right job came along. And it did --- the vice-presidency of a small accounting firm in another state.

When interviewed at age 35, Robert had been there for a most enjoyable five years:

> *The president seldom tells me what to do, and he respects my opinions. Often an important client will call, and when the secretary asks whom he would like to talk, the president or me, the person will say it does not matter. I'm really looking forward to the presidency when he retires.*

Although he enjoyed the decisions that he must make after a careful consideration of all the facts involved, Robert relished even more the opportunity his work gave him to help people and to contribute to the well-being of the entire community. One would be hard put to disagree with the assessment he made of his situation.

> *I could sit with this firm for the rest of my life and continue to progress, both monetarily and socially. I'm objective. I never make a rash judgment. That's probably why I've made so few bad business decisions. At the office they call me "Mr. Cool." The other day my secretary said that if the place were burning down I'd calmly go out and find a fire extinguisher and put it out.*

Another asset was his genuine interest in people:

> *Whatever the situation, I try to help people. I'll pick up hitchhikers and stop to help people with flat tires. In the*

office, I talk to clients on their own level and make myself available to them, regardless of the size of their account.

In his early 40s, Robert's job, as vice-president of a successful accounting firm, allowed him to enjoy the home that he and his wife purchased at a modest price, remodeling and redecorating it over the years with his increasing income. Their improvements have included the addition of a great room, an outside deck, and a ceramic studio where his wife could turn clay into pottery and sculptures. He was proud of his wife's art work and the way she decorated their home with it. The two of them played tennis frequently, enjoyed swimming, and practiced yoga. Robert was especially pleased with his ten-year-old son, who had just earned his yellow belt in karate, was taking piano lessons, and entertained friends at their home. He spent a good bit of time with his son, and he was as much interested in the things his son did as he was in his work activity. The latter included his above-mentioned position, a stepping-stone to the presidency of an expanding institution, and with it a seat on the Board of Directors who did not disparage his relative youth but instead appreciated the respect he had earned in the community, where he served as a trustee of the local college and on the advisory committee of a local charity. Although Robert used much of his commuting time to mull over what the day would require of him and what remained to be done, he could not help but also savor the distance he had come. His conservative dress, his dignified manner, the positions of responsibility he enjoyed, and his entire style of life would make it difficult for an uninformed person to guess the nature of Robert's origins.

Career Management

At age 42, Robert became president of the firm. During the next decade he greatly expanded the firm's services and twice moved the firm into a bigger building. While adding contracts with larger companies, his firm continued to perform bookkeeping for small businesses and prepare tax returns for individuals. Under Robert's leadership, the firm's annual income had increased tenfold. His success brought tempting offers from highly prosperous financial institutions. He was chosen to represent his State accounting association at a meeting held halfway around the world with numerous world leaders in attendance. Closer to home, he was honored as Citizen of the Year. While the list of honors and accomplishments could be far extended, these were not the chief criteria by which Robert measured success. Rather, he believed that it is the grace with which people live their lives and the manner in which they relate to each other that determine the quality of life. While there are surely strategic elements in what Robert has emphasized throughout his life, the importance he assigned to service goes far beyond the prospect of personal fame and fortune. It permeated his human encounters in relationships chiefly marked by mutual respect.

Those who inhabited Robert's interpersonal environment were no strangers to these characteristics. It seemed as though no employee could fail to be impressed by his accessibility and by his interest in making his employees feel valuable.

> *I say hello to every employee. I know 'em by name. We would not have grown and become so successful without being sensitive to our people's needs and to how we interact with one another. I'm constantly going to different meetings. I go to manager meetings. I go to employee meetings. I can be on the agenda or not on the agenda. It doesn't matter. We have 48 employees, and any one of them can call me direct without going through my secretary. It's this kind of thing that probably accounts for our lack of turnover. Some of my janitors just call me Bob.*

The same spirit pervaded his relationship with the firm's board of directors.

> *They're not only my bosses, they're my friends. I can call any one of them during the day if they're in town or at their place of work and say, "What about this?" or "I need to get a fast approval on that, can we talk about it? Can you come down?" They're all able to converse with me.*

It was the same way with his clients:

> *I go to people's places of business and talk to 'em. They love that. I want to see what the business looks like. I want to see how they handle things. Are things in disarray or are they squared up nice and neat? You meet their bookkeeper. You meet their controller. It's on a first name basis. Most people call me Bob.*

Back inside the office building he was also careful not to appear remote. Instead of an office on the top floor where he could enjoy the view from the penthouse and perhaps impress his visitors with an unmistakable sign of his status, Robert was located on the third floor. Other executives have asked him why he didn't take the top floor. He told them that he did not want to be on the top floor because his clients might react negatively if he were to claim those perquisites upon which others of his rank insist. That's not what had made him successful. He explained that even when he played tennis or racquetball with clients, he never played during the day.

> *I don't want them to think of me as the stereotypical executive who's out on the golf course during the day, who's remote, who can't be bothered, who as much as says, "I'll meet with you when it's convenient for me." Besides, no big deals are made out on the golf course anyway!*

Concerns about his image could be found elsewhere:

> *I would never own a Cadillac. You don't need to ride around in a Cadillac. I drive a company car, a Buick. It does the job! I have peers whom I've grown-up in accounting with throughout the area who are what I call "big men on campus." I may call them, but they won't get back to me until it's convenient for them. They've got their Mercedes. Their wallets are stuffed with $100 bills. They wear gold chains. Sometimes one of their clients will tell me, "So-and-so is wearing so much gold, he can hardly stand up straight!"*

A principal message of Robert's, not lost on his employees, was that the client deserves the firm's respect, should never be treated in a cavalier fashion, and must be served beyond the call of duty, and far beyond what is customary among his competitors:

> *Service makes all the difference. Whatever the size of the account, the response time should be the same. It is important that we get right back to them. I tell my people, even if we're busy, call back everybody that you have a message to call, even if it's six o'clock and they're not there. Leave a message on their answering machine. Or if you catch them, they may say, "It's six o'clock. What are you still doing at the office?" That's service! And that's what separates one firm from another. It's the little things that clients remember. That is why we have more long-lasting clients than our competitors do. They can get hold of me or Ann or Shirley.*
>
> *I tell my people that you gotta treat people with respect. I have one vice-president who loves to be a big deal and put women down. The fact is half my accountants are women. They outshine the men by far, and I let them know that. They're more on the ball, more client-oriented. They want to do what's right. This fellow I'm telling you about might well have been my successor, but he'll never make it. We confronted him, and he changed his tune a little bit, but he's not going to change his inner feelings, so he lost his chance.*

At age 59, Robert stressed the importance of emotional intelligence for one who is in a position of authority, no matter the industry. The best leaders are those who are capable of empathy toward others, whether or not they are highly endowed with whatever it is that is measured by a typical IQ test. Those with emotional intelligence, probably Robert's forte, are capable of getting along with both those above and below them, fostering an interpersonal environment in which constructive feedback can be freely given, and inspiring in others a commitment to their common goals. Their relationships with others, at work and elsewhere, are marked by a mutual respect and caring that are at the foundation of any thriving enterprise.

In every realm of his life we find Robert attending to the welfare of others and indicating how important they are to him. For him, the accountant is somebody who is willing to listen to your problem, not one who deals with people on the basis of some black-and-white formula or policy. A special innovation of his was the firm's internship program for accounting students at the local college. There was the firm's sponsorship of an annual golf outing to benefit a local charity. There was the seed money the firm gave for a senior citizen project. According to Robert, service has become a lost art, but never to him. His promises were always kept. His word can be counted on. He stated that at the end of the day, his chief gratification consisted of having genuinely helped somebody.

It would appear that little has changed since his high school years when his classmates appreciated his friendliness. Another thing that has not changed very much is Robert's competitiveness, an asset to anyone in his particular field. He hates being *second in anything. If he gets beat in one game, he just tries harder the next game.* His present position involves competition with other accounting firms, and he can point with pride to the increase in his firm's profits during the time that he has been there. Attempting to understand his competitiveness and need to excel, he thinks it may have to do with the fact that

> *My parents had it very hard, had so little money, and I'm reaching out to attain something higher, to prove something to myself and maybe to them as well. I'd like to eventually become an authority in accounting, to help others out, to teach them some of the things I've picked up over the years.*

Apart from whatever accounting expertise he could surely share, more than anything else he would have others know and to act upon a dictum etched out by three decades of personal experience:

> *First you have to realize your limitations, whatever they happen to be. Then you have to try to improve on them. If you do this, you'll end up ahead of the game.*

Robert's style of conducting business is congruent with whom he is to the core, and probably began in the company of a deeply caring mother and encouraging father. He remains a man satisfied with how he has conducted himself in the work domain, where his interests and motivations are hardly distinguishable from the rest of his life experiences. He has steered a steady course. He has been a faithful steward. Little wonder that he concludes, *I think that most of my dreams have been fulfilled. Sometimes I'm even in awe of myself.* As well he should be.

PART II

The life portrait of Robert Coyne tells a complex story shaped by multiple influences and forces. In the second half of this chapter, I view the portrait from two different vantage points, first from the perspective of self-construction processes and content and then from the perspective of career construction processes and content.

Self-Construction

How did Robert construct a self that he himself liked? I address this question about self-construction -- or how he shaped who he was and what he became -- by examining the process and content of his self-making (Bruner, 2001). For my purposes herein, *self-constructing processes* broadly comprehended refer to *how* Robert shaped himself as a social actor, motivated agent, and autobiographical author. In comparison, *self-construction content* broadly comprehended refers to *who* Robert became in terms of enduring personal characteristics and motives. Before appraising Robert's personality and reputation, let us first consider the processes that he used to constitute himself.

Self-Construction Processes

Three interwoven processes for self-construction are the social actor's self-organizing, the motivated agent's self-regulating, and the autobiographical author's self-conceiving. As a preview, Robert's secure attachment schema and extroverted, norm-accepting orientation to relationships and rules inclined him to focus on needs for development and self-realization combining promotion and prevention strategies for integrative adapting that in due course sustained an autonomous reflexive schema and the vocational identity of a Pathmaker.

Social Actor. Many prominent psychologists (e.g., Bowlby, 1969, 1973; Maslow, 1955) have concluded that people have a number of fundamental needs, including those pertaining to growth and development as well as those pertaining to safety and protection. Infants and children obtain the nurturance and security required to meet these needs by establishing relationships with parents who support, encourage, protect, and defend them (Brockner & Higgins, 2001). Robert was fortunate in having a family who gratified his attachment needs for both nurturance and security, fostering what would remain in adulthood a relationship pattern in which he was secure in both his agentic independence and cooperative associations.

Perhaps the term that best applies to Robert is "nurturing." His family gave him what he needed to succeed in life. Robert gives what he got; he treats others as he had been treated. His parents were both nurturing and authoritative, exerting a moderate degree of control. Robert felt especially close to his parents who took an interest in him and his activities. He described his mother as *caring* and *very encouraging*. He had a warm relationship his with father whom he called a *guide*. He felt close to an older sister who was *very helpful* and an older brother who *cared* about him. In short, Robert experienced secure attachment relationships with parents who provided nurturance and security, with the subsequent benefits of high self-esteem, rewarding intimate relationships, strong social support, and effective communication skills. Having been held by a loving family, Robert as an adult knew how to hold others when they were in need.

Attachment theory has been promoted by some theorists as a broad theory of personality organization and intrapsychic structure (Shaver & Mikulincer, 2002). The secure attachment schema that Robert practiced in his family interactions shaped his psychosocial disposition and performing strategy as a social actor. During childhood, Robert's secure attachment enabled him to begin to develop a well-integrated personality structure and performing strategy. In Gough's (1990) cuboid model of personality dispositions, Robert resembles the Alpha type in being extroverted in interpersonal orientation and in accepting social norms and cultural values. He exemplifies the characterization of the Alpha disposition as ambitious, productive, goal oriented, task-focused, well-organized, forceful, and dominant (Domino & Domino, 2006; Gough, 1987). Robert usually displayed social poise and dealt effectively with frustration. Functioning at a high level of integration, he was able, as a company president, to fully realize his potential for leadership and management roles.

Motivated Agent. Robert's secure attachment schema supported the development of a strong self-regulation schema and a strategy that enabled him, as he matured, to direct his own thinking, emotions, and behavior towards both promotion and prevention goals. Although everyone is concerned at various times with both promotion and prevention strategies, most people display a predilection for one or the other. However, because promotion and prevention foci are conceptualized as being orthogonal rather than opposite modes of self-regulation (Higgins, 1997), it is possible for an individual to be simultaneously highly promotion-focused and highly prevention-focused (Florack, Keller, & Palcu, 2013). Robert is one of these promotion-prevention "hybrids" who displays double regulatory foci comprised of both positive and negative selves (Grant & Higgins, 2013). Launched by loving parents, he had developed this hybrid regulatory focus by combining his mother's promotion strategy with his father's prevention strategy. This double focus guided his self-advancement in safe ways, a combination that contributed to his high performance (Kurman & Hui, 2011). Robert's outstanding accomplishments and repeated success in diverse contexts coincide with Oyserman and Markus' (1990) explanation of how high levels of functioning may be facilitated by interrelating a positive possible self who one would like to become with a negative possible self who one fears becoming. Robert conceptualized a specific positive possible self that also included an outline of what one might do to avoid a negative possible self. The feared possible self of becoming like his father was motivationally beneficial as a negative representation of what could happen if Robert did not achieve the desired state.

Robert's approach of pursuing self-advancement in cautious ways contributed to his high performance. When Robert's context raised uncertainty or evoked a need to make a career decision, it activated Robert's hybrid focus on challenge and threat as he considered what he might gain and could lose. Robert's habitual preference in forming goals and making career choices effectively integrated his agentic independence and communal interdependence into a generativity that has been both productive and compassionate. On the one hand, he "stood out" by focusing on self-chosen goals that represented his aspirations for who he would like to be and how he would like to behave. On the other hand, he "fit in" by way of his rule-accepting disposition and empathy for others. His was a competiveness oriented to real personal growth and advancement as part of a community, not to a façade of success taken at the expense of others.

With a hybrid regulatory focus, Robert developed general resources that facilitated integrative adaptation. He looked ahead and looked around. In particular, he developed the career adaptability resources that he could engage to improve his career circumstances. When faced with a vocational development task or an occupational transition, Robert's regulatory focus and adaptive readiness motivated him to engage career adaptability resources and make integrative responses. Robert's adaptive readiness for forming his self-chosen goals engaged all four of the adaptability resources highlighted in career construction theory (Savickas, 2013). Regarding *concern* Robert explained that he had always looked ahead and was a downfield planner. He was hopeful and viewed life from a long-term future perspective. He showed *control* by being deliberate and conscientious in taking responsibility for his own future and concentrating on what he wanted to do. Robert demonstrated *curiosity* by engaging in exploration-in-breadth as he was open to many possibilities and searched for potential alternatives that fit his values, goals, and beliefs. Then in due course, he followed-up with exploration-in-depth by gathering pertinent information and talking with knowledgeable others to further evaluate his alternatives. Once Robert committed to an occupational goal, he expected to succeed and made plans that he confidently enacted, effectively solving problems along the way. He eagerly pursued his goals yet remained flexible and open-minded.

Autobiographical Author. Robert's regulatory focus in forming goals and an adaptation strategy for attaining those goals was enhanced by his autonomous reflexivity in conceiving a vocational identity and composing a career narrative. When faced with changes and choices, Robert prepared to act by engaging in purposeful, self-contained, and instrumental deliberation. Although he listened to advice given by his father and mentors, he did not necessarily act on it. Instead, Robert set and relentlessly pursued self-chosen goals after gathering relevant information, learning new things about himself, evaluating that information, making decisions, and forming plans. His reflexive deliberation led directly to action, without the need for validation by parents or other people. At the same time, Robert remained open to new ideas and alert for opportunities to implement his identity and revise his career story. He knew who he was and, even more importantly, how he became that way. Robert's goals gave direction to his life and provided long-term vision and short-term motivation. In this way Robert achieved a clear, stable, and coherent vocational identity, one befitting the career of the Pathmaker that he became. As Robert stated, *You have to look downfield and plan ahead ... I've always been a planner.*

Self-Construction Content

Setting goals and pursuing them with relentless drive have always been two of Robert's outstanding characteristics. In his system for teaching acting, Stanislavsky (1924) emphasized that each character in a play has an overall objective that conditions all of her or his behavior throughout the play. This super-objective welds together all aspects of the role, producing an integrated and purposeful identity (Levin & Levin, 1992). The super-objective is, in a sense, the modus vivendi or arrangement that one works out with life. Robert's three earliest recollections clearly show his modus vivendi. The first early recollection reveals his self-concept, the second early recollection explains his convictions about life, and the third early recollection summarizes how he has arranged the two to concentrate on a super-objective and thereby composed the central motif of his life. The three early recollection explain how Robert conceived himself, what life meant to him, and how he decided to conduct his life. Let us listen to Robert's life theme of goal directedness as he tells us, in the form of personal parables, about his self-concept, life convictions, and super-objective.

Goal Directed. In responding to the Rotter Incomplete Sentences Blank (Rotter & Rafferty, (1950) during the ninth grade, Robert wrote that "My greatest ambition is to build things." and that "People think of me as a boy who does things." Robert's first recollection, building a snowman outside with my brother, reveals his self-concept as a hard worker who engages in constructive projects. The recollection also shows his comfort in working with an older colleague who serves as a reassuring senior partner and mentor. There is no questioning his success in building the snowman, or in expanding his firm. The least that can be said about Robert is that he has always been a hard worker. Never forgetting his mother's example, he remained faithful to her standards. As a high school freshman, in referring to his household chores, he reported that there's no use in doing nothing when there's things to be done. His work enables him to disregard the unfavorable aspects of his competitiveness and to pride himself on his material accomplishments. At the same time his work has become an outlet for that part of him which he is happiest about: his genuine interest in working with people.

Robert's life abounds with successful, rewarding human relationships. His comfort with others, perhaps the most important inheritance of his childhood, was borne out at age 40 in his Minnesota Multiphasic Personality Inventory - 2 (MMPI-2; Butcher, Graham, Tellegen, & Kaemmer, 1989) report:

> This person takes an active, assertive role in dealing with groups. He is likely to be seen by others as sociable, enthusiastic, and outgoing. He expresses self-confidence, affability, and self-acceptance.

His lack of intrapsychic conflict and his consequent affirmation of others empowered him to engage the world successfully and to accomplish with little difficulty the goals he set for himself.

As Robert pursued his goals, such as building a snowman, he benefitted from the guidance of older colleagues. Never was there a time that Robert was without people to guide him along the way and cheer him on. He had a warm relationship with his father. Although Patrick was hardly an example of ambition or success, Robert viewed him as a gentle taskmaster. When asked to describe his father with one word, Robert called Patrick a guide. Robert's sister proved to be the same, the one word he chose as most befitting her was helpful. When she was no longer in a position to play that role in his life, Robert was temporarily dismayed if not immobilized. His older brother cared for him and showed an interest in even the most mundane aspects of his life. As a high school freshman, Robert reported that his brother was sociable like his mother. Robert's mother had hoped that her son would go much farther than she had gone, and throughout his life there were others who hoped the same for him -- including an uncle who wanted him to become an engineer, a brother-in-law who urged him to attend college, and a father-in-law who encouraged him to take the C.P.A. examination. In parochial school there had been teaching nuns who encouraged and disciplined him, and his high school years without them were not nearly as successful. Thus, it is not surprising that he thrived under the tutelage of the company controller who did not let him get away with foolishness and in the accounting firm where he enjoyed the respect of his President and later his Board of Directors. Robert needed the support and interest of such people as well as the limits they set. He enjoyed whatever opportunities there were to prove them right.

Robert's second recollection, an incident that also occurred at age three, shows his conviction that life is unpredictable:

> *Quite vividly I can remember driving, of course I didn't know where I was driving until later, going into the car, but when my brother went into the service it was a long trip. I can remember riding with my mother and father. And I can still picture in my mind my brother*

going into the induction center, wherever it was. I remember wondering, where is he going?

In this recollection, Robert's life is changed dramatically by powerful forces beyond his understanding. As he is swept along for the ride, he can only wonder where he and his family will end up. Maybe this is why he tried to look downfield, anticipate problems, and make plans.

This belief that a smooth ride can become bumpy may have been stamped deeper into his story when in the eighth grade, the family atmosphere changed from balmy to stormy. Overnight the climate in his house became turbulent and chaotic when his brother's children and wife moved in his house. The three kids created *havoc; there was never quiet*. Robert worried a lot as he tried *to get by at home with all the problems. I just couldn't handle all this mess.* On his 12th grade sentence completions, he wrote that "My mind *is gone*" and "My career *is shot.*" He never talked about the chaos to anyone, neither a guidance counselor nor a priest. His solution was *trying to be maybe a little more grown-up than my age was. I acted a lot older than I really was.* This extraordinary change in family climate was a major turning point in his life, one that would for decades to come reverberate like thunder, until he recreated at his firm the balmy climate he had enjoyed as a child.

Robert repeated his conviction that life is bumpy in this third recollection, yet this time he adds a proposed solution, one that becomes his super-objective. He remembers from age five that *we had a cobblestone driveway and I can remember riding on this rough surface and falling down occasionally or quite often because it was not smooth.* Implied in this story is the fact that after falling he gets up and rides some more. His determination to ride, despite the obstacles that life may present, appears to be Robert's super-objective. When life's cobblestones knocked him down, Robert had the courage to concentrate on what must be done next. As he did in high school when he was losing the game, he concentrated more and tried even harder. He got up, solved the problem, and advanced. Robert could not escape chaos, yet he could conquer it with learning and hard work. He concluded that he had to be on his own; nothing would be handed to him on a silver platter. He believes that the challenge of life consists of overcoming inevitable obstacles. His success can be measured by the extent to which he had come from behind to become victorious.

Robert's three earliest recollections may be used to state a syllogism that consists of his major premise about himself, his minor premise about life, and his conclusion or super-objective:

> I am a worker who needs reassurance from mentors who know the game plan.
>
> Life knocks you down no matter how well you plan or how hard you work.
>
> Therefore, I keep picking myself up and just work harder to reach my goals.

These early recollections, as well as Robert's psychometric data, reveal a life theme through which his behavior can be understood. The central motif of Robert's life is the need to overcome formidable obstacles. His humble origins, the difficulties he had to deal with when his brother's children disrupted his familiar world, his mother's sudden death, and his own failure to obtain a college degree in the field of his primary occupational interest were among a number of unwelcome events which might have proven to be his undoing. Instead, he viewed setbacks of any kind as only temporarily unfortunate, regarding them as opportunities to prove that he had what it took to make the best of things. Limitations of any kind were turned into challenges and ultimately into experiences of victory over the fates. In responding to *Thematic Apperception Test* (*TAT;* Murray, 1943*)* card #1, Robert at age 40 recounted the story of a boy who faced with a problem is figuring out how to deal with it. He wants to improve the situation, to perform at the level expected of him, and he will try his best to achieve that end. Although he is in a temporary bind, the boy refuses to quit. In fact, his momentary difficulty makes him even more determined to succeed. He has always been convinced that tragedies need not be lasting as long as he puts his mind to the problem. His resourcefulness is enough to play whatever cards life dealt him.

Setting goals and pursuing them relentlessly has always been one of Robert's outstanding characteristics: *You have to look downfield and plan ahead ... I've always been a planner.* Having found what he really wanted to do, he stuck with it. Robert admired an uncle who *set goals for himself and worked toward them.* As a payroll clerk, he listened intently to an older colleague who advised him to *get a job as an auditor, stay with it five or six years while you finish your training, and then look for a C.P.A. firm that I thought I could handle and to go there even though I would not necessarily be the top man.*

In a moment of deep insight, Robert reflected on his own identity and explained his super-objective when he said *my parents had it very hard, had so little money, and I'm reaching out to attain something higher, to prove something to myself and maybe to them as well.* Robert's compelling interest is in being a faithful steward of his talents, in fulfilling his mother's expectations of him, and in the conduct of his life proving himself to be a parental legacy which fully justified their faith in him and their otherwise unrewarding and unsuccessful lives. Through him, his parents have finally overcome the limitations of their heritage.

Robert' clearly portrayed his identity achievement and goal directedness in his response to *TAT* card 7BM. Robert said that the hero is mulling over his future, taking stock of where he is and where he wants to be. Although he listens to his father's advice, he does not act on it. He comes up with his own plans and accepts responsibility for his decisions. This story is a fairly accurate description of how Robert has experienced himself in the world. He never wanted to simply drift as his father had done, and although his need for certainty and preference for routine may have led to a premature crystallization of views and values and to a life not noted for adventure, Robert clearly made much, if not the most, of what life had offered to him. Not many have done nearly so well.

Drive. A super-objective must be pursued and the arrangement of a life theme must be played. The way in which one pursues goals and plays the theme is called the *modus operandi* or, more simply, the style of living. Robert's life-style matches the description of what Mosak (1977, p. 184) called a *driver*, that is, a man in motion who is almost counter-phobic in his ambitious behavior. But of course, Robert remains the driver, never feeling the self-estrangement of the driven, workaholic. At age 40, Robert's scores on the ten basic scales of the *MMPI-2*, all well within normal limits, testify to his ego-strength and excellent adjustment. According to the *MMPI-2* narrative report, *he describes himself as a competent, self-confident person who takes on too much responsibility.* He is partly driven by perfectionist tendencies. Recalling that his sister always insisted that he do his very best, by early adulthood Robert described himself as liking *to do a good job in everything I do.* The *MMPI-2* description coincides with what he himself believes is very true of him: *He holds to a somewhat perfectionist view of himself.* Another related feature is his strong competitiveness.

Robert has enjoyed the competition involved in his sports activities, even in his late fifties, and he finds a similar enjoyment in the business world: *Competition lends excitement. It also serves as a release from my hostile feelings.* When pursuing his super-objective, Robert feels fully alive because competitiveness adds excitement to his life and gives him a socially acceptable outlet for his hostile feelings. The *MMPI-2* suggests a potential cost to Robert's way of being in the world: *His competitiveness, persuasiveness, and aggressiveness may cause others to see him as an opportunistic and manipulative person.* Whether or not this is the case, Robert has done a good job of sublimating his aggressive impulses, perhaps to an extent that makes him almost entirely unaware of them. His scores on the *Dynamic Personality Inventory* (*DPI*; Grygier & Grygier, 1976) suggest a lack of insight into his own aggressiveness and an inability to articulate it in words. His *Thematic Apperception Test* responses tend to support this assessment. In *TAT* card 3BM Robert saw a set of keys and not the revolver on the floor. In *TAT* card 13MF, it was not the hero but someone else who had killed the hero's wife.

It would be difficult for Robert to acknowledge outright hostility in himself, and although his successful control of such impulses may be useful in his workaday world, it may also account for a lack of spontaneity and creativity that made a good part of his life duller than he would have liked. His *DPI* scores indicate a constriction of ideas and imagination, a lack of creativity that makes him less well-rounded than he might be. The *MMPI-2* report describes him as a *rigid individual who is unable to recognize or acknowledge that he has personal difficulties because he views maladjustment as a psychological weakness, and he has a need to be seen as strong and invulnerable*. Elsewhere the report describes Robert as a person *characterized by a denial of worry and anxiety*. It would appear that the very defenses he has used so successfully to cope with the various problems of his life have cost him a certain kind of vitality and exuberance that would make an otherwise extremely successful life even more livable.

Career Construction

In Robert's life portrait we can see clearly the development of his vocational identity and its implementation in his educational and occupational choices. Robert's life portrait reaffirms the validity of established career choice theories that concentrate on intrapersonal variables such as interests and talents. In addition, by highlighting the role of interpersonal variables in the formation of vocational identity and the dynamics of person-environment fit, Robert's life portrait affirms the importance of recent attempts to construct a relational theory of career development, one rooted in family interaction, childhood attachments, adolescent identifications, and other significant human relationships. In this section which concentrates on Robert's career, I first consider how relationships with significant others helped Robert to construct his career by choosing occupations that expressed his life theme and by working in organizations that fit his life style.

Career Construction Process

Psychologists who are developing career theories rooted in human relationships usually emphasize the family-of-origin, with its interpersonal attachments and bonds. After all, the family environment provides the first context for career (Bradley & Mims, 1992). The family forms a gestalt in which the parts produce an integrated whole with its own emergent properties. The family constellation constitutes the interpersonal *ground* against which an individual's *figure* can be recognized. In this way, Robert's family prefigured, or suggested beforehand, his disposition toward life. When Robert was born, his family already had a 20-year history. Their lives together involved two parents and two siblings with agreed-upon values, practiced patterns of interaction, and a family project. As soon as his parents brought Robert home from the hospital, he began to adapt to this social situation and make sense of life. Robert made a secure place for himself by learning what his family required of him and how he could move among them. Determining both how he fit in and how he stood out enabled Robert to understand his family constellation, an understanding he would use to shape a vocational identity and construct a career. In reviewing Robert's life portrait from a career perspective, let us look at the origin of his vocational identity and his occupational interests from the relational perspective offered by parental types and birth-order position.

Parental influence. In tracing the origins of a client's occupational interests and vocational personality type, Holland (1997) wisely recommended that counselors focus on one easily observed variable in the family, namely parent personality types. Holland (1997) theorized that parents reproduce their own vocational types in their offspring. The personal characteristics shared by Robert's mother and father prescribed Robert's family values, that is, the standards used by both parents for distinguishing what is important. Family values represent the important issues and goals agreed on by both parents. Parents use these values to describe the family's past accomplishments, evaluate its present situation, and guide the family into the future. Because parents agree on them, family values operate as imperatives that cannot be ignored by the children. These values frame the significant issues to which a newcomer must react.

Usually children mimic the family values and over time incorporate them into their own self. Sometimes children rebel against these values and incorporate the opposite into their self. Robert learned to agree with and incorporate three paramount family values. In terms of Holland's (1997) typology, Robert adopted, and may have outdone, his parents' *Conventional*, *Realistic*, and *Enterprising* values.

Robert's parents conformed to *Conventional* values. In Robert's words, the family values were, in order of importance, don't miss Mass on Sunday, don't waste time, and do your homework first. The family accepted societal norms for behavior and emphasized acting responsibly. Devout Catholics, Robert's parents also prized the orderliness and structure brought to their lives by conformity, responsibility, and hard work. In addition to respecting authority, they were accurate, precise, and correct. As Robert once explained, *I think my family, my father, and his brother, my brother all liked things that were definite. They are all very exacting. Julie was very exact.* He remembers that Julie was *meticulous and never hurried*. Robert's father's word was law and Robert learned to rely on Patrick's authoritative guidance. Because of this experience, Robert was comfortable around people in authority. He came to value obedience to rules and conform to social norms because they served as reassuring guidelines. Without clear rules and strong authority, a situation he experienced in high school and college, Robert found it difficult to renounce his impulses.

From his parents' unified message, Robert also absorbed *Realistic* values. They taught him to sublimate his aggressive impulses into hard work. Patrick would not let Robert waste time. Homework had to be done before anything else; then they would work together in the family garden. Every Saturday morning Robert would clean his room. Robert also described his mother as *a very hard-working person* and his brother as a *hard worker*. His family valued practical knowledge and liked activities that were explicit, ordered, and systematic, whether that activity be with machines or numbers. Robert was also *Realistic* as he followed his parents' lead in being genuine and self-effacing as well as in treating people with respect. This family value later manifested itself in Robert's commitment to client service, awards for community service, and contributions to both the youth and the elderly in his community.

Robert's parents showed *Enterprising* values when they insisted that he should get ahead and accomplish more than they had with their own lives. Both parents had been forced by their own parents to quit school after the seventh grade. Because of this, neither of Robert's parents could live the life they had dreamed for themselves. Patrick never became a railroad engineer and Mary never completed high school. They hoped that Robert would go further than they had been allowed. *Mother kept telling me to try to go as far as I possibly could*. His sister urged him to *do a better than average job in anything I do*. Robert's parents emphasized that education and hard work lead to success. A family goal was to have Robert compete and succeed in the conventional world, a world that had all but defeated them. Toward that end, the family equipped Robert with a competitive attitude to accompany his excellent work habits and common sense.

Because Robert closely identified with his parents and admired the nuns, he made their shared values his own. These values structured the core of his vocational personality type: *Conventional-Realistic-Enterprising* (*CRE*). Conventional traits of planfulness, persistence, obedience, orderliness, caution, and conscientiousness characterized his approach to succeeding at practical and Realistic work. Enterprising traits such as competitiveness, ambition, optimism, enthusiasm, and dominance animated his life. As an entrepreneur, however, his goal was not personal aggrandizement; he was genuine in his self-effacing generosity toward the community. He used his position and its power to enrich the community, not creatively but conventionally. His benevolent leadership for the benefit of the community became a matter of conscience for him. Like his mother, he too would become just as good as he could be -- sociable, friendly, helpful, kind, and responsible. He worked hard to manifest these values, and to implement his self-concept in his occupation as well as through community service. Robert integrated his three paramount adaptive strategies to form a consistent and differentiated vocational personality type (*CRE*) with coherent aspirations and congruent preferences.

Sibling influence. In addition to parental influence, there are other easily observed elements in the family constellation that also prefigure children's vocational personality pattern and influence their style of working. One such element, which has been studied extensively by family psychologists but not by vocational psychologists, involves siblings. Birth order, or one's place in the sequence of children, constitutes an important interpersonal element of family constellation. No two children live in the exact same family. For example, a first-born child has no older brother or sister, while a second-born child does. Through sibling interactions children learn how to get along with other people. Children without siblings experience more difficulty learning how to fight and make up, to cooperate and compete, and to lead and to follow. Thus parental personality patterns and birth order provide two distinct yet complementary vantage points from which to view a family constellation.

Robert's interactions with his siblings affirmed and reinforced the script he learned from his parents. When Robert was born, his sister Julie was 18 years old and his brother Gary was 16. Given his position in the family, a counselor immediately wonders whether Robert was a "mistake," constituting a "second family" for his parents, who were just completing their child-rearing. Fortunately, Robert's parents treated him not as a mistake but, in the words of his mother, as a *complete surprise*. It may be just a coincidence, yet it is worth noting that for the rest of his life Robert avoided surprises by *looking downfield and planning ahead*. Of course, being reared by four adults may also have contributed to Robert's planful attention to life's details. From his vantage point, Robert probably felt like a dwarf among giants. When he looked around he saw not just two parents but a second set of parents in his sister and brother. Yet as he stood small among four big adults, Robert certainly occupied a special position. Simultaneously, he was "the baby" and an "only child." Because he had no other children in the home with whom to interact, Robert was psychologically an only child. Nevertheless, he still enjoyed the privileges bestowed on a baby. For our purposes herein, we will use the word "youngest" to denote Robert's psychological position in the family. As a youngest child, Robert received both the doting reserved for the family's baby and the high expectations for responsibility and accomplishment conveyed to an only child. This uncommon mix of indulgence and discipline, combined with encouragement from four adults, often prefigures a vocational personality characterized by charm (baby) and prudence (only). Such a potent blend of competitiveness and caution (cf., promotion-prevention regulation hybrid) often propels youngest children to achieve high office and become leaders. Typically, their occupational positions involve being second-in-command, more often the chief operating officer rather than the chief executive officer (oldest children seem better prepared to be the CEO). When youngest children are the CEO, it is typically in a conservative position such as a superintendent of schools, general officer in the military, or president of a college or financial institution. They then have a strong board of directors, or other higher authority, with whom to consult. Let us more systematically compare Robert's life portrait to the specific predictions made for him by the birth-order literature, namely that this family position will condition him to become achieving, mature, sociable, and cautious.

Robert's position as a youngest child offered rich opportunities. As the youngest child, Robert always retained a special relationship with his parents, who were not distracted by rearing other children, until the chaos erupted with his brother's three children. Thus, they had more time to talk and play, impose high standards, and reward him. As a part of this intensive, uninterrupted contact, Robert's actions received his parents' immediate and consistent reinforcement. The lavish attention and exaggerated encouragement he received from his mother and sister helped to make Robert a *driver*, that is, a child who seeks and achieves early success. For example, at age 25 he was already a manager. As the youngest, he never had to look back; he could always look ahead. He was encouraged toward success, spurred toward it. His mother and sister instilled in him a desire to maximize talent and gravitate to more socially prestigious and "adult" occupations. He learned to compete and push himself to excel. In short, during his early years at home Robert rehearsed a role with high status, good pay, and significant responsibility. This type of rehearsal led Claudy (1984) to predict that a youngest child like Robert would have a high probability of entering a white collar, cerebral occupation.

Robert had the usual share of special opportunities given to youngest children who live in a world of adults. His parents took him on trips and provided him with cultural experiences, and his older siblings were always taking him places. Furthermore, Julie tutored him to succeed in school and Gary coached him to win on the playing field. These advantages came at a cost, however. With solely adult models in the home, Robert felt great pressure for more mature behavior, to always act older than his age. Early on, he learned to be obedient, cultured, and socially sensitive. He helped the nuns as he helped his mother. The nuns recognized his maturity. In the eighth grade, they chose Robert to place milk orders and collect the money from all the classrooms. In high school, he served as homeroom treasurer for three years. During his 12th grade interview, Robert stated that he felt older than the other students because he had experiences the other kids had not. Robert even preferred to dress and act older than his chronological age. For example, at his age 25 interview, Robert looked and dressed ten years older than his peers. He liked his environment orderly, his room clean, and his relationships clearly defined. Toman (1970) could have been describing Robert as the exemplar of a youngest child who likes firm facts and tight concepts, and hates big words.

Robert's relationship orientation of low affiliation and high sociability characterizes youngest children. Lacking siblings his own age, he took Julie and Gary as prototypes for peer relationships with females and males. Because of the age difference, Robert spent many hours alone as he was growing up. He filled his time with reading books, cleaning his room, playing with model trains, and collecting stamps. Often he would study with his mother and sister, or they would play canasta or *Monopoly*. His precocious maturity probably made it hard for him to hang out with the gang, and more comfortable staying in the basement engineering his trains. Usually his peer interaction involved the structured context of competitive sports activities, not just fooling around and goofing off. In grade school Robert enjoyed playing baseball on Saturdays after cleaning his room in the morning. In high school he loved playing basketball and baseball after school. His mother would not allow him to play football because she feared that he might sustain an injury. Robert relished playing sports because it allowed him to compete and practice coming from behind. As an adult, he would proclaim *I am an individualist.* Yet, when he did interact with peers, he showed warm social skills.

Throughout h is life, Robert sought the reassurance of older male mentors such as his brother and father, who were caring yet more distant from him as he was growing up. He needed the reassurance of his elders, a trait common among youngest children. When his elementary teachers provided this structure and reassurance Robert excelled yet when his high school and college teachers left him alone he floundered. After college, Robert found in his firm's president the male mentor and source of reassurance he needed, an older colleague who would not let him slack off. Later, his Board of Directors played this role. The pattern is clear: with reassurance and structure Robert will prevail. After all, he built the snowman with an older male mentor.

Career Construction Content

Having considered the interpersonal influences on Robert's development of his *CRE* vocational personality pattern, let us turn to how he implemented his personality through congruent educational and occupational choices. As Robert's world expanded to include the neighborhood, school, and workplace, his challenge was to match his *CRE* vocational personality pattern to fitting positions, ones that would provide opportunities to learn, work hard, and succeed. In terms of career theory, this matching or decision-making behavior seeks the goal of good person-environment fit, alternatively referred to as congruence (Holland, 1985), correspondence (Lofquist & Dawis, 1991), or incorporation (Super, 1963). In their textbook on career counseling, Lofquist and Dawis (1991) emphasized this point:

> In their development from birth to physical maturity, they [individuals] develop capabilities for responding to environmental requirements and preferences for the stimulus conditions for responding. Individuals seek to replicate in a given environment the positive reinforcing stimulus conditions they have experienced and to avoid negative experiences (p. 1).

As noted in Robert's life portrait, his parents typecast him to pursue a secure occupation in an orderly environment. Their own vocational personality patterns with the resulting family values, household climate, and gender guiding lines all conditioned Robert to develop a vocational identity as a *downfield planner* and vocational interests in *Conventional*, *Realistic*, and *Enterprising* activities. Robert made congruent choices that implemented his self-concept because as an adolescent and young adult he had achieved a clear and stable identity. He knew his talents, values, and interests and kept *looking downfield* as he explored the work world for suitable and viable occupations. Early in childhood, he evinced career adaptability in selecting coherent aspirations and fitting hobbies. Before recounting Robert's aspirations and hobbies, let us consider the most fundamental career choice that an individual makes, that is, the selection of a role model.

Role model. A child's opinions about his or her mother and father establish the norms for male and female sex roles, or what Adlerian psychologists call gender guiding lines (Griffith & Powers, 1984). As a young boy reflecting on the lives of his parents and siblings, Robert may have concluded that neither men nor women achieve their dreams. Men must take whatever jobs are available; then, they temporarily or permanently lose these jobs because of war, bad business, or plant closings. In spite of these difficulties, men should keep quiet, work hard, and support their families. Women may have a little more success in life. They might even finish school. If not, they still will learn what they need to know because they are more ambitious than men who quietly accept their fates.

The male guiding line drawn by his father, and walked by his brother, probably felt like destiny to Robert. Unless he did something about it, he would probably end up similar to his father and brother. Ideas about what exactly he could do about it must come from role models. Someone else, other than his father and brother, had to portray a possible solution. His mother tendered her husband's brother as the role model for Robert. She enjoined Robert to follow the lead of the uncle who was a civil engineer. He had finished his education in night school and struggled long and hard to succeed. Robert learned to admire this favorite uncle, who *set goals and worked toward them*.

Robert occasionally went to work with his uncle, who let Robert draft simple things such as duct work. This uncle became the proposed "solution" to the problems experienced by unambitious males in that he was exact and goal-directed, had finished high school, studied engineering in night school, worked his way up the ladder, and was now earning good pay in a secure job. In other words, this uncle did what Robert's brother and father had not done. In so doing, he became a role model that showed Robert how to actively master what his father and brother had passively suffered.

Expressed interests. As a child, Robert selected congruent hobbies such as collecting stamps, engineering model trains, and playing cards and board games. Early in grade school, Robert had already focused his occupational aspirations; he wanted to do either *something mechanical or something like accounting*. Engineering interests followed his role model and accounting interests followed his mother's guiding line, imitated his sister, and expressed the Conventional family values. In the ninth grade, Robert had refined these two preferences a bit. He said, *I'd like being a constructor or builder, something like that. Or, working with figures --accounting, something like that*. A while later he replaced construction with mechanical or electrical engineering because it involves inside work whereas building trades involve outside work. In particular, he wanted to be either an accountant because it is *more regular, more secure or a mechanical engineer or draftsman*. Prophetically he added, *But if I couldn't get it done, I could get any job around that I'd like or not particularly like at all*.

Occupational researchers using a psychodynamic perspective (Bordin, Nachmann, & Segal, 1963) have concluded that accountants and engineers, the two occupations that appealed to Robert, share many similarities, including a strong identification with their parents. This line of research has shown that engineers are orderly, dispassionate, and planful. They prefer to work within well-defined parameters. Engineers also work well with male authority figures and can be equally successful as a follower or leader (Beall & Bordin, 1964). Segal and Szabo (1964) reported that accountants conform to social norms and have positive attitudes toward their parents and toward people in general. Schlesinger (1963) reported that engineers and accountants both appear to be responsible, conforming, orderly, and competitive. Engineering and accounting both seem to generally fit Robert's personality. By the beginning of the 12th grade, however, Robert had settled on electrical or civil engineering because these occupations involve precise details, definite conclusions, and facts rather than theory. He loved math courses. He planned to study drafting at a community college and then engineering at a suitable university. At age 25, Robert wrote on his sentence completion form that that "I always wanted to be... *an engineer.*" Nevertheless, he wrote that "My greatest ambition... *is attaining a top accounting job*" and "I need... *a few years to attain a fine goal.*

Measured interests. The results from Robert's ninth-grade vocational appraisal battery reflect well his expressed work values, occupational abilities, and vocational interests. In the ninth-grade, his *Work Values Inventory (WVI*; Super, 1970) had a moderately defined profile. His strongest value was a concomitant of work -- he wanted work that was carried out under pleasant conditions, not too dirty nor hot or cold. His concern about working conditions was closely followed by two extrinsic values: security and a livable wage. He subscribed to two intrinsic values, namely, the desire to contribute and develop new ideas. In the twelfth grade, Robert completed the *WVI* again. This profile changed markedly from the ninth-grade profile, a change that reflected the chaos he experienced at home and an increased interest in school. His values profile in the senior year was defined by an outstanding peak on security. Livable wages and creating new ideas remained as strong as they had been in the ninth grade, but two new values emerged: intellectual stimulation (i.e., solve new problems) became his second highest value and achievement (i.e., work where you can see the results and feel a sense of accomplishment) was equal to wages and creativity. At age 35, Robert responded to the *WVI* for a third time. The results returned to a less-defined profile, with security and intellectual stimulation (cf., promotion-prevention regulation hybrid) remaining his highest values, then joined by having the independence of being his own boss and making decisions along with the freedom to choose his own way of life while not at work.

Robert's work values in high school fit his expressed intention to pursue an engineering or accounting career. Furthermore, his well-above average level of intelligence provided the general mental ability required to succeed in training for these careers. Robert scored 117 on a mental ability test (Otis & Lennon, 1967) and at the 80th percentile on a verbal reasoning test (Bennett, Seashore, & Wesman, 1966). He graduated in the top third of his class with a grade average of 80%. Robert showed strong aptitude for both verbal and numerical reasoning, but much lower aptitude for abstract reasoning, the kind useful in an engineering career. This is not surprising in that Robert preferred practical knowledge and *liked things that were definite.*

On the *Kuder Preference Schedule - Vocational Form CH* (Kuder, 1956), taken in the ninth grade, Robert showed an overriding interest in computational and clerical activities (both above 95 %tile) followed by strong interest in mechanical (77%tile) and literary (75%tile) activities. In contrast, he showed little (less than 20%tile) interest in outdoor, scientific, and social service activities. In RIASEC terms (Holland, 1997), Robert's profile showed strong *Conventional* and *Realistic* interests, moderate *Artistic* and *Enterprising* interests, and weak *Investigative* and *Social* interests. His occupational interests on the *Strong Vocational Interest Blank - Revised* (Strong, Campbell, Berdie, & Clark, 1966), also taken in the ninth grade, showed one primary pattern and three secondary patterns. In particular, Robert scored very similar to engineers and production managers; and similar to president of a manufacturing concern, senior C.P.A., aviator, carpenter, printer, and police officer. He scored dissimilar to veterinarian, teacher, minister, musician, and salesperson.

From this vocational assessment, a counselor might conclude that in graduating from high school, Robert would be seeking a secure job that pays a livable wage and offers him the potential to feel a sense of mastery in using his mind to solve problems and meet challenges. That work should be done in an office with nice surroundings. The job should probably be in accounting or possibly in engineering, and it should have a structured career path along which one can move from an entry-level position to a senior position. The position should not involve direct interpersonal contact of the kind required by sales or teaching nor should it demand an artistic flair.

Education. After graduating from high school, Robert attended community college. He studied pre-engineering for two years but did not attain an associate degree because he failed his final math class. He refused to take that course again, fulfilling his destiny as a male who does not finish school. This turning point in his life bears examination. At age 25, Robert explained that pride stopped him from retaking the math class: *Well, I was too proud. I didn't graduate with my class and I didn't want to go back to study with people in the class after mine.* He also explained that retaking the class would be pointless because he did not have money to go on to a university. Accordingly, he decided to go to work at anything he could find, *for about a year,* to save for college. However, *things changed* and instead he started saving money to get married. Of course these explanations make sense, yet at a deeper level one must wonder if Robert was opting out of engineering, with its Investigative-Realistic-Enterprising work activities, to move to a more congruent occupational environment. True, the personalities of engineers and accountants have many similarities; yet, there are two differences that seem relevant to Robert. Engineers use abstract principles and laws to produce concrete products (Beall & Bordin, 1964), and accountants like cleanliness (White, 1963). Robert preferred facts over theory and indoor, clean work over outdoor, dirty work. Thus the switch from engineering to accounting improved Robert's fit with the work environment.

Occupations. Robert's initial positions as a payroll clerk and as a night auditor fit him better than engineering ever would. These two position, both considered to be Conventional-Realistic-Enterprising occupations (Gottfredson & Holland, 1996, p. 262), were completely congruent with his Conventional-Realistic-Enterprising interest pattern. To get ahead, Robert studied accounting. This move was a necessary step in his *downfield plan* to excel as a C.P.A. When he made his major career move he began as a vice-president and then became president of an accounting firm. Work as an accounting executive seems completely congruent with Robert's role in his family-of-origin. The position fully implements his vocational personality and exercises his foremost coping strategies.

Robert loves accounting because it requires that he do what he rehearsed as a child. It is an extension of his first jobs as the milk-money collector in grade school and homeroom treasurer in high school. The job environment has clear rules. As he stated at age 35, *I like things in black and white. I don't like the middle of the road. Public accounting involves making things definite.* When he visits a client, Robert, who cleaned his own room every Saturday, looks to see if things *are in disarray or are they squared up and neat.* Accounting rewards him for carefully deliberating before making decisions; one of his favorite activities is doing financial analyses, as Julie used to do at her job. Robert routinely must make plans for his firm -- *I was always a planner.* And when the plans do not work out, he can remain calm in the middle of chaos, as his mother and father did. Accounting gives him the job security his father and brother never achieved. Unlike his brother, his promises are kept. Accounting also allows him to help people and contribute to the welfare of his community. As company president, he teaches his employees that *service makes a difference.* As his mother taught him, they too must learn to care for other people, not just for the firm. He respects all of his coworkers. Given the bond he forged with his mother and Julie, it is not surprising that he detests sexism and is an advocate for women coworkers and employees. Half of his accountants are women. He proudly reports that *they outshine the men*, maybe as his mother and sister outshone his father and brother. Robert also excels because he remains willing to work harder than the job requires.

Given his experiences with his family, it is no wonder that Robert intermixes with everybody: his Board of Directors, colleagues, employees, and clients. The Board of Directors are not bosses; they are older friends who provide the reassurance that his father and brother once offered him. His mother would be proud to hear him at age 59 say, *There are so many things to learn. I am learning new things every day.* He is not trapped in a rut; he continues to be curious. *I like diversity, I'm not a specialist. I like a little bit of everything.* Most of all, he still loves competition, especially with other accounting firms, and is genuinely proud of how he has guided his firm to excel. Being president of an accounting firm pushes Robert to actualize his potential and be all that he can be, and to be someone that he himself likes.

To this day, accounting continues to enable Robert to pursue his super-objective of *reaching out to attain something higher, to prove something to myself and maybe to them* [his parents]. In 2015, he once again moved his firm to a larger building. His employees and he remain dedicated to providing quality service and committed to their volunteer work in many civic organizations. Most of all, Robert might appreciate that his employees view him as a *nice, genuine guy.* Near the end of his final interview, Robert was asked to reflect on the success, satisfaction, and security that his congruent career has earned him. Then he was asked, *What advice would you give to young people?* Robert answered as one might guess: *The big thing is having a goal and looking ahead, looking downfield.* Maybe this statement makes you too envision a small boy driving down the cobblestone driveway and looking ahead to avoid being thrown from his bike, with his mother smiling and nodding her approval as she watches through the window.

CHAPTER FOUR
The Obligations of a Guardian

The next life portrait illustrates in fine detail what researchers have learned about identity "foreclosure." Individuals shape their identities by actively constructing a coherent viewpoint from which to conceptualize the self and comprehend the world. Once formed, an identity becomes a personal strategy for understanding one's self and making choices. Through these functions, identity mediates the relations between self and social roles. Generally, adolescents construct their identities following a crisis of self-awakening that prompts exploration and experimentation as a means of eventually committing themselves to self-chosen goals. However, some adolescents accept a conferred identity by committing themselves to their parents' goals for them, foregoing exploration of possible selves and experimentation with potential preferences. This normative approach to identity formation can, at its best, lead to opening oneself to choices that benefit the family and community or, at its worst, lead to closing oneself off from occupational dreams.

The distinguishing feature that makes a normative strategy produce identity foreclosure appears to be the quality of relationships with the family-of-origin. A normative strategy combined with healthy family relations may reflect an interdependent pattern of career construction, one in which the collective good of the family becomes the criterion for individual choice. In contrast, Individuals with foreclosed identity strategies hold fast to their commitment to childhood assumptions and values. During adolescence, they do not explore and rethink these beliefs based on their own perspective and experiences. Instead, they opt for certainty and security by committing to goals chosen without a period of exploration that would loosen ties to childhood convictions. They find the certainty they need by staying on a course set by their parents. This identity foreclosure usually results in a personality that is placid and highly responsive to external feedback. Thus, adolescents who accept conferred identities tend to do what parents expect of them, seek social approval from their families, overvalue the opinions of others, and worry about their reputations (Marcia, 1980). In school, they are often diligent, well-behaved, and respected by their teachers.

Individuals with conferred identities usually grow-up in families that constrain self-expression and inhibit exploration. Such families typically focus on tasks not feelings as the father dominates the child and the mother discourages emotional expression. The parents exert pressure and provide reinforcement for conformity to family values, and this is perceived positively by the adolescent. Rather than vent strong feelings, positive or negative, members of these families quash their own preferences and avoid anxiety by staying busy. To avoid crisis and solidify the conferred identity, adolescents must inhibit their own impulses and close themselves to disconfirming evidence. Thus, once set upon a circumscribed path most, yet not all, adolescents live out their conferred identities.

As you read this chapter from the perspective of Career Construction Theory, recognize how William Garrod's anxious-ambivalent attachment schema led him as a social actor to organize and maintain the strategies of an introverted, norm-accepting personality disposition. As a motivated agent using a prevention schema to avoid disappointing others and do what he ought to do, William adapted to vocational situations with strategies for adjustive defending. As an autobiographical author, William deliberated using a communicative reflexivity schema to conceive a Guardian's vocational identity and compose a circumscribed career story. In reading the life portrait, also note how the normative identity-processing strategy used by William differs from the informational identity-processing strategy used by Robert Coyne, the subject of the prior chapter. Robert constructed his vocational identity and became "a driver" whereas William accepted a conferred identity and became "driven." Now consider the details of how William Garrod's circumscribed career construction began with antecedents of family obligations and ended with consequent success and stability marred by discontentment.

PART I

A Life Portrait of William Garrod
The Ties that Bind

Through the 1950s and 1960s, it was not unusual for sons to share in their fathers' field of work. Circumstances and sentiment combined to produce multi-generational families of teachers, doctors, lawyers, and soldiers in addition to those with a family enterprise -- farm or factory -- to tend. By the 1970s, it was becoming generally believed that adolescents should develop an ambition for work they would enjoy. Nevertheless, many fathers still hoped that their children would take advantage of the clientele, patronage, or contacts that they themselves had struggled to establish; yet this was a hope, not an expectation, so that if a child did step into the father's business it was a flattering choice.

However, some families still held to the tradition that the eldest son should follow in his father's wake. On the model of the self-sufficient village, the boy apprenticed to his father would ensure that whatever service the father provided would be available to the next generation of townsfolk, and of course the boy's own future would be secured. For a younger son there might be several options depending upon which neighbors had no sons of their own to train, yet the eldest son was sure to share the father's occupation. This tradition was especially strong among prominent families in small or isolated communities where the practice lingered long past any need for it. In such families the tradition might be modified so that instead of parents assigning the boy his father's occupation, they prescribed for him something grander, often medicine or law. Or if the family was prosperous, the parents might talk of career choice, yet such a choice could sound to the boy as if it were between the unequal alternatives of father's work or some little idea of his own. In either case, the boy inferred that one particular vocation was expected of him. William Garrod was one such young person.

Family

For as long as William could remember there had been a bridled intensity in the air caused by a full engagement in the family business, a flour mill in a Midwestern small town. This mood reflected his family's ardent desire to expand the mill, which had been founded by William's great-great grandfather in 1880. William's great grandfather took over the mill in 1903, followed by William's grandfather 27 years later. William's father, Arthur, took it over in 1954 at the age of 25 when his own father died suddenly.

William himself may not have spent much conscious thought on his family history, yet he could not escape or fail to notice its impact. It was obvious in his parents and relatives. It was especially evident in William's father, Arthur, who at a young age took the reins of the family business to support his widowed mother and two younger brothers. What Arthur remembered of his own father was that *he was a consummate businessman and community leader.* After his father's death, Arthur's mother sustained his goals and emphasized the need for a good education and hard work. Arthur faithfully executed his responsibility to achieve. Three years after graduating from college, he was running the mill. Almost immediately, he began studying for an M.B.A., commuting to the city for classes after a full day at the mill. There was never any question as to where Arthur's priorities lay. William's mother stated, *When he was studying for his M.B.A., I didn't let Billy disturb him.* Nor did Arthur have much time to spend with his family after he had earned the M.B.A. He had to expand the mill as well as serve in many roles as a community leader. His wife organized the family resources to spare his energy for these pursuits. As Arthur achieved greater prosperity and community respect, he fulfilled his own parents' dream. He expected the same from his own children, William and Charles: *I want to see my children complete their education and become happy and successful citizens.*

William himself described his father as carrying *too many burdens at too young an age; he was the sole financial support of his family.* Of course, it was difficult work for a young man. *He did what he had to do, and he did it very well. But, he's looked tired every day of his life ... a man under pressure.*

William's mother, Eliza, for her own part, similarly was encouraged by her parents to excel:

> *To them I was the smartest person in the world, and I wouldn't disappoint them if it meant burning the midnight oil, which I did. I had to work very hard to get the kind of grades that would please my parents.*

At college Eliza majored in French and English and was elected to Phi Beta Kappa.

> *Now my husband is my career. My world is small. Nine-tenths of my day is with my family. As far as I can see, my greatest contribution will be to produce two fine boys.*

Although very active in community organizations, she emphasized her role as homemaker and mother.

> *My children are my hobbies. I run the house, keep it clean, cook nutritious food. I've never been a gadabout. I try to make my husband's life comfortable.*

Unlike her husband, Eliza was always at the service of the family, catering to her husband and sons, protecting them from the world beyond the gates. And like her husband, she had maintained her own parents' dream.

> *When you ask me about the value of an education it is almost as if you were asking what is good about God. Education prepares one for society and for a good life. Education will make Billy the man that I expect he will become.*

The Garrods' expectations for their sons were as real as the formal drapes and furniture in the living room. They were not debatable. They were unquestioned maxims, the basis and direction of their life together and how their children would prosper. William and his brother Charles would not be allowed to squander what their father provided. Even more, the boys were expected to surpass their father's success, a goal toward which they were deliberately prodded.

Career Growth

When William was in the ninth grade, his mother reported that:

> *He's a sweet child, reliable, gets along exceptionally well with people, and has never been a bully. He has a wonderful heart and nature, very responsive to kindness.*

She went on to recall a prominent perception of him:

> *When he was three years old, whenever we had guests in the house he would always insist that they leave with a gift. He wanted to give them something of himself and his hospitality.*

This is not to say that she was entirely pleased with her son:

> *He has better than average ability, but he's inclined to be on the lazy side. I wish he had more persistence, more ambition.*

When asked how she could account for this, she responded: *Maybe I prod him too much. Maybe my standards are too high.* Nevertheless, she saw a puzzling contrast: *My husband doesn't have a lazy bone in his body.* This was a serious disparity.

William's so-called laziness arose from no lack of stimulation. From early childhood his parents attempted to energize him, to make sure that he would perform at an optimal level. Progressing beyond his father's number games, William next played chess with him: *Dad would never take advantage. He'd throw the game more often than not.* In addition to games, Arthur encouraged gemstone collecting by giving his own collection of semi-precious gems to William and helping him add to it. While saving for his son's higher education Arthur also told William about good books to read and demanded excellence in his studies.

> *Father gets mad if I don't do as well as I could in my schoolwork. He doesn't get mad at small things. He just wants me to do my best.*

And he had also begun explicit career shaping, as reported by William:

> *He likes me to help him at the office. He always compliments me on the work I do. Sometimes he takes me along with him when he goes to conventions.*

William's mother combated his lethargic tendency not with activities so much as with subtle yet constant reminders that she expected much of him.

> *When he comes home from school I'm with him; if he needs me I'm with him; if he needs help with schoolwork I'm with him. He's never left alone. It's just up to him to want something, and we'll move heaven and earth to see that he gets it.*

William experienced his mother's attention as tacit urging. He knew that she expected him to achieve, and when he did, she did not go out of her way to dole out compliments; he had simply done what a person of his background would be expected to do. She took it for granted that he would behave as she had during her own formative years.

> *My childhood ambition was to do what my mother and father wanted me to, and to be everything they wanted me to be. I'd come home and do my homework, and then I'd scrub the floor so that my mother wouldn't have to do it.*

As one would expect, William found elementary school dreary, in comparison to the stimulation at home: *I didn't like the routine and the waste of time. I could read, count, add, and subtract by the time I went to kindergarten.* Better-prepared than most of his classmates, he was eager to participate, yet *it got to the point where the teachers wouldn't call on me. It was a frustrating experience.* Another memory reflected his unhappiness in grade school.

> *I used to whoop up all the time if I had to go to school. I was the champion thrower-upper for about three or four years. I wanted to stay home where I could watch television and color and work on my puppets.*

But his mother insisted that he go to school.

William's first days in school also coincided with the birth of his brother, Charles. The extent to which his mother's preoccupation with the new baby seemed connected with his being sent to school may have upset him. In addition, soon there would be someone besides his father to emulate, another "star" in the household. When William was 14, his mother described nine-year old Charles as:

> *a truly amazing child; very, very bright; he enjoys work, no amount is too difficult for him, you never have to tell him to do it; if he gets 98, he thinks should have had 100. Charles is just a humdinger of a boy. He skipped a year in school. He's remarkably talented in all sports. He's just a wonderful, wonderful child. He hasn't the sweetness William has, but he's a darling. He's the more ambitious type. There are no heights Charles cannot reach with his ability and drive.*

As he entered high school, William had close on his heels a younger brother with daunting achievements.

As an adult William made a passing reference to his parents' partiality toward young Charles, yet he denied that there was any rivalry between them: *My parents made sure it never developed. There was rarely any competition between us.* The two boys spent much time together, with William teaching his younger brother how to play pool and ping-pong as well as helping him earn Boy Scout badges. They sometimes talked about eventually working together, as partners in their father's mill. William enjoyed being a big brother who could teach, explain, and help: *Charles had great respect for me for many years.* In his teens, Charles chose to attend the same university as

William had, and asked his advice on what courses to take, how the different fraternities compared, and which aspects of campus life were most important. As an adult William spoke of his brother with pride:

> *I'm glad that as the older brother I didn't have to live up to his standards. I was always a good student; he was always a sensational student -- the top of his class in grade school, third in his class at college, and number one in graduate school. He was a scratch handicap golfer, a great ball player, an all-around top individual. A principle difference between us was that he really wanted to be Number One, which was easier for him to be than it was for me to be Number Ten. He never had to study as much as I did.*

William's insistence to the contrary, it may yet be that his brother's general excellence (academically, socially, and athletically) prompted in him a need to forge ahead in a different way, to establish a different set of criteria for measuring people's abilities and success. As an adult he commented, *Charles was never that spread out*, meaning running the mill was more demanding than his brother's academic position as *a professor in his ivory tower*. Charles was far less practical than William. In light of their parents' values, it would be hard to believe that Charles was not regarded as the more promising of the two, and it would be most surprising if William were not made painfully aware of this. As William himself reported, he was grateful for his place in the birth order, for the fact that he did not have to move in the wake of his brother's outstanding achievements. What he did not report was the kind of energy it took to avoid being swamped by a ship which threatened to overtake him.

Career Exploration

High school was not the assured success for William that grade school had been. Aware that he needed good grades for college, he was unhappy whenever he seemed to be doing less well than he and his parents thought he could. He began to doubt whether he had the ability ascribed to him. At the same time he put little effort into courses he found boring or vocationally irrelevant: I would prefer bookkeeping or typing to geography and science. I'm interested in subjects that can help you.

Vocational goals were often discussed in the Garrod household, with the parents' values and expectations expressed both directly and indirectly. All through his school years, William saw himself doing what his father did. At age 14 William stated:

> *I want to run the mill because my father is, and I just would like to do it. I've been thinking about it for ten years. After college I'll work with Dad to learn the ropes. I don't think I'm as much interested in the production end of the business as in the financial and accounting end of it. Let Charles manage the employees and plant operations; I'll run the business.*

His parents strongly supported these aspirations. William's father affirmed,

> *I would like William to follow my line of work, to step into what I do. Although a profession is all right too if that is what he wants. However, I think he can do well running the mill. A man should do what he is supposed to do.*

And William was fully aware of his parents' feelings:

> *My father wants me to go into the business field because that is his field. He has the mill built-up which I can go into when I'm ready for it. He's happy about the idea. My mother likes the idea too.*

He even knows what it would be like to work for his father:

> *Being in his office has given me opportunity to see what the work entails. I have seen the way he works and the customers he has dealings with. I enjoy working with figures, solving problems, figuring up the expenses of*

> *different projects. This is why I prefer accounting to management; it seems more challenging.*

Only fleetingly did William ever think of doing something else. His mother would have liked one of her sons to be a physician, but William objected, I couldn't see anybody in pain. In passing he had thought of being a musician or a skilled craftsman; he wanted work that would be a source of pride and satisfaction to him. He was sure that he would not enjoy working for anybody else unless it provided a good chance for advancement. In his father's field he would have the satisfaction of having a nice office of my own, a good number of customers, and respect from those who know me.

As a high school senior, William was immersed in extracurricular activities. At his father's office he had progressed to processing accounts payable and receivable as well as typing and filing. At school he did reporting, photography, and layout for the student paper. He was business manager for the yearbook and treasurer of the French club. He formed a gem club. He played in the school band and orchestra and earned extra money with his own jazz band. He won an athletic letter for keeping the statistics for the sports teams: I don't go out for sports because I wouldn't be good at them. Whatever I feel I can do well, I try to do. At graduation he was recognized for his many accomplishments. His grades suffered, in Garrod-family terms: My average is about 90. I missed the Honor Society by less than one percentage point. This was quite a letdown for me. Beyond this, he earned the equivalent of an adult middle-manager's salary each year dealing in gems from his collection. At 25 he recalled this period as hectic:

> *I was always doing too much. I was burning myself out. It was the beginning of a pattern that I followed through graduate school. I'd work for weeks and then collapse over a long weekend because I simply couldn't move. There I was, shaking, short of breath, and with pains in my chest. But I'd charge the batteries, and then off I'd go again.*

This was no longer a boy in need of prodding.

William understood going on to college as inevitable for him, even a responsibility. At age 25 he explained,

> *College was always expected of me. I come from a family where every member save one is a college graduate. When you're brought up in a family like this...*

He had applied to an Ivy League university:

> *If whim had allowed the decision to be made, I would have gone to the University of Florida. But what with the social life and climate, I probably would not have got much work done.*

The idea that life can be enjoyed, not spent only in earnest purpose, had already become alien to him. Despite his good grades, he waited anxiously until his admission to the prestigious college of his choice was confirmed.

His college years, similar to his high school career, were flawed by his disinclination to study his utmost to get the highest grades possible. Looking back, he commented:

> *I didn't devote myself completely to study as I possibly should have. I was above average, but I didn't work that hard. The same way in graduate school. If I'd spent more time at courses, I'd have done much better. I had a certain number of things I wanted to do. This meant sacrificing something, and for me it was the grades.*

He was relieved that he had made it to a good school, so that *I didn't have to prove myself again,* and as before worked very little at required courses outside his interests. He continued his activities in journalism, serving as an editor for the college paper and also writing occasional stories for the city paper and two wire services. He joined a social fraternity but *didn't like the rah-rah fraternity situation. I was more serious.* He preferred the company of one special friend. A new pleasure afforded by college was *freedom to come and go, which I never had at home. In my parents' home there had always been strict hours and accountability.* He enjoyed the chance to develop autonomy, to accomplish things without his parents at his shoulder.

William enrolled in a special program that, by taking extra courses during the academic year and summers, would provide a bachelor's degree in three years. In addition to the heavy course load this required, he took a job selling insurance, continued to expand his gemstone business to include rare and precious gems, and each week put in many hours on his newspaper work. William did not find the coursework to be very challenging. He was especially disappointed in the School of Business:

> *The School just was not up to the standards of the rest of the university. Most of the faculty did not know how to teach. I like to be pushed a little bit, to be shown that my thinking is not complete. I knew more about the practical applications of what they were talking about than they did.*

This experience may have discouraged him yet he completed his degree in accounting and moved to a better university to obtain an M.B.A. As part of his M.B.A. program and with the help of his father, he obtained a summer internship as a Business Associate in the Consumer Foods Division at the corporate headquarters of a major food manufacturer. When William graduated at age 25, the company recruited him and he moved to Philadelphia for his first job. Although William's 60-hour work weeks left him little time for leisure, he enjoyed himself immensely. After three years living alone, he married a hometown girl and brought her to Philadelphia. She found a job working as a high school teacher of English. After one year, she became pregnant with their son, and became a full-time homemaker.

Career Establishment

After completing four years with the company, William received a significant promotion. Unfortunately, in his new position William found himself constantly beset by conflicting orders and assigned to tasks that he disliked. In addition, bad feelings permeated the office:

half of the office didn't talk to the other half. In his two years in this position, William grew disenchanted with urban life in Philadelphia.

> *The city beats me. It's a filthy stinking hole. I'd get home at the end of the day drained and uptight, and I couldn't fall asleep after I went to bed. I finally reviewed the credits and the debits of my situation and found that the give-ups were greater than the gets.*

Some six years out of school, William moved home with his wife and baby son to join his father's business.

In his first year back home, despite tussles with his father and low pay, William's energy and ambition transformed the mill. He expanded the business by attracting new customers and adding modern equipment and stream-lined processes. He increased yearly production and in four years company profits nearly doubled. He felt satisfied with his success *I like to shape things, structure things, put deals together. It demands creativity. I'd be bored with work that was more routine.*

And he was pleased to have *a great effect on the living and well-being in my area.* William's father, bedazzled by his tactics, eventually allowed him free rein. He had once hoped for his other son to join him at the mill, yet as his retirement drew near he had to admit that this would be unlikely, because by this time Charles was content working as a college professor. William's dynamism probably bore little resemblance to his father's notions of what it would be like at that stage of his working life, leaving him relatively passive in the face of a reality so perplexingly different from his dreams. Nevertheless, after William took command of the business, his father kept an office at the mill and still came in every day.

Of course, William felt unsettled and declared that he was *a still man with a tiger by the tail.* He went to the office every day of the week and was away from home on business more evenings than not. He could not adequately explain, at age 35, why he set himself such a demanding pace. Certainly, it was freedom that mattered more than money: *Being my own boss is more important to me than anything else.* It also was not the nature of his work:

> *I can't call my own shots. I'm still dependent on a customer, I can't walk out of that office when I want to. I have to take my free time when it's most convenient for others. I'm constantly under the gun.*

William was soberly aware that his stressful life was dangerous. He had been brought to thoughts of his own fragile mortality when a close friend died. He considered taking on a partner. *When I was choking, just choking!* Occasionally, it crossed his mind to give up the mill, but this would disappoint his parents. Instead, he seemed uneasily resigned to continuing as he was, but:

> *I've never figured it out. Why do I take it out on my own body and especially my mind? I'm not out to conquer the world. I just want to do a job and be recognized for being able to do the job. No one has ever made me run. I guess I have the oldest child syndrome, always on to the next plateau.*

At the age of 35, William appeared in many respects to be functioning in middle age. His sense of himself had no "becoming" to it; he was as he was. He had little idea of play. He did not enjoy vacations for themselves, but only as respites in which to deal with his exhaustion. At age 25 he had boasted of not needing recreation: *I don't want to throw away what God has given me. I want to take full advantage of what abilities I have. I don't like to see people waste themselves.* At age 45, he did play golf and tennis, primarily *to give vent to my anger*. Nor did simpler pleasures have much to offer him.

Career Management

At age 59, William offered an assessment of his circumstances.

> *I've been blessed with the ability to help solve problems. The same ability has been a burden. I've never had the opportunity to enjoy what I like because I've been doing what everybody wants or expects me to do. I don't know why. I am just spent. I've given all I can give. I have taken all the emotional strains and upsets I can*

> take, and I know myself well enough that at this point I say, that's it! Leave me alone! Let me do my thing quietly.

The pain and sadness of these comments reflect William's unhappiness with events he could not predict or control. At age 48, after 20 years his marriage broke up unexpectedly when with virtually no warning his wife left him. His son was a vexing problem, rejecting advice or guidance, seemingly adrift. His daughter was more similar to him in character yet often antagonistic to him. He felt that his father, now dead, restricted his options to a set of obligations, and he resented the demands of his mother, then ill and dependent on him. He was half-consciously jealous of his brother, a renowned professor at a prestigious university. His interpersonal relationships had become marked chiefly by discontent and wrangling. A similar picture emerged from what he had to report about his working life. It was filled with employees and investment partners apt to betray or ruin him by their incompetence. It was peopled by ungrateful customers who strangled him with their claims upon him. Wherever he looked either at himself or those whose company he must keep, he found conflict and edginess.

Long gone were the days when William dreamed of finding joy and satisfaction in business with his much-emulated father. In those days he could revel in the prospect of receiving his father's special blessing for coming into his own as the first-born son who now stood in his father's place, as tradition meant it to be. Somewhere along the way, the dream faltered; his father became less and less an assured guiding line, increasingly nothing but a propounder of obligations. William came to see his life as shaped not by his own decisions but by constraints of the role his family assigned to him in his rompers. William's father died of a heart attack at age 65.

> After my father died, I was left with his estate, which threw another responsibility on me. If I had it to do over again, I probably would not have come back here. If I'd stayed in Philadelphia. I'd have had a more exciting life instead of one so mundane. I didn't like the fact that I felt a fairly big obligation to come back, and I guess I'm the angriest at that. I really didn't get any

> *help from my Father. There is no question but that he took unreasonable advantage of me.*

Meanwhile William's mother, in her lingering illness, struck him as selfishly indifferent to him except as one she could manipulate to her own ends:

> *After my divorce, she lived with me on and off for about three years. That has been a very difficult situation. I never had a good relationship with my mother, and it didn't improve. Once I had a date over the house and my mother told her, "Please leave my door open, dear. I may need William during the night!" This kind of thing shows how self-centered and selfish she has always been. She may do for others, but you can be sure she's always looking for a blanket to cover her. I now realize how much I dislike my mother. Her personality is impossible to live with.*

Some of the major issues and conflicts in William's life and personality were writ large in his maternal relationship. He cannot ameliorate his mother's physical and emotional circumstances. Her manipulative helplessness and his sense that she cares nothing for him and his own needs are all that is required to fuel his conviction that others are out to consume him, to use him up, and then throw him away. She is the archetypical "other" whom he must service, no matter the cost to himself and despite any opposite impulse. Her disabilities may be especially troublesome to him, dramatic examples of how vulnerable and fragile a human being actually may be, and perhaps hound him with the warning of his own mortality. His dislike of her should come as no surprise.

Everyone acquires an array of convictions and techniques to get through childhood; everyone leaves it, even in the best of circumstances, with unsolved issues. The residues of all these make-up one's emotional baggage, which determines marital choice and shows clearly in marital conduct. William's concentration on the domain of work affected his marital style:

One day Alice came to me and said she didn't love me anymore and wanted to separate. On our 20th wedding anniversary, she left. This hit me really out of the blue. There was no advance warning. It was all very painful. The best thing I've done is to treat her as a very eminent psychiatrist advised me to -- like you treat the dead, with respect and nothing more. Our communication is restricted to letters. I think she saw me as very powerful, strong, and domineering, and wanted more power in our relationship. I didn't realize this. Guess I've been more work-directed than family-directed over the years and just wasn't aware of what was going on.

Although he tried to control his wife like his mother had controlled him, he could not manage his wife like he managed the mill. Connecting emotionally with a much-needed loved one, seeking to understand and to be understood behind closed doors, finding rest and refreshment in another's arms and heart, have never been high on William's list of priorities. Intimacy is complex and sometimes baffling, whereas at work both the accomplishments and the rewards are plain to see. Rare as it may be, true success in marriage requires a profound self-comprehension as well as empathy toward one's partner. One must be able to listen, to negotiate, and to relish partner differences. It also requires a fair amount of energy, not to mention time together. Stretched to exhaustion in his work, William could supply neither of these. Unacquainted with himself, he had no concept of discovering his wife's depths. He was accustomed to being in charge, taking responsibility, solving problems, fixing things, and then moving to the next item on his list. He did not conceive of consulting or sharing tasks. His talent lay in quickly divining what needed to be done and devising creative solutions, not in meeting a partner's emotional needs. William has brought the same set of uneven talents, as well as acknowledged ambivalence, into his present relationship. He speaks lucidly of how he and his girlfriend differ:

I make no advance appointments if I can avoid them. I keep everything fluid. That's my lifestyle. Dorothy, on the other hand, is highly organized. She works with a notebook and is driven crazy by my spontaneity. We are diametrically opposite in every single category. She talks things out, while I come to a conclusion very quickly. It makes communicating very hard, especially for her, since she wants to please all the time. She wants to process everything. That's the way she gets to connect. I, on the other hand, go directly from A to Z. Just totally different styles.

These original tensions have exacerbated over time, as is evident in William's narrative:

I'm tired of being badgered. I've become tired of always being put in the position of having to do things for others. It was the same thing in my marriage. I keep thinking, now I have another set of burdens, not pleasures. One of the things I like about dating is when it becomes problematic, it's goodbye Charlie. That is very nice.

Partnerships, marital or otherwise, have not been easy for William. They have brought him problems over the years in his business, his various investment projects, and even his gemstone dealing. There was one employee who, William declared,

was telling people I was incompetent, that he had done all the work in the office, and that they should only deal with him. There was another employee who had run my gem business very badly, non-creatively.

Among his partners in entrepreneurial projects

there was one who stole from me, another who was just obnoxious for the sake of being obnoxious, and still another who was certifiable, as crazy as a bedbug. If I had to describe my faults in the last decade, it would be that I've chosen badly in terms of partners.

Everywhere around William there have been people who betrayed him, abandoned him, or failed to give him the support and appreciation he had expected. He believed that he was left alone to carry out impossibly onerous responsibilities. His father's death entangled him in an assortment of financial demands. His brother Charles relished his opportunities to travel and to be with his family. He suggested that William could develop these opportunities too, yet William saw in his family a succession of restrictive burdens. After his divorce he had to contend by himself with his incorrigible son. Then even with his girlfriend, he found no one to comfort his exhaustion from the daily adversaries he battled alone. Retreating into his silent house,

> *I'll play with my gemstones by myself just moving the pieces around for an hour. I stay away from people because of the pressure I feel, the grabbing on you.*

One of the ways in which he has tried to assure himself of his worth is by associating primarily with those whom he considers to be accomplished and capable, like himself. When he was a child, few of his schoolmates measured up to that standard, so instead he cultivated praise from his teachers. His friends came from families like his own, whom he met through his parents. In high school he dated seldom, limiting himself to girls he considered to be of his own intelligence. At college he sought out professors with national reputations and delighted in relating like a colleague with one or two who were on a first-name basis with the Governor. He became personal friends with the University president on the basis of their shared interest in gem collecting. In graduate school he made himself a confidant of the Dean. He was enthralled by his first employer, who brought him into the company to do important things. He was readily contemptuous of colleagues or customers whom he considered stupid or lazy: *I like to deal with bright, clever people.* His gem dealing has provided him with entrée to the inner circles of interesting and successful people: *Wherever I go I know important people.* It is reassuring to him to be recognized by those he considers elite. In his 30s, he remarked, *Sometimes I wonder if this town is big enough for me.* Clearly, it was a source of pride to him that he was not the typical small-town businessperson.

Throughout his 30s and 40s, William's working life had diversified, so that in his 50s it comprised three fields of roughly equal size, at least in terms of the attention and energy he spent on each of them.

His gem dealing and the mill shared him with a series of real estate developments including a potato chip factory that he bought. In his real estate business he met with setbacks, frustrations, uncertainties, and discouragements. The potato-chip factory, at first something of a lark although it sat upon valuable land, became stale:

> *It became a real struggle. What I thought would be a joy and a fine project has become a nightmare. It went from being one of those very "up" deals to having to hang on by my fingertips in terms of cash flow. I have some assets, but they are ebbing away every day. I bought a factory, and it wound up owning me!*

In his late 50s, William's mill survives but does not bustle. His expensive divorce settlement, together with major reverses in the real-estate market, have forced him to reduce personal expenses.

> *It's not been very much fun. I have no problem earning a good income without killing myself. But, my work is stressful, more psychological than anything else. It involves a lot of hand-holding with people I feel take advantage of me in every way -- emotionally, physically, and financially. I have to hold things in much more than I would like.*

These comments imply that William has relaxed his pace somewhat, but if so, the energy that he saves he puts into working out deals. The land around his potato-chip factory was eventually parceled out for condominiums, yet not before he had worried considerably over the outcome. An out-of-state real-estate project promised an excellent profit but had to be aborted owing to protests in the surrounding community. Most recently he has turned a nice profit in his own town by creating a successful industrial park on property that he and two partners had purchased. Yet despite the sweetness of this particular accomplishment, the overriding flavor of his business ventures remains that of adrenalin.

> *I've always taken on too much. I'm always trying to juggle too many balls. I was able to do that more effectively ten years ago than now. My patience level has*

> *really worn thin. I always say I'm good in crises, but I hate to be tested as often as I seem to be. I have a lot of problems. I handle upwards of two dozen matters a day, and I have to come up with solutions. That's what I do for a living. I've always done that. I take horrible garbage and turn it into something valuable. The process feels like kicking, screaming, getting pushed and shoved, and each project seems to get harder and harder as the boards and all the people I have to deal with get more difficult.*

William's gem business is *not real work*; arising as it had from a hobby, it is fun for him and he has made a considerable amount of money doing it.

> *Sometimes I'll just go downstairs and play with my gems. I might want to keep my hands busy and write a couple of letters, or write an article. Eventually I want to get out of the business and just sell rare pieces. I don't want to sell a zillion gems any more.*

If there is any area of his life in which William feels perfectly independent of others' claims or intrusions, it is with his gem collection. Here he can work (or play) alone, intrinsically satisfied, responsible to no one else's reactions. As one of the few refuges of his life, it has profited him in more than just money: *I never really think about what I want, but if I did, I suppose I'd have to say that the only thing I really want are my gemstones, as crazy as that sounds.* This may represent at least an embryonic agreement with his brother's admonition: *Whatever you want to do, do!*

In the main, though, William's life seems to illustrate a conviction that it is lazy, foolish, and plain wrong to act in accordance with one's dreams. He was discomfited when his son switched his college major from business to music:

> *I think he's capable of much more than that. He tends to go wherever the water flows the easiest, in everything he does. I consider that a chief personality defect.*

As for himself,

> *I put blinders on, go left foot, right foot, left foot, right foot, and one-by-one finish off all the projects on my list. Every day I do another turn at the wheel, while my brother keeps on saying, "Whatever you want to do, do!" Every day I do what I have to do. That's what it really boils down to.*

He traces this life pattern back to his mother's admonitions about duty. And yet, the week after his wife left him,

> *My mother said, "Do whatever you want to do, whatever's good for you. If you want girlfriends, go get any girlfriend you want!" I couldn't believe it came from her mouth! I just listened and thought, "Who's saying this?" With her it's always been "You have an obligation." That's the word I hate the most!*

Only time will tell whether William will retire early, which according to his age-25 sentence completion, he had secretly planned to do. When considering retirement, he dreams of enacting an increasingly recurrent fantasy: *Maybe I'll eventually leave here and move to a beach. I'd like to be on a beach. I guess I'm tired.* One wonders, though, how well he could fit into this fantasy. Could he enjoy idleness? Perhaps he would begin by trying to rent umbrellas to other beachcombers and expand into deck chairs and sun screen, so long as the weather itself did not betray him!

PART II

The life portrait of William Garrod tells a complex story shaped by multiple family influences and social forces. In the second half of this chapter, I view his portrait from two different vantage points, first from the perspective of self-construction processes and content and then from the perspective of career construction processes and content.

Self-Construction

The most outstanding impression of William has been that of a driven man, a person who devoted his entire energy to the workaday world, who was carried away by a host of obligations, whose impulses had been bridled by a sense of duty, and whose life had become increasingly joyless. What can explain his unusual expenditure of energy, his driven state during adolescence when he deliberately sought no rest from an endless list of extracurricular activities and which, according to his school counselor, threatened to undo him? How are we to understand the tempo of his life in young adulthood when he would periodically collapse in exhaustion from the responsibilities he embraced? The same question arises with respect to middle adulthood during which vacations were taken, most uneasily and then only as *cures* for his exhaustion. Indeed, he has asked himself what drives him, yet not so seriously that the conduct of his life has changed one whit from what was observed about him more than four decades ago.

I address these questions about self-construction -- or how William shaped who he was and what he became -- by examining the process and content of his self-making (Bruner, 2001). For my purposes herein, *self-constructing processes* broadly comprehended refer to how Robert shaped himself as a social actor, motivated agent, and narrative author. In comparison, *self-construction content* broadly comprehended refers to *who* William became in terms of enduring personal characteristics and motives. Before appraising William's personality and reputation, let us first consider the processes that he used to constitute himself.

Self-Construction Processes

Three interwoven processes for self-construction are the social actor's self-organizing, the motivated agent's self-regulating, and the autobiographical author's self-conceiving. As a preview, William's anxious-ambivalent attachment style and introverted, norm-accepting orientation to relationships and rules inclined him to focus on needs for security and safety using a prevention strategy for adjustive defending that in due course shaped a communicative reflexive schema and a vocational identity strategy of a Guardian.

Social Actor. William's approach to life began with an anxious-ambivalent attachment schema. High anxiety coupled with low avoidance made William simultaneously attracted and repelled by parental aspirations. Nevertheless, William perceived this pressure positively and sought reinforcement for conforming to family values. The Garrods' expectations for William were not debatable. They were unquestioned maxims, the basis and direction of the family's life together. He could not free himself from childhood beliefs and values, thus he remained attuned and firmly tied to what his parents told him he ought to do. His goals were always clear because they were *ingrained by my family*. He did what his parents expected of him as he once explained: *My childhood ambition was to do what my mother and father wanted me to, and to be everything they wanted me to be.*

Fearing abandonment if he drifted from their vision for him, William became preoccupied by his relationship to them. In addition to seeking parental approval, William overvalued the opinions of others and worried about his reputation. Beginning in grade school and continuing through graduate school, William earned the respect of his teachers by being diligent and well-behaved. Later in life, he experienced great stress produced by a conflict between his wish to be autonomous and his need to please others. In the end, both contained and constrained by his parents' finalized account of who he should become, William did what he was supposed to do. He ignored impulses, fantasies, and feelings that might challenge the inner certainty provided by adherence to that account.

It seems that William's insecure attachment schema, one of anxious preoccupation, emerged from relating to a mother who was both protective and demanding. She was the archetypical "other" whom he must service, no matter the cost to himself and despite any opposite impulse. Once her own needs were met, she attended to William yet met his needs only on her own terms. Later in life William stated that she cared nothing for him and his needs. He claimed that he never liked her. In his early years, William emulated his father. He needed his father yet Arthur was at work and unavailable to William. Arthur's main role seems to have been to connect William to work at the family mill. William learned from Arthur how to relate to others in terms of work, not in terms of a relationship itself.

Together, William's parents constrained his self-exploration. They focused on tasks not feelings and discouraged emotional expression. William tried to repress his emotions yet he could still feel them if not deal with them (Fosha, 2003). William ignored his own preferences and endeavored to believe that he really was the person his parents wanted him to be.

Preoccupied with maintaining parental approval, William developed psychological needs for certainty and reassurance and then devised a working model of relationships by which to meet these needs and quell his anxiety. This working model and repeated rehearsal of its strategies organized a personality structure and firmed core characteristics that Gough (1987) referred to as a Beta disposition. This means that William combined an extroverted orientation to other people and interpersonal experience with a norm-accepting orientation toward rules and conventional values. Similarly to Robert Coyne in the previous chapter, William respected rules. However, being introverted rather than extroverted, William was more reserved and less active than Robert Coyne. Closely fitting the characterization of a Beta personality disposition, William saw himself as ethical, methodical, conscientious, dependable, modest, persevering, and responsible. William honed these admirable characteristics through interacting with his parents, yet the cost of submitting to his parents' expectations was a conformity in which he lacked assertiveness and put the needs of others before his own. Being so good at delaying gratification and handling frustration, he lived without adventure. Of course, his conscientiousness and consistency led other people to view him as stable, predictable, careful, reserved, inhibited, conforming, and submissive. As a social actor, William performed a role that preserved the family tradition. At his best, he knew himself as a conscientious caretaker; at his worst he knew himself as a rigid conformist who lived in denial of his own needs.

Motivated Agent. William's interaction with his parents focused his career motives on conferred goals aimed at duties, obligations, and responsibilities that he ought to fulfill rather than self-chosen goals aimed at his own ideals, wishes, and aspirations (Higgins, 1997). William's parents, in prescribing an occupational goal, continually emphasized responsibility, family harmony, and doing what one ought to do. Accordingly, out of a sense of duty William felt compelled to avoid disappointing his family and follow the career path they charted for him. As he stated, *A man should do what he is supposed to do.* William did what he ought to do as a way of maintaining the status quo, avoiding adverse circumstances, preventing feared outcomes, and protecting himself from psychological harm and occupational failure (Carver & Scheier, 1998). William typically approached goals that aligned his actual self-concept with an "ought self-concept" and standards rather than an "ideal self-concept" (Higgins, Roney, Crowe, & Hymes, 1994).

Beginning late in middle childhood, William began to form a career adaptability strategy for dealing with the educational choices that he would face in preparing for his career. Consistent with his preoccupied attachment style, William believed that he must avoid failing in the opportunities presented by his father, after all *a father's need requires a son's deed.* This avoidance orientation led Robert to a prevention focus on security, safety, and responsibility in accepting his occupational inheritance and following a predestined career path. To avoid failing to fulfill his duties and obligations, William vigilantly focused on what he ought to do, rather than eagerly focus on what he wanted to do (Higgins, Roney, Crowe, & Hymes, 1994). He played not to lose rather than to win.

Valuing security and tradition, William adopted the goals and internalized the standards promulgated by his parents without examining or questioning them. He adapted to what was available within the constraints imposed by obligation, legacy, and duty (Grotevant, 1992). In Career Construction Theory (Savickas, 2013), adaptability refers to how individuals select goals, particularly in terms of looking ahead and looking around. William had no need to look around to explore his context for possible options; he just needed to look ahead and plan how to achieve the goals laid out for him by his family. He did develop adaptability resources including concern, control, curiosity, and confidence yet used these psychosocial resources differently than Robert Coyne, the participant in Chapter 3. Rather than use these resources to broadly explore possible selves and occupational options, William deployed these resources to explore in-depth a conferred occupational choice and ideas taken from significant others (Eryigit & Kerpelmann, 2011).

William knew his purpose and focused his ambition on goals that he crystallized without exploring alternatives. Given his beliefs about obligation, William narrowed his focus to concentrate on alternatives that seemed most certain, maintained the status quo, did not disappoint his parents, and fit with what his family taught him he ought to do. He restricted occupational exploration to investigating only how he would someday manage the family mill. His concern about the future, and disciplined self-control in preparing for it, concentrated on running the mill and developing the confidence that he could do it well. Early in life he began to conscientiously develop the attitudes and skills that managing the mill would require. Along the way, he was decisive, committed, certain, and careful. Remaining vigilant in his prevention focus, he closed himself off to disconfirming evidence and alternative courses of action.

Autobiographical Author. William avoided the tasks of conceiving a self-authored identity, choosing instead to respect parental expectations and conform to their aspirations for him. William saw his vocational identity as shaped not by his own decisions but by constraints of the role his family assigned to him in his rompers. William's conferred goals and prevention focus for attaining those goals prepared him to adopt what Berzonsky (1989) termed a normative style of processing identity-relevant issues. The normative processing-style begins with the commitment already made; the identity outcome was prescribed not self-chosen. William's normative style of identity formation began with a foreclosed vocational identity, that is, a commitment to goals chosen by others. Based on an insecure, preoccupied attachment to his parents, life was obligation not opportunity. The inculcation of goals, the dangers in the outside world, and the safety of family strongly influenced William as he was making up his mind about life. William's controlling family did not allow him to be independent or to make decisions. He could not explore his preferences, let alone choose for himself. His parents made the choices, and they were emphatically not negotiable. William's part was to listen respectfully, accept the conferred identity, and commit himself to an obligation. William did not explore his own career options in-breadth, which may have loosened ties to his childhood sense of certainty and convictions about his family obligations. Instead, he formed his identity by using in-depth exploration of goals set by his parents. He made commitments and plans rather than choices.

Throughout life, William was unacquainted with himself. He denied his own ambitions -- maybe for music or journalism -- for fear of abandonment. He experienced life as an ongoing series of obligations and crises that were painful and sometimes overwhelming in intensity. For a time, William escaped the crucible of family tradition by moving to a job in a distant city. However, ultimately his conscience prompted him to return home. After all, *a father's need requires a son's deed.*

Self-Construction Content

To fulfill his *obligations*, William crafted a character armor woven from the busyness of a Type A behavior pattern and reinforced by a repression that converted feelings into bodily concerns.

Type A Behavior Pattern. It seems quite likely that being busy, or exhausted, or busy and exhausted together, have served to keep William from experiencing his feelings and exploring his options for just one more day, over and over again, too busy and too tired to start any self-exploration. In his 30s he seemed the archetypical Type A personality, "... aggressively involved in a chronic, incessant struggle to achieve more and more in less and less time, and if required to do so, against the opposing efforts of other things or people" (Friedman & Rosenman, 1974, p. 67). Individuals who display a Type A behavior pattern generally hold responsible jobs, meet family obligations, and fulfill community commitments. They enjoy challenges, deadlines, and pressures, which seldom seem to provoke anxiety or depression. When people who display Type A behavior patterns encounter problems, they typically experience physical symptoms and trouble sleeping.

William seems to have adopted Type A work habits and attitudes during childhood, as a means of coping with the loss of control he experienced in his family (Glass, 1977; Mathews & Siegel, 1982). William's work addiction emerged from a crucible of family tradition, in terms both of family values and his parents' experiences. It seems that the world frightened his mother, so that she subsequently tried to protect her children as her parents had protected her. William reported, *She did not like me being around crowds of kids or going into too many kids' houses, because I was cold-prone and she was worried about diseases.* At age 59, he stated,

> *There are not many people I will talk with about my stresses. I've never felt safe, and I guess my parents always told me that is something you have to be very careful talking about. Out of your mouth and you lose control, and I've always believed in that.*

His first early recollection shows William accepting the responsibility when parental figures transmit their agenda to him. He remembers at age 2-1/2 or 3,

> *Playing ball in my backyard with my grandfather and father. Just swinging the bat. They're both throwing the ball to me. That's the first thing I can remember.*

In his second memory, William indicates how the dangers of the outside world can intrude on the family:

> *I can remember very clearly, sitting on a Sunday afternoon in the sun parlor with my grandparents and my parents. The radio was on, and there was this shock, you know, the announcement that the garage next to the family mill had exploded, and my parents turning stone . . . stone white. I didn't know what it really meant, but I still remember sitting in the sun parlor listening to that.*

In his third early recollection, from age six, the outside world again brought problems into the parlor:

> *I remember vividly our next-door neighbor coming in to announce that JFK had been killed, and then going into hysterics in the living room; in the sun parlor rather.*

Among the many explanations for William's Type A behavior pattern are the messages he received from his parents: to excel, to follow their examples of achievement, to carry on, and to validate their hallowed tradition of hard work and notable accomplishment. His father's insistence on the family values surely contributed to William's early and constant strivings for success. His mother's prodding, together with her own example of academic excellence, were no less influential. William claimed that neither parent actually threatened punishment were he not to act in accordance with their dreams; he knew perfectly well what they had in mind: *You didn't have to ask. You knew what was expected of you.* Life in the Garrod household was geared to the serious business of achievement. There was no time for nonsense; even games and conversation had to serve a constructive purpose.

One of William's favorite stories, which he read over and over again as a young boy, was *The Little Engine That Could* (Piper, 1930), about the locomotive that *carried the Christmas toys over the mountain when the big engine could not.* He is not sure exactly what significance that story has for him. He thinks it may have something to do with a need to prove to himself and to others that he has what it takes to make it on his own. As early as the ninth grade, William stated, *Things must be worthwhile. Activities must be worthwhile. I look at myself constantly to see if I may not be doing the best I'm capable of.*

Many of the things that William said about himself over the years shed some light on how he developed a frenetic work pace. First, his tendency to drive himself too hard is not new. During adolescence he was careful to go to bed early in preparation for the next day's demands. At the age of 25 he observed:

> *When I was 13 years old I seemed to always have more drive than others, an abnormal, maybe unusual drive. I always took on more than I could handle. The guidance counselor once told my parents that all the activities would be the death of me, that I'd burn myself out. High school was terrible. There was always this feeling that I had to do it, had to do it. I push myself in too*

many directions, cut down on sleep and outside pleasures. I will not shirk my responsibility. I haven't had a vacation save when I was 13 years old. I don't want to throw away what God has given to me. I want to take full advantage of what abilities I have. I don't like to see people waste themselves.

These family injunctions came through strongly at age 25 when he wrote on the *Rotter Incomplete Sentences Blank* (Rotter & Rafferty, 1960): "My mind...*operates best under pressure.*" "I am best when...*under pressure.*" "Sometimes I...*waste too much time.*" "What pains me...*is wasted effort and ability.*"

At age 35, William worked during most of his waking hours, six and a half days and four nights a week. When asked what makes him drive himself so hard? William responded with:

I don't know. I never knew because I've always run so fast and too hard and I've done it my whole life. I've never been able to figure it out. There's no reason for me to run the way I run other than I guess I want to. But I think it has something to do with proving yourself. But after you do, it's on to the next one and proving yourself again. It happens whenever an opportunity comes.

Whatever the reasons for William's frenetic pace, its outcomes have cost him more than he may care to realize. His fearful state includes an enslavement to customers whom he cannot tell to *go fly a kite*, an absence of close friends, and a marital relationship that always took a back seat to his other responsibilities. The fact that he has been too busy to pursue intimate exchanges with others may of course be just the point. In high school and college he was well-nigh friendless, and later his interpersonal relationships were satisfying only to the extent that he could prove his persuasive ability and solve problems. There was no mutual exchange and never any comfort in all but highly structured contacts. *A man on the run* has no time for play, no room for people who expect more of him. It is a lifestyle which inevitably increased William's loneliness, made for self-estrangement, and finally led to his fundamental fear that he is hardly alive at all. As long as he remains too busy with too many things, he can avoid intimate relationships with others and prevent a genuine confrontation with himself.

At age 59, William said that his goals were always clear because they were *ingrained by my family*. Another filament in the binding tie appears when, later in this same interview, William was asked for anything he resented during childhood.

> *I resented the amount of time my father had to work, and I think that's my consistent complaint, that my father had to work such long hours, and I find myself in the same position, so that what I resented then, unfortunately, I'm involved in myself.*

During the same interview, William commented on his brother's catch-phrase:

> *"Do what you want." Mine is "do whatever you could do." He keeps telling me to do whatever you want to do. I do what I have to do, and I try more.*

This approximates an understanding of his super-objective in life. In addition to proving himself competent and autonomous, William uses busyness to tie himself up, so as to follow his obligation. As we have seen, however, an important part of William has been his determination never to be whole-hearted in doing what his parents wanted. He has always struggled to maintain some little degree of autonomy. William's conflict over his wish to be autonomous and his need to please others and be appreciated by them has caused him great stress. This conflict has been evident throughout his life, beginning with his relations to parents. Although he was entirely aware of their expectations for him, academically and vocationally, by age 14 he did not wholly endorse them.

William's response to Card 1 of the *Thematic Apperception Test* (*TAT*; Morgan & Murray, 1943) may reveal much of how he experienced his original household. At age 14, he saw a young boy pressured by his parents to accept a challenge. He supposed that the "hero" will eventually yield to his parents' expectations, but only grudgingly.

Maybe he will go through the motions of accommodation yet not work nearly as hard as his parents would like. He will obey but he will not enjoy it. In fact, William at 14 did not accuse his parents of any wrongdoing in how he was reared, nor did he try to explore any resentment he might have about it. He believed that the circumstances he described for *TAT* Card 1 were not his own. Much of the time William appeared to accede to his parents' wishes, yet he never did so entirely. Despite their concern about grades, he did not study as much as they expected and, in fact, reported that grades were not important to him. He took piano lessons for 13 years because his mother wanted him to, yet he practiced only after constant urging, preferring to play trumpet and drums in his own band. Throughout his school life he immersed himself in activities although it sometimes dismayed his parents. He also did not share his grandparents' and parents' deep religious convictions yet as an adult he went to church on Sunday and Holy Days. Again and again we find William balancing precariously between outward conformity to his parents' value system and the demands of personal integrity.

More than anything else William would like to be, and to think of himself as being, his own man. However, he needs so badly to achieve and to be acclaimed for it that his work has enslaved him. He cannot tell off an importunate customer; he cannot even get up from his desk and walk away whenever he pleases. At age 25 he complained:

> *I get to the point where the pressure is too great from too many sources. At times I'd just like to go off and sit. Then I say, "All right, you're dreaming; get back to reality." But I'm tempted to find out what it would be like, particularly since I've never done it.*

> *In middle age, William did not admit this temptation so freely; he might have his regrets, but it would not be practical to indulge himself.*

Repression. Although William sometimes wonders about the reasons for his self-inflicted punishments, he is too defensive for more than just an occasional glance at who he is and what he means by the way he is living his life. In this regard, his response at age 40 to *TAT* Card 17BM may be most revealing. Referring, to the acrobatic figure in the card, he says, *What he's looking at I don't know, what he's thinking I don't know, and what he's doing I don't know.* William would rather not know too much about himself, would prefer to remain out of touch with the deepest aspects of himself. This, together with a relatively drab interpersonal existence, has resulted in a boredom which can be only momentarily relieved by new business ventures, by the excitement of new challenges in a world which rewards him hardly enough for his self-denial. William's normative style and foreclosed identity, in addition to the distractions of his pace, prompts him to deliberately close himself off to the world.

William's responses to structured personality inventories clearly reflected his closed character. His *Minnesota Multiphasic Personality Inventory* (*MMPI-2;* Butcher, Graham, Tellegen, & Kaemmer, 1989), taken at age 40, showed scores all within the normal range. Still, the profile configuration, defined by an inverted V in the first three scales, suggests that William remained free of psychological symptoms by using repression to handle anxiety, avoid conflict, and bury emotional difficulties. Individuals who score a "conversion valley" profile on the *MMPI-2* usually take a rational view of problems: they might be depressed but would not admit it, they have little insight, and displace psychological problems onto body functioning. Accordingly, William's *MMPI-2* narrative report described *a lack of insight and difficulties establishing interpersonal relationships*, referring to *a rigid person who may express his anxiety in compulsive behavior and rumination*, and to one who is *chronically worried and tense* yet at the same time *shows an extreme denial of emotional problems*. William at age 35 had said,

> *I keep my emotions pent up. I have got to sit calm and quiet and be unemotional. Under high pressure I shake physically, and have tension, chest pains, shortage of breath. I'm uptight, but my mind is always working and I don't sleep well.*

He has practiced this style since childhood: placid on the outside like mother and intense on the inside like father.

> Mother tried to keep everything as quiet as possible. Keep the upsets to a minimum. Mother was very cautious. Father was a bastion of silence... I do not ever remember disagreeing with my father or mother in any way.

William's scores on the *MMPI-2* scales also suggested that he was likely to keep to himself and that he was dependable, reliable, and able to accomplish goals despite lacking inner motivation and experiencing chronic depression. He appeared to be dominant, ambitious, responsible, foresightful, progressive, conscientious, tense, alert, and not given to self-criticism.

William's scores on the *Dynamic Personality Inventory* (*DPI*; Grygier & Grygier, 1976), again all in the normal range, suggested stubborn, clinging persistence, along with conscious enjoyment of attention and admiration, need for freedom of movement, and desire for emotional independence as a reaction against dependency needs. The *DPI* profile also indicated a tendency to plan, manage, and organize. These inventory scores, as an aggregate, seemed to accord quite well with the picture of William as an adult closed off from himself by the constraints of the obligation his parents set upon him.

In many respects William appeared to grow old too soon. His constant pushing himself required him to renounce feelings and fantasies that might threaten the pursuit of his goals, although for most of his working life those goals had little real meaning for him. At age 35 he listed his assets: *a nice home, nice friends, good affiliations, and the fact that I'm really respected.* But as he aged he seemed to regret the price he had paid for these things. At age 59, William remained caught up in a way of life which, although it threatens to literally destroy him, is sufficiently viable that he need not examine too closely some of its unfavorable consequences. He can continue to view his pressure-filled life as inevitable for a man of his gifts and position, to deny any envy of those without such burdens, and to imagine only occasionally what it might be like to escape an existence circumscribed by duty and worry. When asked what inscription might be most appropriately put on his tombstone, he replied, "Here lies the man who would rather collect gemstones than women." You see, if *you add a gem to your collection you don't get into trouble, but if you add a woman you can get into big trouble.*

Career Construction

From the time of his first interview, William exemplified a stable career pattern (Super, 1957) but it was in an occupation chosen for him. He chose nothing, decided nothing. In his case, stability came from binding himself to obligations at the cost of self-expression. William's life portrait provides an unusually clear view of what may happen when one accepts an assigned identity and a conferred career. In this section, I examine how a normative style of career construction and foreclosed vocational identity shaped both the process and then the content of William's career construction.

Career Construction Process

Occupational choice should result from a "chain of decisions" (Ginzberg, Ginsburg, Axelrad, & Herma, 1951) in which one's past choices and experiences shape one's present choices. But instead of a chain of decisions, William forged a chain of plans. His parents made the choice and assigned it to him. He committed himself to their choice before he had the emotional and intellectual resources to decide for himself. He planned his life so as to discharge the obligation imposed by his parents. To preserve his commitment, he learned to keep his own impulses deeply buried. In terms of career theory, William displayed pseudo-crystallization (Ginzberg et al., 1951), or what the developmental psychology literature calls identity foreclosure (Marcia, 1980). That is to say, he hardened at a time of life when he should have been still flexible, curious, and tentative enough to explore and experiment.

William internalized his parents' conviction that it is one's *duty to appreciate what you have.* Moreover, he has learned not to question that duty: *I can't accept those who deviate from their upbringing.* He explained that he never allowed himself to say, *Well, I don't like it, I'm not going to do it.* Foreclosed children view their parents as accepting, involved, and child centered. The comfort and security this affords has been termed the "foreclosure halo." William clearly adopted the "foreclosure halo" to describe his upbringing as uniformly beneficent. When asked at age 14 to give his reaction to his father, William said,

> *He gets mad if I don't do as well as I can. He wants me to do the best I can do and not fool around. He gets angry if I'm taking it easy and not trying my best. He is doing the right thing -- making me work. I'll get in the habit.*

In his earlier interviews William spoke highly of his parents. At age 25, he said,

> *They both want me to do the same thing. The mill was expected of me. I never thought of not doing it. The mill gives me the protection and background I desire. It won't be taken away from me.*

During college, the closeness to my parents changed but the respect did not lessen. I saw I could make it on my own, which was always important to me, and I think that is why I did so many activities. When he decided to return home, to be available to his father, he stated, A father in need requires a son's deed. But the halo eventually faded. At age 59 William reported being very angry that my mother and father took unreasonable advantage of me.

In his interviews, William often referred to his career as an obligation. At age 35, he said, Dad was very devoted to a cause, an obligation. He was under tremendous pressure running the mill. At age 59, he described the bitterness of obligation.

> *Work ties me up and ties me down, both in terms of mental and emotional commitment. I'm emotionally exhausted. I guess at this point, what I'd like to do is not have everyone pulling on me. Not have the pressures. That has really become more and more of a thing. I've been tired of always being put in the position of always having to do things for everybody. Always another set of burdens, not pleasures. I stay away from people, be-*

> *cause I feel the pressure, the grabbing on you. In looking back, I succumbed to the easiest route. I felt a really big obligation. I guess I am angry at that. I'm really angriest at that. My mother and father took unreasonable advantage of me. It's always been "you have an obligation." I am tired of that word! There is no word I hate more than obligation. I don't want the obligation. I do not look at it as a privilege. It leaves me holding the bag, as always. I've never really had the opportunity to enjoy what I like, 'cause I've been doing what everybody wants or expects me to do, which I do!*

The word "obligation" is related to the medical "ligature," a tie, and it carries an intensifying prefix: to obligate people is to bind them, to tie them off from what otherwise they might choose to do. In imposing obligation upon him, William's parents constrained him to a particular mode of life. They used bonds of affection and support as the ligature, so that if he broke their constraint he would break the bonds. In his compliance, William bound his own ideas and feelings tightly within himself and constructed an "obliging" personality, one that is courteous, accommodating, and helpful. He swallowed the obligations and they swallowed him.

The dissipation of the foreclosure halo, which William had placed on his parents, shows that it is possible to escape the constraints of foreclosed identity, yet it seldom happens. People in the position of foreclosure accustom themselves to making decisions and plans without consulting their feelings, and because of this disregard, it typically takes them years to realize that they feel any dissatisfaction with their lives (Ginzberg et al., 1951). To re-open themselves, to take cognizance of the fact that there still exists a variety of options, is so difficult a task that it rarely occurs. What is involved requires considerable self-exploration to learn who they really are and to trace, understand, and resolve conflicts with their parents. Berzonsky (1985) speculated that those few foreclosed individuals who can eventually strike out on their own paths may be better able to accept and make use of changing circumstances; he labeled these as developmental foreclosures, in contrast to the firm type, much more numerous, who do not waver from the parental strictures that they have made their own.

According to the hypothesis of Kroger (1995), William's foreclosure is a firm one. Kroger reported that adolescents whose early recollections involved "proximity to significant others in a familiar setting" (p. 324) were more likely to form a firm foreclosure. William's three early recollections reported memories of being at home with family members. He should thus find it difficult to shift to a self-chosen course after his father and grandfather threw him the ball. The difficulties involved may be noted when, at age 35, William managed to reopen his foreclosed identity long enough to question it:

> *Sometimes I ask myself why I should run the mill. Tune-in in about two years and I'll tell you where I am going. I'd like changes to appear in my freedom and I'd like to spend a little more time with my family. I am not happy with the situation that I find myself in I'm really grossly unhappy with the pressure. I am unhappy because I am locked in. I get to a point where I am choking, just choking. I don't know what to do. I really don't know what to do. I have often thought of going down to the local university to take their career tests. What should I be? I need guidance in sorting out my opportunities. I would like to test out a few other things that I would like to do. I've toyed with the idea of changing careers; but it would be a great disappointment to my mother and father. I just have not made up my mind about where I am going. I know where I have been and I think that I have accomplished everything I've ever wanted to accomplish. But is it worth it in terms of what you give up?*

These doubts came to William at a time when he was shocked by the death of a close friend. His doubts express renewal (Williams & Savickas, 1990) in that he reawakened the self-questioning that foreclosure had stilled. He resolved this particular crisis by deciding to maintain what he had established, holding on rather than innovating his occupation or breaking new ground in his career

Career Construction Content

William's foreclosed vocational identity drew the lines between which he constructed his conferred career. He adapted to what was available within the constraints imposed by obligation and legacy duty (Grotevant, 1992), becoming interested in those activities that allowed him to actively deal with what he had passively experienced in his family. His interest in gemstones enabled him to turn tension into intention and private preoccupation into public occupation (Savickas, 1995). His attempts at active mastery are readily evident in his role model, favorite story, and hobbies as well as clearly recognizable in his educational and vocational choices.

Role model. William's controlling family did not allow him to be independent or to make decisions. He could not explore his preferences, let alone choose for himself. His parents made the choices, and they were emphatically not negotiable. William's part was to listen respectfully, accept the conferred career, and commit himself to an obligation. So the needs that were the impetus for his movement through life caused him to seek mastery of this issue by becoming autonomous and persuasive. But his developmental environment neither modeled nor supported these goals, so William looked for inspiration elsewhere. He found his solution in literature that offered a role model, *Tom Sawyer* (Twain, 1884). Of course, William was strongly influenced by his father's guiding line, and even went regularly to work with him. But when he read about Tom Sawyer and imagined being like him, he was consciously choosing his own role model, one that addressed the problems propounded by his guiding line. This choice had the effect of strengthening William's self-image as he pictured himself having Tom's adventures. Tom was something of a schemer and a hustler, always trying to strike it rich, an imaginative and venturesome boy whose exploits culminated in insouciant flight from the dreary respectability of his village. Yet ultimately his conscience prompted him to return home. William, somewhat similarly, "escaped" to the city for a time, yet he came back to make his father's need a son's deed. William's hobbies also showed an early effort in his lifelong struggle to become his own man.

Hobbies. As a ninth-grader, William's first interview began by discussing what he did after school. William replied that he made puppets and put on puppet shows at school, writing the scripts, recruiting five or six schoolmates as puppeteers, and organizing the presentation. When asked how he became interested in puppets, William said that in sixth grade he had to write a book report and he *stumbled over this book on puppets and found it very interesting.* He then began watching television series that used marionettes, especially the *Thunderbirds* and *Stingray*. He said that he began making marionettes like those used in these shows. He explained that *a puppet controlled from above by strings is called a "marionette," and the puppeteer is called a "manipulator."* William's interest in marionettes illustrates how a hobby can provide a means and context for constructing one's self. William transforms himself from being his parents' puppet to being the puppet manipulator. It is really a sound course of play therapy, even if he just *stumbled* upon it. He had been the passive recipient of parental shaping and scripting; then, with his puppets, he became the impresario who managed the show. He delegated the work to a team he organized, just as later in adulthood he devised the deal and then recruited investors. As he said, he did not do the detail work in puppeteering or in business transactions. He is the hand and not the tool.

Gem collecting has been a life-long hobby, one conferred by his father when he gave William his collection and then helped him add to it. By his teens, William was a dealer:

> *At age 15, I was running a gem business and sending out 75 to 100 letters a week. I didn't need the money. I just always wanted to have a great gem collection.*

In college he made good money at it and by age 35 the collection was worth several hundred thousand dollars.

A third hobby was music. At his mother's insistence, William took piano lessons for 13 years. Yet for fun he played the trumpet and drums. In high school and college he organized his own jazz band that played gigs for money. Although he has not played in public for over 30 years, to this day he still maintains active membership in a musicians' union. A fourth avocation was writing. He was a reporter and editor for his high school, college, and city newspapers; a stringer for national news services; and author of many articles in gem magazines.

William's hobbies of making puppets, writing, collecting gemstones, and practicing music each involve solitary, aesthetic activities. In due course, he turned each aesthetic hobby into an instrumental business activity: being a puppet theater impresario, editing articles by other writers, working for newspapers, booking his band into gigs, and running a gem business. His aesthetic hobbies may have started as expressive outlets but they became jobs; in each instance, what had started for enjoyment became a subsidiary vocation.

Favorite story. Although his avocational interests were clearly aesthetic and self-expressive, William's favorite story provided a script to fit the legacy duty imposed by his parents. To fulfill his obligation and repress his feelings, William kept busy. The story of *The Little Engine That Could* (Piper, 1954) showed him that he should seize challenges and stay busy. Moreover, this cultural script provided William with an exemplar of achievement through self-confidence and utmost effort, rewarded by social recognition. At age 40 William said, *I still get a thrill out of the story "The Little Engine That Could." I like being "The Little Engine That Could," especially when the big engines cannot*. At age 59 he said,

> *I had five or six projects going two years ago. I'd taken on too much, like I always do, but this time it caught me. I took my "Little Engine That Could" book, which I found in a Walmart, put it out and said: "Okay, here's a list of what has to be accomplished," and put blinders on so each project got my attention, set up a goal and accomplished it; took the next goal and accomplished it, accomplished it, and accomplished it. Now I am almost at the end of the various projects.*

The Little Engine That Could provided William with a script that was focused, busy, achieving, and struggling to be autonomous, *to be my own man*.

Expressed interests. In the ninth grade, William stated that he *wanted to be a tax consultant and accountant -- combined*. He elaborated that *I could then do the books for my father's mill*. When asked why this occupation attracted him, he answered, *because I want to*. On his ninth-grade *Rotter Incomplete Sentence Blank* (Rotter & Rafferty, 1950) he wrote that his greatest ambition is to be an accountant, yet he also wrote that he secretly wanted to be a novelty and toy inventor. At age 25, his *Rotter Incomplete Sentence Blank* revealed that his greatest ambition was to be a business executive. He noted that his career is foremost in his mind, his standards are high, his drive is great but his full abilities are yet to be determined and the future is uncertain. He also wrote that he secretly planned to retire early.

Measured interests. In the ninth-grade, William's *Work Values Inventory* (*WVI*; Super, 1970) had a well-defined profile. His strongest value was extrinsic to work itself; he wanted good pay. Given that, he then valued freedom to be the type of person he chooses. On the job he wanted the autonomy to work in his own way and off the job he wanted the independence to live his own way. In addition to laying out his own duties, William valued positions in which he had the authority to plan and lay out work for other people. In the twelfth grade, William took the *WVI* again. This profile, also well-defined, changed markedly from his ninth-grade profile. His values profile as a high school senior was defined by a peak on esthetics, meaning work that allows one to make beautiful things. This high score on aesthetics was followed closely by creativity and then security. In the ninth grade, aesthetics, creativity, and variety had been his lowest scores. In the twelfth grade, management and achievement -- both high in the ninth-grade -- became his least preferred values. This inversion may reflect a developmental effort by William as a high school senior to become independent of parents and other authority figures and not conform to social roles and rules. Valuing both creativity and security coincides with the possibility of an independence-dependence conflict. It is difficult to find a job that both offers security and invites self-expression. More often, the price of self-expression is uncertainty as to the outcomes. At age 35, Robert responded to the *WVI* for a third time. The resulting profile, again well-defined, showed esthetics very low but creativity, independence, way of life, and intellectual stimulation very high. Security had become much less important, replaced by seeking prestige earned through doing one's work well.

William's work values in high school, certainly in grade 12, did not fit his expressed intention to pursue an accounting degree. In contrast, his superior level of intelligence provided the general mental ability required to succeed in training for a profession. He also showed strong aptitude for both numerical and abstract reasoning, as well as above average clerical speed and accuracy. He showed significantly less, yet still above average aptitude for verbal reasoning. It not surprising, given his subsequent career, that in high school his occupational aptitude pattern resembled those for engineering, science, and accounting rather than the pattern for verbal-linguistic occupations. On the *Kuder Preference Schedule-Vocational Form CH* (Kuder, 1956), taken in the ninth grade, Robert's vocational interest profile, again well-defined, showed an intense conflict between activities that involved autonomous self-expression and activities that require heteronomous adherence to rules. On the one hand, William scored above the 95th percentile for both computational and clerical activities. On the other hand, he scored at the 94th percentile for musical activities, 75th percentile for literary activities, and 56th percentile for artistic activities. This inconsistent profile indicates that William preferred routine activities, requiring attention to details coupled with conscientious, deferential, and responsible behavior. At the same time, he liked creative and imaginative activities that allowed him to be rebellious and to impose individuality on his work. To fit these two opposing tendencies together, William seems to have preferred activities that require little sociability or emotional involvement as well as permit a cynical and disillusioned attitude. His *Kuder* profile indicated above average interest in persuasive activities (68th percentile) and little (less than 20th percentile) interest in outdoor, mechanical, and scientific activities, with no interest in social service activities. In RIASEC (Holland, 1997) terms, William's profile showed strong resemblance to Artistic and Conventional types, moderate resemblance to the Enterprising type, and minimal resemblance to Realistic, Investigative, and Social types. His code would be Artistic-Conventional-Enterprising (ACE) or maybe Conventional-

Artistic-Enterprising (CAE). This code may reflect his struggles with a foreclosed vocational identity in that parents wanted him to be Conventional and he wanted to be Artistic.

William's occupational interests on the *Strong Vocational Interest Blank (Revised)* (Strong, Campbell, Berdie, & Clark, 1966), also taken in the ninth grade, showed the same ACE code. He had one primary pattern, music, along with two tertiary patterns, business detail and business contact. On the occupational scales, he scored A for Musician; B+ for C.P.A. partner, senior C.P.A., and office worker; and B for accountant and real estate sales. He scored C for Investigative and Realistic occupations (psychologist, physician, chemist, physicist, engineer, production manager, and veterinarian), as well as C for Social occupations (teacher, minister, YMCA director, public administration, and school superintendent).

William was intellectually talented, scoring 120 on the *Otis Mental Ability Test* (Otis & Lennon, 1967) and at the 63rd percentile on the Verbal Reasoning test of the *Differential Aptitude Tests* (Bennett, Seashore, & Wesman, 1966). From this vocational assessment, a counselor might conclude that in graduating from high school, William was intellectually talented yet psychologically conflicted because he was attracted to both creative and conventional occupations. Given his work values and vocational interests, a counselor would probably focus on how William could integrate his opposing tendencies into one job. A counselor might suggest that William explore artistic businesses such as museum curator, special collections librarian, archivist, critic, photojournalist, antique dealer, newspaper reporter, book editor, art historian, and even jeweler. These types of occupations would allow William to work in creative and artistic environments yet offer him the security of a well-defined role that required conscientiousness and attention to details. The position should not require extensive interpersonal contact of the kind required by sales or teaching nor should it involve any mechanical or scientific tasks. The ideal job would bring forward his conformity to family rules as well as his need for creative self-expression. In short, it would allow him to be creative in a structured environment. One cannot help but notice that William's position as a gem dealer meets all of the antithetical specifications.

William's vocational assessment clearly shows that a career counselor must take pains to distinguish identity achievement with commitment to self-chosen goals from identity foreclosure with commitment to parental goals. It is easy to confuse the two because both show a stable vocational identity and strong commitment to goals. Moreover, clients usually do not realize their identities are foreclosed. A few researchers have used objective measures to try to distinguish between self-constructed and conferred identities, with little success (Brisbin & Savickas, 1994), probably because of client denial and lack of self-reflection. William's life portrait suggests an interesting alternative: the use of projective techniques to diagnose foreclosure. These techniques bypass consciousness and may subvert defensive safeguards such as denial and repression. Although projective techniques are rarely used by career counselors, they certainly seemed useful in William's case. They may even be particularly useful to administer to individuals who display inconsistent vocational interest profiles (Nauta & Kahn, 2007).

Glimpses of his foreclosed identity abound in his responses to the *TAT* in the ninth grade, William responded to *TAT* Card 1 by saying that *the boy is disgusted with having to play the instrument, but he'll go to his teacher and have her work on him.* To *TAT* Card 2 he said,

> *Daughter is back from college and kinda looking disgusted at the farm. She most likely went to the city and saw how they did things there. She looks kinda disgusted about having to come home to this.*

To *TAT* Card 4 he responded,

> *The girl is wanting to go someplace and the hero doesn't want her to. She's trying to hold him back.*

To *TAT* card 6BM he said,

> *He didn't want to do what his mother said. The occupation his mother had wanted him to. He could have been a big disappointment to his mother. She says she is not going to forgive him. He looks pretty sad about it, but*

> he might be glad about what he did. Or just think about changing his ways. Maybe he stuck to his ways, though.

Three years later, in the 12th grade he responds to this same card:

> It looks like the man in the picture has done something he has been dreading, and he has informed his mother I imagine, and he is unsure of what she is going to say about what he has done. It seems to me that she is just keeping silent and not saying anything about him taking some course of action on it.

At age 25, this was his response to *TAT* card 1:

> He's had some problems in his studies or he's trying to figure out whether he's interested in facing the challenge of an instrument. It doesn't look like he's very happy about what he is thinking about.

Asked how the boy got into this position, William said,

> My guess is that he was placed there by his parents and it does not look like he is very happy about being in the position. He looks serious enough worried about it that he will probably give in -- yield and learn. Whether he will work hard is another story. He'll probably resign himself to it.

If counselors could diagnose the presence of foreclosure, and that is a big if because foreclosed individuals are not inclined to seek counseling and when they do their denial and commitment misleads counselors, then counselors have available an extensive repertoire of useful interventions including self-exploration, values clarification, attribution retraining, decision-making instruction, and assertiveness training.

Education. From high school forward, William exhibited attempts to enact his RIASEC profile of ACE in activities that integrated his inconsistent interests. The fulcrum for this integration seems to have been his persuasive talents. He used his negotiation skills to integrate opposing forces, whether they be within himself or in the environment. In high school, William's favorite subjects were bookkeeping and typing. Although he thought seriously about becoming a musician, he decided to attend college to study accounting. Extracurricular activities had come to include numerous outlets for him to practice organizing, persuading, and negotiating. He held office in several school organizations, played in the band, wrote for the newspaper, edited the newspaper, kept statistics for sports teams, formed a gem club, and directed fund-raising projects. These activities were typically characterized as Artistic because they involved music, writing, or cultural artifacts. His Conventional interests led him to impose structure on these activities through editing, collecting, and record keeping. The Enterprising style he displayed in organizing and directing these activities showed his Tom Sawyer spirit and that, indeed, he was a *Little Engine That Could.*

Occupation. The career that William first envisioned in thoughts of *Tom Sawyer* and the script provided by the *Little Engine*, and later rehearsed in hobbies and school activities, cohered in his occupational aspirations. He saw himself as a negotiator. At 25 he aspired to *a position that will give me success, will give me prestige, will give me the ability to work with people, to solve their problems, to have them want me to solve their problems.* He saw himself as a negotiator, as he could not be with his parents when they placed obligations upon him.

By his 50s he had created his niché, one that integrated his Conventional, Artistic, and Enterprising talents. He used Conventional attributes in running the mill. He used Artistic attributes in his gem business and writing articles for gemstone magazines. He used Enterprising attributes to structure innovative real estate deals and develop new investment opportunities.

> *I structure major land and real-estate transactions from a tax and business point of view. I have a unique ability, a knack, for making business transactions. I like to shape things, I like to structure things. I like to put deals together. The creativity is in structuring the deal, not closing it. I am interested in the negotiation*

> *phase. I have the ability to stimulate confidence in others.*

Through his negotiating he could now do what he once could not; he had actively mastered what he once passively experienced. How had he adapted to obligation and foreclosed choices? There are two prominent ways. First, he accepted his parents' occupational choice, yet shaped it to suit himself. This could occur because, fortunately for William, the occupation of business owner is role-flexible, allowing executives to enact their positions differently, as opposed to a role-rigid occupation in which everyone must work in the same way. As mill owner, William emphasized his role as negotiator with major customers. On the side, he structured real estate deals in which he could be a negotiator. He arranged his occupational activities to maximize his autonomy, working alone as much as he could. In the process, he transformed what he passively experienced in his family into a strength. He could not negotiate with parents, so he learned to be a negotiator with the world.

In his avocation or second occupation, we see even more clearly the manifestation of William's self-concept as a negotiator (Super, 1940). William started building his gem collection in the ninth grade, with help and encouragement from his father, and by adulthood it had become a small business in which he bought and sold rare specimens and collections.

> *I enjoy selling. Actually I enjoy buying and negotiating; I don't enjoy the physical act of selling and buying. It's the negotiating.*

He found gemstones that people wanted, and selling those gemstones to them made them happy. In addition to fulfilling his values for autonomy and negotiating, he achieved social recognition here as well. He was nationally and internationally known for the articles that he had written on gemstone collecting, and he had made the acquaintance of socially prominent collectors. Dealing in and writing about gemstones fully implements all aspects of William's vocational personality type. He collects (Conventional) gemstones, writes (Artistic) articles about them, and deals (Enterprising) in them. Furthermore, the avocation

> *mainly fills the moods. It relaxes me, which is the major reason for a hobby. When I get angry, I do not say anything, I go do my gems. It is recreational. I can sit down and lose myself in a problem without any pressure other than my own. When under pressure, I go downstairs and play with gems.*

Writing articles about gemstones brings us back to the issue of William's foreclosed vocational identity. William did well in his newspaper work. Given a free choice of occupation, would he have chosen journalism rather than business? It seems that William's values would have fit him well for either of these, but since he persisted in journalism throughout college and still writes today, perhaps this was his road not taken. At age 59, William said during the final interview,

> *I am so accustomed to reacting in situations that I don't do any thinking. I will continue to run the mill. Every day I do what I have to do. That's really what it boils down to.*

That statement provides a vivid precis of what William's foreclosed vocational identity has wrought.

CHAPTER FIVE
The Adventures of a Searcher

If I am not for myself who will be for me? If I am only for myself, what will I be? These profound two questions are ascribed to Hillel, the famous Rabbi who lived from 70BC to 10AD. His first question concentrates on agency, or the sense that one can produce intended outcomes. The second question concentrates on communion, or the sense that one must form partnerships with other people. As a pair, the questions prompt us to reflect on the dual modes of being human and how we blend agency and union in our own lives. Of course the moral imperative is to integrate agency and union into a generativity that is both productive and compassionate. Unfortunately, not everyone is able to integrate agency and communion so as to become an agent who cooperates with and contributes to the community. The lives of some people are seriously compromised by events and circumstance that lead them to over-emphasize agency. The life narratives of individualistic actors emphasize restiveness, competiveness, independence, and opposition to authority. These qualities can produce occupational success, yet sometime without much enjoyment or personal satisfaction.

The next life portrait illustrates how unmitigated agency can be expressed at work. In Paul Dempsey's life portrait we encounter someone who compulsively sought new adventures whenever an employer tried to control him. Paul's need to control his own destiny first emerges when his mother dies, leaving him on his own -- depriving him of a safe haven and secure base. Initially unable to form new partnerships, he was forced to rely only on himself. Paul spent decades competing with others to show both them and himself that he could stand alone. He used activity and adventure to conceal, from himself and others, his unrequited needs for connection and cooperation. When coworkers and employers moved too close or threatened his autonomy, Paul found a way to move to a new adventure. Fortunately for Paul, his need for control at work was modulated at home by the deep union and affection he felt for his wife and children.

As you read this chapter from the perspective of Career Construction Theory, recognize how Paul *dismissive-avoidant attachment schema* enabled him as a social actor to organize and maintain an *extroverted, norm-doubting personality disposition*. Pay particular attention to how a family tragedy disrupted what was once a secure attachment. This perspective on Paul's life yields insights into and hypotheses about the life-long consequences of a dismissive-avoidant attachment schema. One consequence forged by his need for freedom and flexibility being his adaptation strategy of avoiding commitments and demanding freedom. As a motivated agent, he met challenges and made choices by using a *promotion schema* and *adustive defending* to, as he said, "take things as they come" and "just wait and deal with problems as they arise." As an autobiographical author, Paul deliberated with *meta-reflexive schema* to conceive an oppositional vocational identity and compose a career story of a *Searcher* who experienced a perpetual moratorium (cf., Marcia, 2002).

You might also consider how Paul Dempsey's dismissive attachment schema differs from the secure attachment schema of Robert Coyne (Chapter 3) and the preoccupied attachment schema of William Garrod (Chapter 4). Robert conceived his identity and became "a driver" whereas William accepted a conferred identity and became "driven." Paul concocted a restive identity, without a specific direction or destination, and kept "driving." He improvised a career by skillfully driving through a series of adventures, with each new adventure enabling him to both compose himself and control threats to his autonomy. Now, let us allow Paul Dempsey to generously and forthrightly instruct us in how a man who, as an adolescent, believed that he belonged only to himself adapted successfully to the social challenges of work and marriage.

PART I

A Life Portrait of Paul Dempsey:
Not a Job, an Adventure

When Paul was in primary school, he lost his mother to a heart condition. This traumatic loss accounts for far more about him as a young boy and later as an adult than even he could possibly realize. In middle age he remembered just enough about his mother to make the impact of her death sufficiently apparent:

> *She was tall and slender with blonde hair like mine. She was good at sewing and would make me costumes for the school plays. In fact she made most of my clothes as long as she was able to. I'd go places with her. We spent a lot of time with my aunt, her sister, and with my grandparents who lived nearby. I always felt very much loved by her. We were very close. She always hugged me and managed to take care of me even though she was ill all along and would look very tired. The last recollection I have of her was of her lying on the couch sick while I trimmed the Christmas tree. I cried a lot when she died, I couldn't really understand what had happened.*

As a ninth grader, Paul described the close relationship with his mother, and remembered that she worried about him a lot. *She did not want me to do things like sports and learn how to swim. She was afraid all of the time.*

Family

Paul's parents married when they were both in their mid-30s. His mother continued to work as a secretary for several years until ill-health forced her to quit. Paul recalled at age 40 how lonely his mother seemed to be: *My father was never around to help with anything. He wasn't there.* He described their relationship as cold:

> *They were not as loving toward each other as I felt they should be. They never argued but they never kissed or embraced either. They were just two people who happened to live under the same roof. I saw other children whose parents were together and they were going places together, and doing things together and I couldn't understand why we couldn't do those things.*

From Paul's description of his parents' relationship one cannot determine the extent to which he might have held his father responsible for what occurred and if her death fostered the resentment which he reported having toward his father over the ensuing years. All he knew was that he was closer to her than to him and that when she died he felt as if he no longer had anyone to care about him, *I was on my own*. Paul did admire his aunt, *a free thinker*, who worked as a nurse. Unfortunately, Paul rarely saw her because s*he traveled all over the country. She worked at a place until she got tired of it and then she would just move on.*

Paul's father had always been a virtual stranger to him. Having worked at a variety of jobs from the time he completed the eighth grade, Paul's father managed to purchase a small diner around the time Paul was born and had remained there ever since. Although there were advantages to owning an enterprise, it required that he be at his post from dawn until dark on every day except Monday.

> *I really can't remember much about my father during my early childhood. He was working all the time. He'd already be at the diner by the time I got up in the morning and would not get back at night until after I'd gone to bed.*

Paul's father, carrying on the tradition of his own youth, was essentially uninvolved with his family. Interviewed during Paul's ninth grade in high school, Paul's father referred to his origins.

> *My father was a poor man. This meant we all had to work hard. All of us had to go out and hustle for what we got. Nothing was handed to us on a silver platter. Whatever pennies were earned were saved. It was a struggle. Instead of going on to high school, I had to settle for the college of hard knocks.*

Looking back at age 35, Paul reported that: *It's a funny thing to say, but I really feel that because he wasn't there during those early years is probably the reason why it is the way it is.*

After his wife's death, Paul's father arranged for a widow who lived next door to work a few hours a day keeping house and caring for Paul. As Paul stated during his ninth-grade interview:

> *She's not quite as friendly as my mother was. Certainly it's not the most wonderful arrangement in the world, but I get along with her all right. She is quite old and doesn't like children. Even at that young age I could see that I really wasn't wanted there; that I was just in her way. Things just weren't the same.*

Until the middle of his freshman year in high school Paul was subjected to the domineering housekeeper whose word went unchallenged by his father.

> *She was always there watching everything I did. This really tied me down. I never felt I could do a lot of the things the other kids could do. I was stifled. She had all kinds of old-fashioned ideas. For example, I had to wear a heavy coat until the middle of June. It was always a matter of "you shouldn't do this, you shouldn't do that." I always felt pressure because she was always watching. It made me a little rebellious. I think the more "don'ts" you put on a person the more they want what they are forbidden to have. Besides, here I was looking for acceptance and nothing I did seemed to please her or my father.*

Paul had to get home early and not stay up too late. The housekeeper forced him to attend Sunday school where the medals he won for perfect attendance hardly compensated for *the unfair obligation they placed on me.*

Looking back at age 40, Paul described his father's reactions to him during adolescence as *detached, cold, non-protective, unfair,* and *uptight.* Another important restriction placed on Paul about a year after his mother's death and continuing into his first year in high school was his father's insistence that he work at the diner every day after school and on the weekends as well. Whatever money he earned was not to be spent. Despite the 25 dollars a week which he earned for his work, he reported at age 14 that he also disliked this obligation:

> *I can't go skiing. There's no fun after school. I have to have all my fun after dark. I've got a lot of other things I could do. I didn't want to be there, to be tied down like that, I wanted to be with my friends, and I especially didn't want to be under my father's supervision. I felt like I had to run away from everything to do what I wanted to do.*

Career Growth

Unhappy over the relationship he has with his father, resistant to his father's periodic attempts to control his behavior from afar, feeling unaccepted by a domineering housekeeper, disengaged from grandparents who were too old to take care of themselves, and uncertain about where and to whom he really belonged, Paul yearned for a closeness and acceptance he could not find among his kin. The elementary school teachers did not make things any better.

> *The elementary school I went to had a cold, clinical atmosphere. The kids got very little personal attention. I could never really get close to any of the teachers.*

These circumstances changed, however, when his seventh-grade class moved into a smaller building:

> *Being there gave me a comfortable feeling. It wasn't all concrete and steel. The teacher took an interest in each student. I could really get close to her.*

Paul's junior high school years were happy ones for him:

> *I really got along well with the teachers. My grades were excellent. In fact, I got in the high 90s in every subject. One male teacher was into hunting and fishing, and I was active in the hunting club.*

The hunting club focused his attention on marksmanship and archery. He had already enjoyed fishing, setting traps, making zip guns, and shooting his air rifle. In high school he added clay target shooting and then became a student leader in the hunting and trapping club. Another source of happiness and stability during Paul's junior high school years was his friendship with peers who shared his interests and enthusiasms:

> *We built model airplanes, went to the same church, walked to and from school together. We would play football and baseball. We were inseparable. Wherever they were I was. Wherever I went they went. We saw things the same way. I could relate to my friends, a group I could be close to. I became dependent on friends rather than family. I felt that I belonged more with them than my family.*

As he reported many years later -- Everybody has to belong to something, to someone. He even attributed his good grades to the relationship he had with his friends.

Unfortunately for Paul, he lost contact with his friends just as he was about to enter high school. His father bought a house in a neighborhood closer to the diner and with a better high school. Paul was quite sad. Once again Paul felt alone, an outsider at home, in school, and among his new peers. Paul's resentment toward his father re-emerged as he stated his chief problem as follows: My family doesn't take enough interest in me. He wished his father would spend more time with him and, because he did not, Paul began to reject him as a mentor and confidant:

> *I wouldn't go to him to talk over my problems. He's like a stranger to me. He bawls me out every once in a while, but that doesn't bother me. I figure he never took an interest in me, so why should I worry about what he has to say? He gives me a little money but not enough to support me.*

At age 25 Paul reported,

> *I would have wanted my father to spend more time with me. It's important, especially for a boy, to have a*

> *father's influence. I always look for guidance from older men because I didn't have this guidance when I was a boy.*

As an example, Paul said that he admired *my wife's uncle because he has a business of his own. He taught me a lot about mechanics.* Paul did not have trouble with authority figures as shown by another example. He said there were two part-time police officers and three state troopers in town. At age sixteen, he enjoyed drinking with the three troopers, having no trouble being served because he was with them and acted older than his age.

Career Exploration

Paul's interests and the energy to pursue them seem boundless during his junior and senior high school years. During the ninth-grade interview, his father complained:

> *Well, he needs to do one thing and stick with it more than he does. He's inclined to jump from one thing to another. Of course, if he gets older he might concentrate on one thing and be good at it. I think it is a matter of age. I mean, I think he will eventually settle on something. I don't think it will go on that way.*

His father continued by saying: He goes from one thing to the other. What he does is clever, but he loses interest.

There is photography and even his own darkroom in the cellar of his father's house where he spends a good deal of time although it is not homey, no one is ever there. Accordingly, most of his hobbies find him on the move or deal with traveling fast, consistent with his earliest memory: On holidays we would go for a ride to my grandparent's house about 25 miles away. I felt very happy. His special hobby was making model airplanes which he entered into races as a member of a club devoted to that activity. Paul also made model racing cars and played with a railroad set. He made his own soap-box racing car and participated in local derbies. Although he had no special interest in sports, he learned how to skate and to swim and was pleased by these new accomplishments. In the winter he went skiing and in the summer he liked to take hikes in the woods. At age twelve he learned to drive a car, by age fourteen he owned a flatbed truck, and by age sixteen he drove a tractor-trailer truck.

During his initial interview, Paul explained how he was saving money from his job at the diner to take a trip to Montana over Easter break. He would go with his aunt to visit a cousin. *I want to take the trip very bad.* When asked "Why?" Paul responded: *Just to get an adventure, I guess. I like to do things like that just to do it.* Asked for other examples, he replied: *I really can't say. I mean, make new achievements, do things I've never done and all that. It sort of gives you the feeling of superiority I guess you'd say.*

In addition to being on the move, Paul delighted in reading mystery stories and any books having to do with electricity, one of his chief interests:

> *When I was just a little kid I saw my mother plugging a switch. When I pushed a hairpin into the switch, it gave me a little shock. From that time on I wondered what made it jump like that. It stuck in my mind. Although nobody paid much attention to my little electrical experiments with plugs and sockets and batteries, as time went on I made progress, got to know more about it. You can never learn enough about electricity.*

Before entering high school, he looked forward to college where he planned to earn a degree in electrical engineering: *I figure I might just as well try for the highest in electricity, shoot for the sky.* His father had promised to give him all the education he could possibly afford. In the ninth grade, Paul selected a pre-college curriculum and wanted to study *electrical engineering or electrical science in college.* When asked what would be a successful life for him, Paul responded prophetically: *You are successful if you do what you want to do.* During his ninth-grade interview Paul said that if he did not do something with electricity, he would probably do sales but *it would not be in a store where I would be cooped up all day waiting for people to come in. Instead I would go out to sell, then I could come and go as I please.*

By the time Paul reached his senior year in high school he was totally alienated from his academic surrounding: *I do as much work as I can, and what I don't get done doesn't bother me. If I feel like coming to school, I do, and if I don't feel like it I don't.* Although he enjoyed mechanical drawing and auto shop, he had ceased caring about his grades and considered school irrelevant for his pared-down vocational objectives:

> *So maybe I don't talk perfect, but I should worry about that? I don't try exceptionally hard. It's a little bit late for that. I can't see where school is going to do me any good. It's here, and I gotta go, so I go. That's about it.*

The vice-principal, who chided him about his long hair and for wearing boots and dungarees, warned him, *If you step out of line one more time, I'm going to throw you out.* Paul stayed away from home as much as he could.

> *I'm just there long enough to eat and sleep. My father is not home very much, and I figure I have nobody to worry about but myself. I was out on the streets all the time. I spent my afternoons with the crowd down at the corner talking about girls, did some drinking, played cards for money in back of the bowling alley, went to bars.*

As he put it 20 years later,

> *I was doing whatever I wanted to do, and nobody stopped me. My father wasn't around so he really didn't know what was going on. After my mother had died, I became thoroughly confused, I didn't know what direction to go in. I didn't know where I belonged. Eventually I became closer to my peers than to my family, I felt cut off like a poor relative. I was looking for my father to be more involved with me, to intercede when I needed it, but he never did. I felt like something tacked on to his life. Finally I decided I only belonged to myself, and I wasn't about to go to him for anything. I guess I was looking for companionship like I had with my*

friends before we moved away, somebody I could be really close to. But I could never find that again. That's probably the reason I got married so young.

In many respects an adult before his time, self-reliant by necessity and out of a resentful rebellion, Paul learned a lot *out on the streets* where he smoked, drank, and shot zip guns. He acted and looked older than his age. At age 25 Paul said that in high school he *majored in girls*. He became coitally active by the age of fourteen: *I went through eighteen girl friends in one year!* When asked how he had felt about dating, he replied that as a teenager he took girls t*o motels rather than movies.* By the age of sixteen he began to drive a tractor-trailer truck without a license and hauled produce to the city where he spent his early morning hours drinking in bars, surrounded by women much older than he. His father still was willing to pay for college but Paul had given up those plans saying that: *I just don't want to have to go.* Moreover, *electrical engineering is mostly inside work*, a place he did not want to be. When asked as a high school senior to describe himself Paul stated:

> *I'm kind of a general goof-off. I do what I want to do. I run my own life and I feel that everybody else should run theirs. If I really want to do something, I carry through with it. If I really didn't want to do it in the first place, why, I don't do it or I just make a half-hearted attempt at it. Otherwise, to tell you the truth, I just never stop to think. The way I feel, thinkin's bad for you. So I never do it. I stick to my own business and I let everybody else mind theirs.*

As graduation approached, Paul thought that after a trip by car around the United States, he would enter the Air Force: *An ambition of mine is to travel and see the country. I have a real urge to travel.* As a senior he put a thousand miles a week on his car. His fascination with cars, along with his exceptional aptitude for building and repairing machines, prompted his interest in becoming a mechanic and in eventually owning his own garage, yet even these aspirations were muted somewhat by the fact that only a high school senior, he already was making 300 hundred dollars a week as a truck driver. As a senior, he summarized his outlook on the future by saying, *just wait and deal with problems as they arise.*

During his senior year, Paul met a girl who was a year older than he. She was fascinated by a high school boy so well acquainted with the ways of the world: *I acted much older than I was, I'd been around. I could do anything I wanted to do without restriction, I guess she saw me as adventurous.* Important to Paul was the fact that he *could sit and talk to her hours on end, there was a real openness.* His new close friend talked him into finishing high school, and they were married right after graduation:

> *At first it was really a ball. We were into fast cars, drinking, partying. We were both working, but we had lots of time for each other. We'd eat out whenever we felt like it.*

Their life-style changed with the arrival of their daughter, and hardly more than a year later, with the birth of a son. Working as a mechanic for an automobile dealership and with his wife at home with the children, Paul relished his new circumstances:

> *It was like belonging to a family group again, I felt secure. There was something solid about what we had.*

The only fly in the ointment was Paul's dissatisfaction with his work. During the first five years of his marriage, Paul worked first as a truck driver and then as a mechanic for the State Highway Patrol. Because of his superb mechanical skills, the garage manager made him also responsible for keeping large amounts of equipment in working order. Given these extra responsibilities, Paul became dissatisfied with his pay that barely allowed him to meet his mortgage and automobile payments. Efforts to augment his income included working as a mechanic in a local garage and as a chef for a catering service. Supplementary jobs such as these continued even after he resigned his position with the State and went to work as an apprentice roofer. This new full-time position turned out to be almost as unpalatable as his previous job.

At the age of twenty-five, Paul found himself on a seasonal layoff and collecting unemployment. He saw very little chance for advancement, complained about the *dirty work*, felt looked down upon by the home owners, and especially resented his bosses' disregard for him: *No one has even patted me on the back and told me what a nice job I've done.* His family was barely able to make ends meet, sometimes being forced to eat whatever food he could bring back from a hunting trip. Tensions mounted between him and his wife, and for a short time Paul moved out of the house. The fact that he and his wife were trying to run their own firearms and hunting supplies store on the side contributed to their deteriorating situation: *It demanded weekends. It demanded evenings.* He attributed the stomach trouble he began to experience to the pressure of a business which had become too large to be pursued on a part-time basis. Recalling the price his father had to pay for *living his business six days a week*, Paul sold his entire inventory and decided to strike out in a new direction, one where he could feel free.

> *I could not work inside. I'd rather be outside where I can move around and feel free. It seems much nicer. I do not want to tie myself to anyone's apron string.*

Career Establishment

Convinced long ago that his home town had little to offer them, Paul and his wife sold their house and moved across the country:

> *It was the best thing I ever did. There was the thrill of moving into a new area, a new house, and eventually a new job. It was really an exciting year.*

Within a short time he was hired by a tree removal service in the area. Pleased with his work, the company first gave him the job of crew chief and then the job of foreman for all the crews. At age 35, he accounted for his promotions as follows:

> *You just go on and do whatever you have to do. I don't know enough to quit. One thing for sure, I don't take anything too seriously. I don't see things that happen*

> as a matter of life or death. When the winter weather got tough I just shut down the office and took a two-week vacation in Hawaii. You can't take life that seriously. Above everything else, you can't let yourself lose your confidence. You have to believe in yourself, regardless of what happens. Things are always gonna change. You have to be able to take what's at hand and make whatever you can out of it.

He was finally awarded the job of company manager and was pleased with almost every aspect of his work: the fact that it was permanent and that every day offered a variety of challenges. He reported: *The day goes by fast. There's no time for sitting around. I'm learning new tricks every day. It's a whole new ball game every time I go to work*. What he especially appreciated was that *if there's a problem, I can go right to the owner. He listens to you, tries to understand your point of view*. He also enjoyed the relationship he had with the 75 men who worked for him. He tried not to *lord it over them* and believed that their respect for him was prompted not so much by his formal authority but by how he behaved with them. There was pressure, to be sure, yet

> when it got too much, I would do something wild to relieve it. For example, I'd drive a truck around the yard for half an hour. Some evenings I'd take my motorcycle and ride the power lines for a while.

As important as his job was to him, it clearly took a back seat to his home and family with whom he enjoyed innumerable avocational interests. He and his wife went on a cruise every year. The entire family spent much of their time out in the woods with their snowmobiles. They owned a travel trailer and went camping throughout the United States. He delighted in some of the *adventures* he and buddies were apt to do, *like going almost a 100 miles away just for a cup of coffee* or *getting in the car with no particular destination in mind and winding up somewhere new*. Paul continued to derive deep satisfactions from his marriage, was pleased with the relationship he had with his wife who *doesn't henpeck or tie me down*, and was proud of his children's accomplishments. As a father, he *tried not to say no to my children.* The early years, when he was forced to spend too much time away from home on an assortment of poor paying jobs, were like a bad dream:

> *I only wish I hadn't missed so much of my children's childhood the way my father did mine. I hope I caught myself in time from doing the same thing to them that he did to me. I feel cheated. I really do. I feel as though part of my childhood was stolen because no one was there to help me enjoy it.*

Although a leader in his community -- he was Justice of the Peace and Chairman of the Town Committee -- and a highly regarded employee in an expanding business which had seen fit to give him increasing responsibilities, Paul's main quest remained what it has always been, for a freedom and a childlike joy he never knew in his youth. He reported at age 40, *I don't let people dominate me.* He looked forward to retirement in 15 or 20 years when he would *sell the house, buy a small motor home, and go traveling with my wife.* He wanted *to be able to change my life anytime I want and go off in a different direction*, totally unfettered by convention, the opposite of his father whose life amounted to little more than a barren survival for him and an anguish for his son: *I try to enjoy myself to the fullest as long as it doesn't injure someone else.* Examples of this were the times he got on his motorcycle or his snowmobile to escape a milieu which always threatened to undo him:

> *I get out into the wilderness where nobody is around, where nothing is near, just complete silence. You look around and can see the deer running through the woods. There can be this fantastic free feeling when you're not tied down to windows and doors.*

For reasons not too difficult to understand, he refused to be chained by anything or anyone, would not jump through hoops which were not of his own making, in his not altogether unsuccessful effort to claim for himself at least as much as what he had often been denied.

Career Management

Unfortunately, after nine years at the tree service, Paul was fired from a job in which he had been highly successful, replaced by two people whose combined salaries amounted to far less than his. Needless to say, it came as a shock:

> *I was very upset that day. I sat in a chair and said to myself, "Here I am, 40-whatever years old, and I don't have a job. I'm in serious trouble here. How am I going to pay my bills? Let's look at this thing realistically. It's not the end of the world. I'll get another job." So I started doing numbers. Given the fact that I didn't have to do all this driving to work and having my clothes dry-cleaned every day, and that I wouldn't have to pay any taxes on the unemployment insurance and that I had eight weeks severance pay in my pocket, by the time I got done and figured out what I had left, I actually made money! So I said, "Well, I think I'll take the summer off and spend it with the kids," which is what I did. My son and I rode motorcycles all summer out in the woods. My daughter and I visited museums and did all kinds of things together. We had a very good time over the summer. Then the kids were back to school, and I said, "O.K. Now it's time for me to go to work." When I went out into industry, I was either under-qualified or over-qualified. I was either too young or too old. So here I found myself unemployable, and I said, "I'll see what I can do."*

A good friend came to his aid with a job as a bus mechanic which lasted only three months, followed by a job as an agent for a freight brokerage that went bankrupt after four months while owing him a lot of money: "Here we are. Now what do we do? I said, "Well, let's play this out and see how far we can carry it."

He carried it far enough to take what he learned from the bankrupt brokerage that owed him back pay to become an agent representing two different freight brokers. He worked on commission as an independent contractor who matched shipping customers to motor carriers. He loved the variety and freedom. He could work out of his car as he solicited new customers, sourced carriers, matched shippers to carriers, negotiated with shippers and carriers, dispatched trucks, scheduled deliveries, solved problems, and managed conflicts.

One day he received a call from the president of the larger brokerage:

> *"Hey, I got a problem. I gotta see you right away. Get the next plane outta there and get down here. I gotta talk to you." I figured this is trouble. His dispatcher picked me up at the airport and brought me to the office. I said, "Gee, Charlie, what's the problem?" He said, "I don't even want to talk to you about this. We'll get to it after lunch." So we had this big fancy lunch, came back to the office, and sat there while his secretary brought in coffee. I said to him, "O.K., now what's the problem?" He said, "I've got some big problems, some of which you've heard of, some of which you haven't. I've got 50 agents working for me, and I got trouble with 49 of 'em. You're the only one I don't have any trouble with. You're the only agent who has ever turned a profit for me."*

The profit which the president mentioned had resulted from Paul's ingenuity. He had figured a way to haul a certain kind of insulation material down the road. Everyone was pleased:

> *More guys were doing two trips a week, knocking down some big bucks. These drivers really made some money on this. They're getting a percentage of this. I'm getting a percentage. Smith keeps feeding me with leads and loads and what have you. We're doing real well!*

At this point Paul was working out of his house. He had more business than he could handle by himself, so he took on a partner.

> *We worked weekends for about three months, sorting all this out with these guys and getting him money for*

> *'em. Now they're committed to us. The reputation spread. Trucking companies get very hungry. They're always looking for more work, more work, more work. I took on several more trucking companies.*

Another example of Paul's ingenuity was when he learned that a certain large paper company was three months behind in their deliveries. They needed six railway cars or 18 truckloads of paper delivered as quickly as possible. His proposal that refrigerated trailer trucks be used was met with an initial skepticism:

> *He says,"Naa, I can't use them because they have corrugations in the floor." I said, Look, fine. How 'bout if we plywood the floor to the trailers? He said, "What do you mean?" I said, "Well, I got some thoughts in mind. Okay, time to put the cards on the table. I know why you need me now. You got 15 feet of snow and they can't move a rail car anywhere. But what happens when the switches thaw and the ice melts and the roads are bare and dry?" So he says, "I'll make this commitment to you: whatever percentage of my freight you handle out of here during the winter, I'll give you in the summer." So I said, "O.K., we'll give it a try."*

But how will he get the paneling he needed to cover the floors?

> *I stopped in to see this guy in a brand new lumber company sitting off on the side of the road. I said to him, "Look, if I send a trailer truck in here it's gonna take 40 feet, or ten sheets, of plywood to do the floor of the trailer. But the trailer isn't 8 feet wide, so we'll have to cut these off." He says to me, "I'll tell you what. Since you're gonna be using a lot of this, I'll cut 'em for you free!" I said, "Great! No problem at all!" The guy was so happy at the lumber yard that he'd cut the sheets ahead of time and have the plywood settin' out in front, layin' on the ground so that when the guys came through in the middle of the night, they'd just grab 10 sheets of plywood, throw 'em in the back of the truck,*

and go on. In the meantime, trailers were very improved and instead of having corrugated floors, they started makin' what they called a 'T-bar' floor. So all of a sudden, I said to this guy upstate, "You might want to look at some of these. Some of these may not need plywood." He said, "O.K., before you plywood any more of these, let me take a look at 'em." So, all of a sudden, it went from a point where they would never load any refrigerated trailers to a point where he would load nothing but refrigerated trailers! I'll tell you, I destroyed the candy industry and the fish industry in the region. Those guys wouldn't begin to haul fish or candy when they could haul paper. We turned that into a $6.5 million a year traffic lane move. Remember, I was getting between 8% and 10% of that money. We really made some serious money on this!

Paul was exactly where he wanted to be. His business was flourishing. He had approximately 60 trucks at his beck and call. He was the biggest hauler of bronze, brass, copper, and machinery in his region. He had moved his office out of his house because he had more than a dozen people working for him. His telephone bills alone had mounted to $25,000 a year. The one drawback was that he was unhappy being so busy in his office and not out on the road. He decided to cut back. One of the unwelcome pressures was his competition. Others could not help but notice his success and so they tried to emulate it.

When you're successful, everyone tries to copy what you do. They feel they could do it just as well without my involvement. They tried to undercut my rate, chopped it down. I still held on for several years. As far as I was concerned, they could have all the freight they wanted, but if you can't get trucks to haul it, eventually you'll have to call us! I told the customers, "Hey, you guys are cute. You're learning. You're doing what you have to do, but when you get stuck, call me and then we'll discuss what I'm gonna charge you to move it. But remember, if you don't call me first, my rates double before you get out the door!" Sometimes they'd have a minor heart attack. They'd swallow real hard and finally say, "O.K., come and get it. We gotta get it out of here!" I irritated the hell out of a lot of people, but what did I care?

There were other flies in the ointment as well.

There are a lot of crass individuals out there driving trucks. They're tired, very tired 'cause they're putting in some really long hours. They're frustrated. They're irritated. They're aggravated. They tend to take it all out on people they come in contact with. Their language can be pretty nasty. Things could get a little hairy once in a while!

In an effort to counteract whatever calumnies people were too ready to believe about him, Paul decided that he must be entirely up front with everyone. Whether they were truck drivers, employees, or Department of Transportation investigators, Paul was scrupulously honest and kept careful records of his transactions.

Agents, brokers, whatever, have the most horrible reputations in the world. Everybody who's ever dealt with 'em thinks they're a bunch of crooks. Not true. Not true in my case. I'm too stupid to be!

Asked at age 54 to describe this strategy, he explained:

I try to be as honest as possible, and that's not always easy. I'm outgoing, sometimes too outgoing. Sometimes I'm an agitator. Whatever you say you have to be ready to live with. I never really thought of myself as competitive. I never prostituted myself to outdo someone else. In the trucking business I knew what I had to charge to make a comfortable living for myself and my drivers, and I made that known up front. I didn't care what other people were doing. I might have made more money if I'd been more competitive, but I didn't want to do it that way!

Meanwhile, business began to slow down. Dozens of trucking companies that had been in business for years had folded. The competition had become so intense that only the biggest companies, which made money in other ways, were able to absorb the money lost on hauling freight. Paul, characteristically, took stock of the situation and made a decision.

> *I took a couple of years off! I started working on boats and playin' around up near the ocean. I started delivering boats up and down the coast. That's part of what I'm doing now. But I got tired of sitting around doin' nothing, so I went back to work again, this time for the company that had originally fired me ten years before. At this point they were losing about $500,000 a year. Between me and the President we turned it all around in six months. So it was now a profit making organization. Then his three brothers fired him!*

Paul continued for a while with this company although he saw the handwriting on the wall:

> *The Executive Vice-President and I didn't get along. He was a real idiot, one of those guys who was running trucking companies all over the country. He'd been with other companies and got thrown out of them because he was so bad. To show you how shortsighted he was, once he said to me, "I can't sign your expense account this week." And I said, "What seems to be the problem?" He answered, "We don't rent Cadillacs when we travel." I replied, "Oh, I do! What do you rent?" He said, "We rent Fords." I said, "Oh, that's nice. I don't get into those things really good. I need something big." We discussed the rate for each car, only a six-dollar difference, and then the fact that on the last trip I drove 200 miles and he only drove six. As I told him, I needed to be comfortable, I needed to impress some people, and I needed to get there in a hurry. It also turned out that he paid 40 cents a mile, while I had no mileage charge whatsoever! He threw the expense account at me and*

> wouldn't sign it. So I carried it into the President's office and said, "You gotta do something about this idiot!" So he calls in the Office Manager and says, "Look, from now on, if I'm not here, he can sign his own expense account. Just pay him. Don't worry about it. I'll take care of it." That was it. From there on out, there was never any question. Later, when the jerk took over the company, he tried to pick my brains for a while, and when I refused to cooperate, I was out the door.

Paul was now "retired" again yet not content to putter around the house. So when he was offered a job as a supervisor for a bottled gas company down South to work full-time for the six busy months of the year, he grabbed it. Within the week he and his wife put up their house for sale, and within the month they bought the house where they have lived ever since. After three years, Paul purchased a firearms store and took it over. This venture was successful yet not appealing enough to keep him from the work with boats he had always enjoyed. With his master's license, Paul was offered a job as a marine mechanic. He has kept it ever since:

> We do everything. We do plumbing. We do electrical. We do generators and diesel and gas engines. It's really good. Some people will bring real big boats out from the Bahamas for the winter and take them back in April. It's just a lot of fun. We have a good time doing it. We bring a lot of boats in right here, right behind my own boat at my dock.

Beside the time he spends out in the small lagoon where his boat is anchored, only 50 feet from a spacious back porch where he can view the comings and goings of other boats, sometimes filing complaints against those who disregard the speed limits and leave wakes that trouble smaller craft, Paul has taken on another venture. He had just begun training police officers in the use of firearms, another love of his. He intended to sell training equipment to local police departments, so that trainees can practice on guns equipped with highly sophisticated accessories. Why this new turn?

> *People give you ideas. Most of 'em won't make any money. Most will never pan out. But hey! We can discuss it. You just kind of fall into it and say, "This is not gonna be a job, it will be an adventure!"*

Even a turn of events that threatened to end that *adventure* is taken in stride:

> *The very day after my wife got herself a full-time job, and we now had full health insurance coverage, I had a heart attack. Neither of us had any medical problems. I'd quit smoking and put on forty pounds between June and October. Maybe that had something to do with it. The heart attack was so strong that the heart got torn loose from the lining around the heart. You could hear the heart rubbing as it beat against the lining. I've got one artery that's blocked 100%, two that are blocked about 75% or something, and one that's pretty much open. I've been on medication and a diet ever since. I've also developed diabetes on top of that.*

Despite this change in his circumstances, they have slowed him down only a bit. At age 59, he remains active in various civic duties and volunteer associations and continues to have an optimistic outlook:

> *There seems to be no end in sight. I'd like to travel more. We'd like to take our boat and go up the East Coast, through the Great Lakes, and down the Mississippi. We have friends all up and down the coast, in Charleston, in Norfolk, in Baltimore. As soon as my wife retires we'll be on our way. I see us in pretty good shape at that point in time.*

His outlook is evident in how he describes his father's life to the end:

> *He worked right up to a week before he died at 84. When he sold the diner he went to work driving a taxi. It was great! He loved it! He could talk to his buddies and be out and about, and he thought this was great. But after he had several accidents with his car, the cab*

> company decided they didn't want him to drive any more, and they put him to work in the garage. He loved that too. It gave him something to do every day. Like he said, "I gotta have some reason to get up in the morning, right?

Paul's description of his father's work-life surely includes a similar feeling about how he himself has handled the various transitions in his own life. Each of them has required a flexibility that finds him still on his own two feet, permitting him to continue on unfazed. In the hands of a person like Paul life becomes very much like a game of chess, a challenge that never ends even when a particular game ends in checkmate. There will always be another game to play with new moves and different outcomes. As Paul described what his working life has been like for him and recounts experiences other people might find harrowing, one's chief impression is that he is a person who is not defined by events. His energetic involvement in the world of work does not appear to betoken unresolved issues from the past. His sense of self-worth does not seem to depend on any particular outcome. He is not propelled by a self-doubt that can make momentary failures into the abyss of despair or momentary successes into the flight of Seraphim. Mistakes can always be remedied; victories always yield place to setbacks. This is not to say that the time he spends at work is devoid of passion but rather that, out of a lack of anxiety, he can be passionate about many things. His energy is not wasted on dread and therefore can be expended to serve the goals of the moment. Despite a trail of uncertainties when the next step to take was not at all clear, Paul never appears to have been undone, at a loss, or in any way desperate. That trail has included being fired as company manager of a tree service, being dismissed again after three months at another company, losing a four-month job for a company that went bankrupt, years of self-employment as a freight agent that finally ended as the entire industry began to falter, short-lived employment as a mechanic at a bus company until he was fired again, and finally his return to living and working around boats in a work situation he finds entirely pleasing.

How can this be the work history of a man who reports that his career has been gratifying? There are several reasons. He has been no stranger to financial fortune. He has enjoyed respect and admiration in his community and beyond. He has raised a family who have enjoyed their life together in ways he never knew in his own boyhood. He has ventured to take risks his father never did and embraced life as his mother never could, much to her son's dismay. If we look deeply enough we can find in Paul what might be termed an indomitable spirit, an uncommon ability to step back and survey his options without panic, a refusal ever to view himself as victim, and an insatiable curiosity about what each new chapter of his life might bring. As he said as a twelfth grader, *just wait and deal with problems as they arise.*

Paul has been a steady-eyed analyst whose decisions were not made in frantic haste, whose plans have always included steps and passages prepared by lessons previously learned, whether painfully or with little effort. His creativity was not fanciful, the risks he took were never foolhardy. He has an air of confidence about him, both in guiding human relationships and in coaxing recalcitrant boat engines. Like the man who is convinced that the darkest moments only herald the dawn, Paul has been certain that new challenges will appear on the horizon, and that lemons will sooner or later be made into lemonade. He has learned enough to know that in the most distressing situation, one can always make do. It is a view to which his wife has grown accustomed. It is a lesson he has demonstrated to his children. Perhaps even more than they, his primary audience has been his father, who lacked Paul's sense of perspective and who would have benefitted most of all from his hard-won wisdom.

Perhaps in time, Paul will lay aside his youthful notions about what life requires. Even now he is able to say, *I'm proud I survived this long. I have found a peace within myself. I'm not fighting myself anymore.* And as long as his marriage endures, as long as his safety valves from a pressure-filled existence remain available to him, and as long as he can continue to act in accordance with just a few of his dreams, Paul will continue to relish his adventures.

PART II

The life portrait of Paul Dempsey tells a complex story shaped by multiple influences and forces. In the second half of this chapter, I view the portrait from two different vantage points, first from the perspective of self-construction processes and content and then from the perspective of career construction processes and content.

Self-Construction

How did Paul construct a self to survive the cold and isolated environment of his youth? I address this question about self-construction -- or how he shaped who he was and what he became -- by examining the process and content of his self-making (Bruner, 2001). For our purposes herein, *self-constructing processes* broadly comprehended refer to *how* Paul constructed himself as a social actor, motivated agent, and autobiographical author. In contrast, *self-construction content* broadly comprehended refers to *who* Paul became, that is, the outcomes of self-construction in terms of in terms of enduring personal characteristics and motives. Before appraising Robert's personality and motives, let us first consider the processes that he used to constitute himself.

Self-Construction Processes

Three interwoven processes for self-construction are the social actor's self-organizing, the motivated agent's self-regulating, and the autobiographical author's self-conceiving. As a preview, Paul's dismissive-avoidant attachment schema and extroverted, norm-doubting orientation to relationships and rules inclined him to a promotion focus on advancement and adventure using a present-oriented adaptation strategy that in due course shaped a meta-reflexive schema and the vocational identity strategy of a Searcher.

Social Actor. Researchers have noted that early loss of a parent often predicts an avoidant attachment schema in midlife (Klohnen & Bera, 1998), even more so for only children because they do not have siblings with whom to forge relatively immediate and safe attachment bonds. The outlines of Paul's life portrait closely resemble the conceptual description of the dismissive-avoidant prototype first described by Bartholomew (1990). For example, Paul idealized his mother yet could not provide clear narratives of specific episodes that supported that glowing assessment. Furthermore, Paul described his parents in polarized terms; idealizing his warm mother while disparaging his cold father. Unable to acknowledge both negative and positive traits of each parent, he exaggerated one-sided descriptions of them. This behavior matches closely Fraley, Davis, and Shaver's (1998) observation that dismissing adults may avoid feeling attachment emotions by not noticing, elaborating, or remembering attachment-related experiences.

Paul may have already formed a secure attachment schema before the death of his beloved mother ripped away his primary attachment figure. Paul then appeared to suffer an intense childhood bereavement, during which he first searched for closeness and then became emotionally detached, which is not unusual when death disrupts a primary connection and the survivor is unsuccessful in getting what she or he deeply needs. Paul briefly grappled for support and sought closeness to others before giving up. He struggled to maintain contact with his father, an attachment figure who could not be counted on for emotional support. However, Paul rather quickly stopped seeking comfort from his cold, insensitive, and rejecting father because he knew that none would be forthcoming. When, as an adult, he declared, *I never wanted anything from my father, and I never asked for anything*, he can be forgiven his deliberate disregard for the many times he surely yearned for affection and help from an ungiving father. And when he added, *I can make it on my own*, it is reasonable to suppose that at least a part of this statement amounted to "whistling in the dark." Paul renounced a father who *tried to rule me with a heavy hand*, who *never let me know when he was pleased by anything I did*. In due course, Paul rejected his father's advice and told his father to get out of his life and *never come back again*. The hurt over his father's rejection was too painful for Paul to acknowledge so he concealed his distress beneath a veneer of rebellion and animosity. His father's failure to comfort Paul may have been even more traumatic than his mother's death. She was gone but his father could have been there; yet he chose to be physically and emotionally unavailable to Paul.

Failing to secure emotional support from his father, Paul looked to grandparents who were unresponsive because they were frail; then turned to an aunt who was responsive yet lived far away. In Paul's family, his mother had been the only one who was not rejecting, insensitive, or unavailable. Experiencing contentious relationships with his father and the unavailability of relatives, Paul lost confidence that he had access inside the family to a supportive caregiver. Next he turned to a moralizing caretaker, a housekeeper who gave sermons rather than hugs. Then in his uncommon search for closeness, Paul looked outside the house. He found it, temporarily, in a peer group before moving to a new neighborhood. For a while he connected to a teacher in elementary school and then another in junior high school. These two teachers' interest in him probably meant more to Paul then he was willing to acknowledge. Eventually, he bonded with his wife, a woman who helped him to feel deeply connected to both her and their children.

Yet there was the time, before marrying her, when Paul knew too well the extent of his dependency. His mother's death which was so immobilizing, his wish for a father who could take her place, and his anguish over moving away from his friends each took its toll and coalesced into a deep desire to avoid emotional dependence on anyone. This loss of faith deactivated his secure attachment to his mother. As a young adolescent, Paul stopped looking for emotional support and then organized his interpersonal behavior around the assumption that others would continue to reject him. To avoid further abandonment, Paul refrained from intimacy and shunned affection in interpersonal encounters. Instead, Paul invested intense effort into maintaining an aloofness that manifested indifference to relationships and disinterest in intimacy.

Paul emerged from his formative years with one overriding conclusion: *I only belong to myself.* Of course, he came by this fear honestly. He believed that he must make it on his own or else never make it. Like other grand convictions, this one entailed subsidiary conclusions, especially: *If I depend on others I am asking for betrayal* and *If I am successful, it be on my own.* Accordingly, Paul felt discomfort with interpersonal closeness and dependency, preferring neglect to punitive attention. Paul "could deal but not feel," in contrast to William Garrod (Chapter 4) who "could feel but not deal" (Fosha, 2003, p. 221). Paul's avoidance, being particularly low in anxiety, produced in him at first a counter-dependency that was dismissive of intimacy and closeness, then a compulsive drive for self-reliance, and eventually a confident sense of independence and self-control. As he had said: *You can't let yourself lose your confidence. You have to believe in yourself, regardless of what happens.* Somewhere, maybe even unbeknownst to himself, there was a fear of ever re-experiencing his feelings of helplessness in the face of his mother's death or of ever depending too much upon another for guidance or nurturance. With so little rewarding interpersonal closeness, Paul settled for a working model of relationships that shielded him from unmet needs by thinking too well of himself and too little of other people.

As a social actor, Paul left childhood with a personality structure that Gough (1987) called a Gamma orientation to relationships and rules. This means that Paul combined an extroverted orientation to other people and interpersonal experience with a norm-questioning orientation toward social norms and conventional values. Paul knew himself to be innovative, forthright, versatile, and clever. He judged himself to be strong and competent yet tended to devalue others as weak and incompetent. Because of this attitude, employers and supervisors believed him to be impulsive, disruptive, rebellious, headstrong, and intolerant -- especially when Paul pointed out flaws in traditional norms and absurdities in established routines. Fortunately for Paul, his skepticism fostered a creativity that enabled him to produce new ideas, products, and services as well as earn him a reputation as one of the most innovative managers in his field.

Motivated Agent. Paul may have learned to regulate himself in relation to promotion-focus ideals from interactions with his mother and later to repudiate prevention-focus oughts and cautionary tales from an uptight father. Paul focused on what he wanted to do. He chose promotion goals to bring about new situations and adventures, not prevention goals to maintain some currently stable yet unsatisfactory situation. His strategy prioritized flexibility, open-mindedness, curiosity, and creativity yet did so by sacrificing commitment, certainty, and careful, vigilant analysis.

Paul suppressed his need for interpersonal comfort by concentrating on external activities. He found consolation in actions that brought "distr-action" as he went from being "immobilized to mobile." Individuals such as Paul who prefer movement and action often describe themselves "as a traveler" (Blatt & Levy, 2003, p. 114). As Paul traveled through life, he encountered a series of challenges that repeatedly tested his fitness for what he viewed as contests in a dog-eat-dog world. In adjusting defensively to these challenges and transitions, he lacked the foresight of a future-oriented and planful career concern. He eschewed strategic planning and preparation in favor of day-to-day tactical maneuvering and ingenuity. Paul's stance was to *take things as they come.* As a senior, he summarized his outlook on the future by saying, *just wait and deal with problems as they arise ... I just never stop to think. The way I feel, thinkin's bad for you. So I never do it.* Viewing life from a present-oriented time perspective, Paul showed little career concern and curiosity. Paul avoided the anxiety, uncertainty, and personal responsibility associated with planful decision making by delaying choices until the situation demanded a new course of action. Instead, he adjusted using strong career control and confidence when the time came to look around for solutions, sometimes responding in a reactive, impulsive, or indifferent fashion with his choices dictated by hedonistic desires or immediate gratification. Dictated by situational demands and consequences, his strategy was a non-reflective approach to solving specific problems in particular situations. His life course was shaped by external pressures and fortuitous circumstances, not experienced as completely deliberate nor fully intended. Absent was a sense of having chosen, although of course he made choices -- often based on the defensive adjustments of wishful thinking and tension reduction.

Autobiographical Author. Throughout his life, Paul encountered a multiplicity of career and life options without a basis for choosing because he viewed his circumstances as predetermined by fate and factors beyond his control. Following a choice, he did not make a commitment to an identity stance, focusing instead on his reputation. Going through life as a Searcher (Josselson, 1996), Paul's strategy resembled what Berzonsky (1989) termed an avoidant style of identity-processing in which he prioritized freedom to move, unlike a father who rigidly remained in place. Paul dis-identified with a father who provided a negative guiding line for how to travel through life.

In an attempt to resist his father's intrusions and retain some self-control, Paul acted out his father's worst fears concerning his son. He became a free spirit of sorts by hanging out with the wrong crowd, staying out all night, one-night stands with numerous girls, and escapades at school. When possible, he withdraw to places where he could neither see nor hear other people; there he was free to do his own thing and to be his own person, oblivious to a world that could consume him. This behavior pattern is not unique to Paul. Individuals with a negative identity usually grow up in a developmental environment that prompts feelings of anxiety and isolation. Also, they usually have distant and detached fathers (Marcia, 1980). Recall that when asked to describe his father in one word, Paul answered: *detached, cold, non-protective, unfair,* and *uptight*. Unwilling to become like his father, Paul may have viewed the choice of a negative identity as the only available option. Although painful and confusing to both Paul and his father, the resulting dis-identification was consciously or unconsciously chosen as a survival strategy. Paul's rebellion and his determination to forge an identity apart from his father's wishes paid off in a specious autonomy yet cost him more than he will ever know.

Paul's negative identity strategy meant that, even after he had made decisions, he had "no set occupational or ideological direction" (Marcia, 1980, p. 181). He lived in a perpetual moratorium, making only short-term commitments after a brief exploration of the context, not of himself (Berzonsky, 2004). Paul's negative identity and perpetual moratorium thwarted active self-regulation by forming life goals, planning a future densely populated with anticipated events, and interpreting experiences through a coherent and integrated structure for making meaning.

Self-Construction Content

The large residual of feeling associated with his father's attempt to dominate him from afar and with his caretaker's continuing efforts to restrict his coming and going account for much of the way in which Paul has lived his life. Not only did he resent these original experiences of others' intrusiveness, but each episode of confrontation and rebellion reminded Paul of his mother's abandonment through death and a vulnerability he tried his best to deny. His resentment led to a resolve which permeated Paul's entire life, to be his own because he thought that no one else would have him.

Self-reliance. As a high school senior Paul could rightly claim, *I run my own life.* And his high scores on the *Dynamic Personality Inventory* (*DPI*; Grygier & Grygier, 1976) Self-Reliance and Initiative Scales, taken at age 40, support this proclamation. In the *Thematic Apperception Test* (*TAT*; Morgan & Murray, 1943), also taken at age 40, Paul describes a bull-headed hero who calls his own shots (Card 4), another hero who goes his separate way despite its effect upon another who needs his companionship (Card 6BM), a rebellious, head-strong son who refuses to heed his father's advice (Card 7BM), and another hero who goes her own way and is destroyed in the process (Card 13MF). Each of these figures, regardless of the cost, is compelled to make certain that no one else will determine their lot. Much of Paul's life can be understood as an attempt to maintain a safe distance from his father by means of dis-identification. This motif was evident in Paul's response, at age 40, to *TAT* Card 8BM in which a son vows that, unlike his father, he will not be done in by life. His survival will depend upon the extent to which the son insures a dissimilarity between himself and his father. Paul's dis-identification extended beyond the family to the world-of-work wherein he generalized it to supervisors and employers, who often felt the brunt of Paul's disappointment in them.

Paul's positive view of self and negative view of others produced a paradox in the view a psychologist who read a draft of Paul's life portrait: "Paul seems to be going through a struggle with breaking away from dependency type behavior, yet it's not clear on whom he was dependent." Confusion may arise because Paul did not appear to be suppressing attachment-related feelings and behaviors. Instead of suppressing feelings about people, Paul deactivated them and felt a cool, aloof indifference. Paul was emotionally inexpressive because his mental processes and self-regulation of affect were designed to avoid creating feelings, not because he repressed his feelings. He blocked emotional responses, he did not conceal them. Furthermore, he minimized his chances of anxiety and rejection by restricting contact with people and never placing himself in situations where he had to rely on others more than on himself. His high score on *DPI* Seclusion Scale indicated that he kept away from people as a defense. Thus, Paul actually experienced very little distress. When feelings of anxiety or rejection did arise, Paul used hyperkinetic behavior to disengage and distract himself.

Hyperkinetic Competitiveness. Paul used movement to escape the cauldron of pressure at work and elsewhere. When he felt pressure he wheeled a truck around the parking lot, drove his snowmobile through the woods, road his motorcycle out in the country, or took a trip. The automated interpretation for Paul's *Minnesota Multiphasic Personality Inventory* (*MMPI-2;* Butcher, Graham, Tellegen, & Kaemmer, 1989) profile (scale 9 =100, low scores on K, 2, and 7), taken at age 40, described him as a hyperkinetic person who organizes life around competition that he finds self-enhancing when it allows him to demonstrate his own strength and others' weakness. The narrative described Paul as an:

> *energetic person with broad interests and a tendency to be involved in a variety of activities. He is restless, enjoys change, and has little tolerance for monotony. He makes up his mind fast, changes it frequently, and generally maintains a high level of activity, sometimes to the point of exhaustion.*

The interpretation explained that this form of avoidance is likely to prompt an over-concern with performance standards, success, power, and control. The interpretation also suggested that if forced into a submissive or dependent position, Paul would feel threatened.

Paul's scores on the *DPI* at age 40 would lead one to regard him as impulsive and changeable. He will not stay put, with a vengeance. He was also irritable and showed insufficient inhibitory capacity. Ambiguity, uncertainty, and indecisiveness were intolerable to him. On the one hand, Paul's competitiveness made him keenly aware of how others perform in comparison to himself (*TAT* Card BM). On the other hand, he was not altogether certain that he had what it took to handle the new responsibilities he was assigned on the basis of his superior work performance (*TAT* Card 14). He was not sure that the rewards of devotion to tasks, of toeing the line, were worth the cost (*TAT*, Card 1). Frequently he was sustained by fantasies of what life would be like when duties imposed by others came to an end, when the workday was over, and once again he could be free to move at this own pace and in his own way (*TAT* Card 9). According to the *MMPI* narrative report, Paul "spends a great deal of time in personal fantasy and dreams." This interpretation coincides with his high scores on the *DPI* scales that suggest vivid imagination (Ph) and fantasy-tinged aspirations (Pi).

Somatization. If Paul could not move on, he somatized. The pressures he had experienced as well as their effects were evident in his *MMPI* responses, which included such complaints as dizziness, nausea, and problems with memory and concentration. He was described further as a "disoriented, perplexed, restless and hyperactive person and as someone who "in the face of emotional stress and pressures may tend to develop somatic complaints." When pressures mounted and Paul could not move on, he was forced to deal with them through somatizing. His *MMPI* profile suggested this pattern in having modest elevations on scales 1 and 3 with an intervening valley on 2, the so-called conversion V. Some psychologists interpret this pattern as reflecting a psychological conflict arising from a reluctance to admit to intense dependency needs (Bradley, Prokop, Margolis, & Gentry, 1978). Individuals with this conflict can sustain activity and effort for long periods by binding their affect so emotional conflict is not apparent. For example, when Paul and his wife conducted their part-time firearms and hunting supplies business, he eventually landed in a hospital with various somatic complaints. He reported afterwards, *I'm to the point where I'd just rather relax, do things I want, not be like my father who lived his business.* In middle adulthood he had become displeased about an increasing number of responsibilities at work: *I'm not looking for advancement. I wish there were fewer duties and responsibilities involved.* His wish for a less stressful life already appeared in what he reported as a high school senior: *Someday I want to be able to sit back and relax and just let the world go by as it wants to.* In short, the personality that Paul developed to adapt to work and coworkers used avoidance strategies, compulsive self-reliance, distracting maneuvers, and somatization to meet the expectation that other people are unreliable. With regard to intimate relationships, this type of personality has been linked to early reproductive maturity and short-term mating strategies during adolescence (Fraley, Davis, & Shaffer, 1998); recall that Paul reported having 18 different sexual partners in one year. Paul's relationship style could have led to a preference for multiple partners, belief in sex without love, and minimal affection during sex. Instead, Paul was very fortunate in marrying a woman who made herself available to him in ways which did not threaten his autonomy. His spouse provided a stable relationship, and truly enjoyed their many activities and adventures. She was the answer to the twin question life posed him: "If I am not for myself, who will be for me? If I am only for myself, what will I be?" (Hillel, 1897, p. 26). His wife has been a partner who imbues him with courage (*TAT* Card 4) and accepts his need to make it on his own while still searching for closeness (*TAT* Card 3BM). She created a home wherein Paul always felt welcome and rooted. This same security and stability were less evident in Paul's career.

Career Construction

In this section I examine how Paul manifested his personality in the world-of-work, focusing first on the process by which he developed his career and then on the content of that career. In considering the process, I concentrate on how Paul's personality with its avoidance of commitment, self-reliant competitiveness, and restless energy led him to a series of jobs, each of which he viewed as an adventure. Paul's life portrait provides an unusually clear view of what happens when an avoidant attachment schema shapes a work life, leading to an avoidant-processing strategy of career construction and a perpetual identity moratorium.

Career Construction Process

Paul's career, although quite successful from an objective perspective, could be called insecure and unstable. Miller and Form (1951) characterized career patterns as either secure or insecure. Secure career patterns are stable and conventional, showing an orderly movement from one occupational level to another or from one position to another. In contrast, insecure career patterns are unstable, showing multiple trial periods as an individual moves through a series of jobs and occupations, some unrelated. Paul's career pattern consists of a repeating sequence of entering positions in a potentially life-time job yet after a trial period he chooses to drift to another position.

The wandering pattern of multiple trials in Paul's career took shape from his use of "experimenting" as a main career coping behavior. Super, Kowalski, and Gotkin (1967) identified experimenting as positive coping behavior in late adolescence and early adulthood, in contrast to the negative behaviors of drifting, floundering, and stagnating. "Experimenting" means trial movement from one related job to another in a process of elimination or zeroing in on a position. It typically results in "stabilizing" or settling into a more-or less permanent position. However, for Paul experimenting did not lead to stabilizing in young adulthood; rather, it continued throughout his life course and composed his career story as a Searcher.

Although he continually experimented, Paul experienced significant objective success and subjective satisfaction from this movement because it effectively implemented his self-conception as an adventurer and his character arc of moving from being immobilized to mobile. From a subjective perspective, Paul's recognized in his career pattern a coherent theme, one that he himself articulated at the end of his final interview when he said:

> *I've had quite a few jobs and yet I've been, at least I think, I've been fairly stable as far as jobs are concerned. I've had about four major jobs in my life, mostly connected with the trucking industry.*

He further explained that his principal attraction to trucking was the fact that *I enjoyed being alone on the road where I was my own boss*. Parsing this thematic sentence into three phrases-- *alone, my own boss*, and *on the road*—unfolds the meaning of the controlling ideas.

Alone. Paul based his career on the illusion that all men are islands. Recall that in his early teens he *decided I only belonged to myself*. Paul felt extremely threatened in work situations where supervisors expected submission or dependence. He organized his work life around competitive self-enhancement, not cooperative partnerships. He reveled in extracting a grudging submission from coworkers and employers. This pattern of elevating his own self-esteem at the expense of others manifested his attachment schema in which he positioned himself as positive and others as negative. He enacted this working model of relationships with a competitive and compulsive approach to activity that served to elude other people, create conflict with colleagues, and minimize time for friends or social events, (Hazan & Shaver, 1990; Hardy & Barkham, 1994). In other words, Paul used work to avoid relationships and be alone.

My own boss. As a consequence of feeling alone in the world, except for his wife and children, Paul exhibited a compelling need to be his own man. He asserted that *you are successful if you do what you want*. To remain unscathed by others' claims on him, Paul took complete and total responsibility for his own career. Furthermore, he sought jobs where he was in control -- the one who made the decisions. He was intolerant of ambiguity, uncertainty, and indecisiveness because they made him feel out of control. And Paul prided himself on his ability to make split second decisions, *as many as 200 per day*. Obviously his restive self-concept, and its vocational implementation at work, made it difficult for supervisors to manage him. Paul complained at age 25 that *No one has even patted me on the back and told me what a nice job I've done*. This recurring complaint can be traced to his adolescence in that relationships with authority figures at work resurfaced Paul's anger and resentment toward his father. Paul's incantation against authority figures was first formulated in his complaints about his caretaker's style of supervision. Recall that Paul complained that she was *always there watching everything I did*. She *stifled* him with her *old-fashioned ideas*. In his mind he wanted acceptance yet nothing he did seemed to please his father or the housekeeper. He reacted to them, and all subsequent supervisors, with rebellion.

On the road. To stay alone and autonomous Paul avoided making commitments. He preferred to just keep moving. During his high school years, he encountered academic difficulties because he could not sit still long enough to study. He already exhibited what was to be a life-long pattern of hyperkinetic energy, psychomotor acceleration, emotional expansiveness, and boredom with routine. Paul's need for freedom was ubiquitous; he hated feeling trapped. As an adult he recalled, *My favorite room was the sun porch* where he slept even in the winter. There *I didn't feel all confined. I felt more free.* He refused to join his father's business because, *I'd rather be outside where I can move around and feel free.* At work he wanted to come and go as he pleased: *My most important need is to be free.* In his career, Paul refused to be tied to the apron strings of any employer. He was unwilling, or maybe unable, to make commitments that would bind him to an employer or occupation.

In sum, Paul's life motif of unfettered movement constitutes a coherent subjective career theme that elucidates a successful yet unstable and insecure objective career pattern. His restive theme might be aptly expressed by the aphorism "My way or the highway." Paul jumped from job to job in pursuit of autonomy and excitement, not security nor permanence. In contrast to his father, Paul made sure that his own work would never become monotonous. The loathing for his father's regimented life was in part responsible for Paul's unfettered movement toward new adventures. As a high school freshman he reported a liking for adventure, *to do things that I have never done before.* Paul followed his impulses and would get enthusiastic about something for a short time and then move to the next thing. He never seemed to settle down, preferring to move on rather than hold on. He remembered what his father had settled for and vowed that the same would never be true of him. Paul's unstable career pattern was foreseen in comments made by his father when Paul was 14 years old*:*

> He needs to do one thing and stick with it more than he does. He goes from one thing to another. What he does is clever, but he loses interest.

Career Construction Content

In considering career content, the reader may consider how Paul's jobs might be strung like beads on the string of adventure. Paul constructed his own career by seizing opportunities to engage in new ventures. As early as the ninth grade, he announced this intention when during his first interview at age 14 he declared:

I'm an adventure type boy. I like to do things just to do it. I mean, make new achievements, do things I've never done before and all that. It gives you the feeling off superiority, I guess you'd say, if you know how to do things. In the ninth grade Paul identified his role model as John Wayne. When asked why he admired Wayne, Paul responded that he is "an adventurer." Paul also greatly admired his widowed aunt, a *free thinker* who *had been all over the country, traveling and working until she got tired of it and she would just move on.* Employed as a nurse, she modeled an approach to work that could meet Paul's needs for autonomy, activity, and adventure. Although in grade school he said he thought of becoming a doctor, he did not follow his aunt into the medical field.

Aptitudes and interests. The results from a vocational test battery administered to Paul in the ninth grade depicted a very talented young man. His score on the *Otis Mental Ability Test* (Otis & Lennon, 1969) placed him at the 95th percentile on national norms and 14th in his class of 468 students. On the *Differential Aptitude Tests (*Bennett, Seashore, & Wesman, 1956) he showed strong aptitude for scientific and technical occupations as suggested by the following scores: mechanical reasoning at the 95th percentile, abstract reasoning at the 82nd percentile, spatial relations at the 80th percentile, verbal reasoning at the 80th percentile, and numerical ability at the 65th percentile. He scored at the 81st percentile on *Nelson-Denny Reading Test* (Nelson, Denny, & Brown, 1960).

On the *Work Values Inventory* (*WVI*; Super, 1970) Paul's scores showed a consistency across three administrations, one focused on variety and economic return. The first *WVI*, taken in the ninth grade, indicated his highest values as creativity, fair supervisors, and friendly associates. In the twelfth grade, the *WVI* showed the same trio of work values, then joined by a new appreciation for economic return and independence. At age 35, his *WVI* still showed a strong value on economic return for his labor, along with a desire for both a sense of mastery on his own part and recognition from others for his accomplishments. He also seemed to become even more concerned with freedom to choose his own way of life.

Results on the *Strong Vocational Interest Blank - Revised* (*SVIB*; Strong, Campbell, Berdie, & Clark, 1966) indicated that Paul's interests resembled those of men employed as chemists, engineers, aviators, carpenters, and production managers. He scored quite dissimilar to men employed in social service and clerical occupations. His results on the *Kuder Preference Schedule - Vocational Form CH* (Kuder, 1956), indicated strong interest in mechanical (95th percentile), persuasive (83th percentile), and scientific (78th percentile) activities along with a disinclination for musical (6th percentile), outdoor (17th percentile), artistic (27th percentile), and clerical (36th percentile) activities. His *Kuder* profile produced a RIASEC code of Realistic-Enterprising-Investigative (REI), reflecting an entrepreneur in the concrete world of mechanics, machines and tools, not in the abstract world of finance or science. The REI code accurately predicted his lifelong interest in working as a leader or an independent consultant who solved practical problems and managed crises. The *Occupations Finder - Form R* (Holland, 1994) listed a single occupation for his REI code, at his ability level (VI): ship captain. At ability level V, the list of occupations included materials engineer, general supervisor, production manager, project manager, and traffic technician. Level IV included diesel mechanic and ship pilot, whereas level III included boat outfitter. It is easy to conclude that the battery of aptitude tests and interest inventories clearly anticipated jobs and projects that Paul would eventually occupy. His expressed interests also pointed to Realistic and Entrepreneurial occupations.

Expressed interests. In grade school, Paul thought of becoming a doctor yet later described that as *a passing fancy*. In the ninth grade Paul showed Enterprising interests in stating that he wanted to be home-room president and eventually class president. Also in the ninth grade, he showed Realistic interests in stating that he would like to do electrical engineering because *electricity has always proved interesting* and *the job pays pretty well*. If he became an electrical engineer, he hoped to enter the communications field, maybe working in a television studio, or work on the railroad. He explained that if he did not get into electrical engineering, he would *probably get a job with an electrical contractor or an electrician*. If he did not do something with electricity, he would probably teach shop or do sales. On *Rotter Incomplete Sentence Blank (*Rotter & Rafferty, 1950) taken in the ninth grade, Paul wrote that he liked *electricity*, he always wanted to be *an electrician*, and his greatest *ambition is to become an electrical engineer*. In the 12th grade he wrote that he likes *driving, fishing, and hunting* and that he always wanted to *be an auto mechanic* and wanted to know more about *working on cars.*

Concordant with his adventurous role model of John Wayne, Paul's expressed interests always centered on the search for new adventures. As he accurately predicted on his 12th grade *Rotter Incomplete Sentence Blank (*Rotter & Rafferty, 1950), my future *will hold many thrills for me.* Accordingly, most of his hobbies had him on the move, traveling fast. His earliest memory announced this career theme of taking a ride: *On Sundays we would go for a ride to my grandmother's house about 25 miles away. I felt very happy.* At age twelve he learned to drive a car, by age fourteen he owned a truck, and by age sixteen he drove a tractor-trailer truck. During his first interview at age 14, Paul explained how he was saving money from his job to take a trip to Montana over Easter break. He wanted to go with his aunt to visit a cousin. *I want to take the trip very bad.* When asked "Why?" Paul responded: *Just to get an adventure, I guess. I like to do things like that just to do it.* Asked for other examples, he replied:

> *I really can't say. I mean, make new achievements, do things I've never done and all that. It sort of gives you the feeling of superiority I guess you'd say.*

Paul showed an enduring interest in adventure. According to Campbell, Hyne, and Nilsen (1992), who identified seven distinct career orientations, an interest in adventuring is expressed in taking risks, competing with others, and physical activities. Adventurers often seek excitement. "They enjoy winning, but they also are resilient in defeat" (Campbell, Hyne, & Nilsen, 1992, p. 55). Paul showed secondary orientations toward the two interest groups most closely aligned to Adventuring, namely Influencing and Producing (resembling to some degree the RIASEC types of Enterprising and Realistic). Influencing, which emphasizes leadership rather than sales, involves taking charge and accepting responsibility for the results. Similar to Paul, Influencers "enjoy the give and take of verbal jousting" (Campbell, Hyne, & Nilsen, 1992, p. 53). Producing involves outdoor work where one can see concrete results. So, Paul showed an enduring career orientation toward adventure, which he implemented through influencing people to produce tangible results.

Paul may have best manifested his interest in adventure when he traveled. Moving about the country, even on short trips, satisfied his craving for novelty and change, and more. Recall that as a ninth grader he had explained that he liked to travel *just to get an adventure...do things I've never done...it sort of gives you the feeling of superiority*. As a twelfth grader Paul stated: *An ambition of mine is to travel and see the country. I have a real urge to travel*. It would have been a surprise if Paul had not become involved in a "travel industry" that allowed him to move while making other things move. Paul was always attracted to moving objects. As a youngster, he competed in the soap box derby, operated a railroad set, and built model airplanes and race cars. As an adult, he owned motorcycles, snowmobiles, trucks, cars, and a camper. He loved to drive, skate, swim, ski, hike, and take cruises. In short, Paul implemented his enduring interest in adventure by staying on the move, both in his jobs and in his hobbies.

Education. Paul did not find any adventure at school, a place where he had to sit still and do as he was told. Unlike the practical world in which he thrived, school did not spark Paul's interests or engage his talents. By the time Paul reached his senior year in high school he was totally alienated from his academic surroundings: *I do as much work as I can, and what I don't get done doesn't bother me. If I feel like coming to school, I do, and if I don't feel like it I don't*. Although he enjoyed mechanical drawing and shop, he had ceased caring about his grades and considered school irrelevant for his pared-down vocational objectives.

Occupations. Paul seems to have actively mastered feeling trapped by his father's views by earning to relish change and adventure. Similar to many before him, Paul transformed his torment into his element. At age 35, when asked "What are you proudest of in your life today?" he replied:

> That I've survived this long. The trucking industry is a changing industry, it changes every day. There is great change in jobs. There is no permanence but there is a great availability of jobs. You have to be flexible I've tried other things, I have always come back to trucking. It's been, perhaps, the easiest road to follow and yet the

> *most challenging. I have found greater challenges there than in other jobs. I've had other jobs that I have just been completely bored with so I've tried other things.*

Objective observers of Paul's career see an insecure and unstable pattern. In contrast, the subjective perspective of a career theme, reveals that Paul steered a steady course toward adventure and challenge and away from routine and permanence. Paul committed himself to being his own man, unsure that anyone else, except his wife, would have him. Through adventure, he repeatedly proved to himself and others that he could make it alone, unfettered by dependence on anyone or anything. This purposeful quest for adventure and self-completion made Paul's career unstable yet highly successful.

Asked at the end of his final interview whether anything important had been missed. Paul replied by talking about the one area where he had bonded and committed himself fully, not to a job but to his children. He gave them what he lost when his mother died.

> *My children are very important to me and their viewpoints are very important to me though sometimes, like I say, I'm probably a little bit more strict than I should be -- I really do, you know, hold them down pretty close, but yet I feel that there has to be ... some sort of balance between freedom and discipline because if there isn't, then the same things may happen to them as almost happened to me. And I was very fortunate in the fact that I didn't get into trouble or that I didn't have big problems when I was young because I didn't have any restrictions.*

While sitting on the deck of Paul's attractive home, looking out at the channel only 50 feet away where his boat is moored, and listening to the cheerful chatter of a loving couple as they prepare lunch in the kitchen, it is hard to imagine the many storms through which he has sailed. Paul has weathered losing his mother at an early age, feeling unwanted at home, moving aimlessly without guiding lines, and not belonging anywhere too much of the time. Paul's grief and loneliness surely must have caused him to lose his bearings on many a dark night. And yet out of this journey came a resolve and resiliency that led him to success not only in the world-of-work but at his own hearth. Broken yet never vanquished, Paul had every right to smile in satisfaction as he reviewed the life he lived against all odds. Refusing to be a prisoner of his pain, he had set his own course at every juncture, never defeated by momentary setbacks nor beholden to others for a single scrap.

CHAPTER SIX
The Disquiet of a Drifter

The poet Samuel Taylor Coleridge used the metaphor of a garden to explain his views on fostering human development. A visitor to Coleridge's home had asserted that parents should raise their children by giving them complete freedom, thus letting them develop their full potential. Coleridge did not debate the point as he led the visitor to his neglected flower garden where upon the visitor asked why it was overrun with weeds. "Well, you see," said Coleridge, "I did not wish to infringe on the liberty of the garden in any way. I was just giving the garden a chance to express itself and choose its own production" (Fadiman & Bernard, 2000, p. 134). Left to evolve by themselves, children cannot reach their full potential. Similar to other living organisms, children require a hospitable environment in which to grow, an ecological niche described so elegantly by Erikson (1968) who insisted that the psychosocial roots of human development rest in the hope that emerges when children learn to trust their parents. Children need to attach themselves to loving and empathic caregivers who welcome them into the world and assure them that they belong in their family. When these dependable caregivers meet most of a child's needs, that child learns to trust other people and face the future with optimism. Children who experience their home as a safe haven develop a sense of hope and venture forth to explore a world made coherent by family values and ideological commitments. Children who lack a secure base of operations, understandably, find it much more threatening to explore their environments and to encounter strangers.

The psychosocial capacity to have faith in people and hope for the future also kindles career construction. The confidence and optimism with which one meets the world engenders an interest in work and what life will be like in the future, prompting an attitude of career concern --the cardinal dimension in career adaptability. Career concern encompasses the forward-looking vocational attitudes that career theorists have denoted with a variety of terms such as future time perspective (Ginzberg, Ginsburg, Axelrad, & Herma, 1951), planfulness (Super & Overstreet, 1960), anticipation (Tiedeman &

O'Hara, 1963), orientation (Crites, 1978), awareness (Harren, 1979), and aspiration (Holland, 1985).

The next life portrait illustrates how career concern can fail to develop. In the story of the Montgomery family, we encounter two parents who seem detached, indifferent, and rejecting. Their inadequate parenting resulted in Fred forming a fearful-disorganized attachment schema, making it nearly impossible for him to connect to other people. A persistent crisis of trust fueled Fred's lifelong struggle to connect with other people who would accept and comfort him. Fred began his life with little sense of hope and began his career without prior planning because his parents failed to tend the "child garden." Given such a barren soil from which to extract nurturance, Fred could not be expected to blossom early. Growing up in the primordial chaos of a disorganized, deleterious, and distressing home, Fred responded by feeling confused, acting cautiously, and seeking safety. Furthermore, he lacked a clear vision of the future and his place in it. Only through his eventual success in creating a workplace where he felt somewhat secure was he finally able to begin to blossom late in life.

As you read this chapter from the perspective of Career Construction Theory, recognize how Fred's *fearful-disorganized attachment schema* and *introverted, norm-accepting personality disposition* led him as a motivated agent to make occupational choices and meet vocational situations with at best *prevention strategies* and at worst with *maladaptive fragmenting*. Fred rarely paused as an autobiographical author to consider himself, and when he did it was with a *fractured* reflexivity schema that did not properly address the career circumstances nor design a purposeful course of action. Absent a coherent vocational identity, his vaguely conceived career story as a *Drifter* was thematically underdeveloped and lacked substance. Loosely rooted in the sands of mistrust, the narrative provided little sustenance for making positive meaning out of negative events nor for directing his career moves. Now consider the details of how Fred Montgomery's wandering career began with antecedents of family neglect and ended with consequent stagnation and frustration.

PART I

A Life Portrait of Fred Montgomery:
Sometimes It Hurts

It was her idea that we look at each other. She said she wanted to look at me, that if I showed her me she would show me her. After whispering back and forth about what we were going to do, she turned off the lights, got up and closed the door, turned the light back on and sat on the bed in kind of an Indian fashion. We both pulled down our pajamas, and she looked at me first. She didn't touch me or anything, she just looked. Then I said, "Now show me yours." Here I was, ten years old and had never seen a girl's nude body. When I asked her to show me her's, I was expecting to see a penis. After she pulled her pants down low enough where I could see her, I said "Well, where is it?" So she put her fingers in there, I guess to open it up. Then I looked her right in the face and said, "How come you don't have a dinky? Did someone cut it off?" I just sat there a moment or two dumfounded. Then we pulled up our pants, turned off the light, crawled under the covers, and went to sleep. I couldn't wait to tell this older boy I knew and admired all about what happened. A couple of days later I got together with him and when I told him, all he did was laugh. It made me feel like such a little kid!

Fred's memory of both incidents, reported at age 40, summarizes much of how he experienced himself during his childhood and adolescence: uncertain in his relationships with females, embarrassed by sexual situations of any kind, feeling an object of ridicule, a naive child unprepared for life's realities and unable, on his own, to do very much about them. Things had changed for the better over the years that he has been seeing a psychiatrist. Fred no longer harbored the feelings of resentment that he once had toward his parents. Nevertheless, he still recalled their inability to listen to him when he needed to be heard, to insist that he do more than get by at school, and to teach him how to function reasonably well in the outside world. Of course, these accusations involved Fred's unrealistic insistence that his parents not be the kind of people they were, victims themselves of relatively impoverished backgrounds.

Family

Fred's father was almost 50 years old when his son was born. The oldest of seven children, he had to quit school and go to work at the age of 16, soon after his father died. After helping out on the family farm he went to work for the railroad where he laid rails, installed ties, and built up tracks. After 17 years of such labor, he and his wife returned to farming, the work he knew best and much preferred although neither the farm nor their small living quarters were his own. Twelve years later, he and his family moved into the city where he worked at a low wage as a laborer for a construction company. Close to retirement when his son entered his first year of high school, the company closed leaving his father unemployed and with the vitality knocked out of him by a life of drudgery. He then spent the rest of his days at home where he took over the household chores for his wife who worked full-time as a waitress. When Fred's father was not making the beds or washing the dishes, he played solitaire and used an old television set to distract himself from his dull existence.

Fred worried about his father, pitying an aging man who had never had an easy time of it, and wished that he could quit school and go to work for the family as his father had done so many years before. As a ninth grader Fred said, *My father is old, and I'm young. He's done more than his share of work*. During his senior year Fred reported: *My Dad just sits around all the time and gets fed up with everything. We get into arguments awful easy*. There was little a young son could do for a father who had worked hard all his life but in the end had to live on an income so meager that he had to depend on his wife's earnings. At his interview, Fred's father, then already an elderly man prepared to die said: *There isn't much left for me, ain't much use planning anymore*. Fred did bring his neighborhood friends into the house after school, and his *kind-hearted* father was able to enjoy their company. During his senior year Fred reported:

> *All the guys seem to think I have the best family going. We have regular social gatherings at my house, play pinochle with my father. My father always enjoyed kids, no matter how old they were.*

That enjoyment included his son as well. The two played pranks on Fred's mother and exchanged dirty jokes during Fred's teenage years. They shared a love for music, for verse and song, as well as an empathy for those who suffered and barely survived. As both grew older, however, their good times together occurred less frequently. Fred's father was more often alone with memories which embittered him, not in a position to act upon his hope that life would somehow be different for his son.

> *I don't care what he does as long as he can make a career for himself. I'd hate to see him end up like me. I've been a slave for somebody all my life, and I ask you, why should he be?*

He added, *Fred has all the opportunities in the world that I didn't have.* His son may not have agreed. The first strike against him was the image of a father whose dreams led nowhere, whose real interests which occasionally enlivened him were often forfeited along the way. He was not surprised to learn, after his father's death that his mother had married him out of pity.

> *She felt sorry for him. He was getting up in years and had no family of his own. After he died she married the man she'd broken up with as a teenager in order to marry my father.*

It was easier for her than for her son to experience a new life. Marriages, unlike a father-son relationship, can sometimes be viewed as an unfortunate mistake rather than an irreparable misfortune.

Fred's mother, like his father, also had to work all her life. As the oldest of twelve children, she discarded her dreams of becoming a school teacher when at age 17 she was forced to leave high school before her senior year to settle for, at least initially, the role of homemaker on a farm. From an early age she had been accustomed to parents made weary by their chores; to the distance which separated farm households from each other and which forced family members to rely on each other and not neighborhood friends for social contact; to standing by helplessly as one year a barn, the next year the house, burnt to the ground; to *the simple things* of life like sewing classes at Four-H and Friday night dances; and, to a financial poverty which ruled out movies in town or the little luxuries others her age enjoyed.

Fred's mother, with a husband 20 years older than she, found married life differed little from everything she had ever known. Like her mother before, she never complained, explaining that: *My father was always the head of our family.* She quietly supported her hardworking husband, went along with his decisions, and accepted her subordinate position in the household. She was delighted with her kitchen, located in the cellar of the small house, where the wood stove was used for baking and for heating the rest of their crowded quarters. She had no neighbors with which to contend; no outsiders of any age upset her usual routine of watching her small son cutting out pictures of tractors he found in various farm journals, waiting for her older daughter's school bus to return in the late afternoon, serving the children cookies and milk or hot chocolate, and then going out to help her husband with the milking before the family finally sat down for supper. When her husband decided to take a job in the big city, she reluctantly agreed: *It took me an awful long time to get used to living in the city. I was used to open spaces. The houses here seemed so close together.* Because she no longer needed to help her husband with his chores, she went to work as a waitress. She spent her one day off a week washing her family's clothes and trying to straighten up the normally unattended five-room apartment. As a high school freshman, Fred complained:

> *My mother and I don't have time to do anything together. On her day off she kicks me out of the house. She doesn't want nobody around when she does the washing and the housework. She says she can't concentrate on what she's doing. She likes things quiet.*

Four years later, Fred gave a similar report.

> It's all I can do to get her attention. She has this amazing habit of appearing to listen to what I'm saying and just when I get to the most important part right in the middle of a sentence, she'll start talking to somebody else, as though she wasn't listening at all. This kind of thing has gone on since the time I was three years old. Sometimes I wonder if she knows I'm alive.

At age 25, Fred said that he was his parents' favorite child because he was so quiet and *only spoke when they asked him a question*. He remembered his mother discouraging him from *bettering himself* and noted again his parents' lack of involvement with him, their apparent unconcern about his present or future whereabouts: *When I was 11 years old I slept outside with a gang of guys every night of the week during the summer. Nobody ever knew what we were doing.* This lack of parental supervision included, of course, Fred's educational pursuits.

> My parents were always too lenient. My sister and I had them wrapped around our little fingers. We could always get out of anything we were supposed to do, especially homework. If things had been different, I'd have gotten better grades, would have completed my education. My parents let me get away with just doing enough to get by.

During Fred's childhood and adolescence, except for the evening meal, there were few family gatherings, no time together playing games or attending sports events or going on picnics. With a mother who was away at work most of the time and with a father who was a casualty of advancing age as well as unemployment, Fred was on his own during late childhood and throughout his teenage years. At age 35, reported that as a child, *I think I was tolerated.*

When asked, at age 40, to relate some of his early recollections about his family, Fred recounted a story about sibling rivalry.

> My sister is four years older than me. When I was born she was resentful because she was Daddy's little girl. When I was about a month old she tried to get rid of me.

> We lived near a railroad track and she was going to take me down and put me on the railroad tracks. She got caught before she got down there, but for a few minutes my mother and father were quite uptight about where she had disappeared with the baby.

Nevertheless, his sister was the one person in Fred's household with whom he was truly involved during childhood. She was not only his first playmate but also his surrogate mother:

> She has always been one of the most important people in my life. My mother worked long hours, did a lot of overtime, and just didn't have the time to bring us up. My sister is the one who raised me. She taught me how to cut up pictures out of magazines. The two of us spent a lot of time playing with her dolls. Sometimes we'd spend our afternoons looking through catalogues and picking out the things we'd like to have.

Once, when his sister went off to visit their grandmother who lived 12 miles away, Fred became so upset that his parents took him to a physician.

> After the doctor heard what was going on, he told my father that I was homesick. My father said, "How could that be? He's home with us." Then the doctor said, "Bring that girl of yours home, and this boy will be all right."

During the first 12 years of life Fred enjoyed his sister's company, relied on her interest in him, and trusted her judgment of things. When she reached the age 16, however, she quit school to work in a factory. A year later she married and moved out of the house. This sequence of events caused Fred to feel abandoned by the one dependable person in his life, and prompted him to reach out for support from his male peers and eventually from new female acquaintances.

Career Growth

Life with others outside the family circle had never been easy for Fred, as he explained at age 25: *I wasn't used to mingling with other people. I was smaller than other kids my age and felt pretty secluded from the rest of the class.* His uneasiness away from home was reflected in what he recalled about his first days in school:

> *My sister would take me into the class. When she started to leave, I'd start to cry and hold on to her for dear life. The teacher would then tell her to sit down with me until I'd settled down. This went on for about two weeks until my sister started getting bawled out for being late to her own class. When her teacher sent home a note, my father asked my sister why she had been late for class, and when she told him, he said, "That will be enough of that. Fred, you just go into your classroom and stay there by yourself."*

Although Fred abided by this directive, his elementary school years continued to be stressful, marked by difficulties with academic subjects.

Even more problematic was his special fascination with and fearful feelings about members of the opposite sex: *In the second grade I had an awful crush on my teacher. Whenever I was detained after school, her boyfriend would come in, and they'd kiss right up there at the blackboard.* At home, where nudity was proscribed, his mother had never allowed conversations about sex. Fred was uncertain about male-female differences, and whatever curiosity he might have had about them remained unsatisfied. His aunt's attempt to discourage him from playing with his sister's dolls made him vaguely aware of certain differences between boys and girls, yet much remained a mystery even at age 40.

> *For some reason I couldn't talk to the girls in my class. I didn't know what to say. I knew they were different somehow from boys, but the whole business was never really explained to me.*

> *He remembered a special girlfriend in the first grade: We wrote love notes back and forth. Then one day I saw her picking buggers out of her nose and eating them. From then on she wasn't my girlfriend no more.*

Three years later he has a crush on another girl which continued into the eighth grade: *I never let her know how I felt about her, and when she moved away, I never saw her again.* The next year, as a freshman in high school, Fred experienced another romantic attachment.

> *I had a crush on one of my friend's sisters. I walked her home from school, if you can call it that. Actually she was on one side of the street, and I was on the other side, much too bashful to go over there and walk beside her.*

His extreme discomfort around the very person he found so attractive continued for about a year. The tenuous "relationship" finally ended on a predictably painful note:

> *I had managed to ask her out to the movies, but the next afternoon when I went to pick her up her, she wasn't there. She'd gone to her girlfriend's house. Well, her mother called and made her come back and go to the movies with me. I didn't like that at all. I'd just as soon not have a date with her than have her mother make her go. During the movie we didn't say a word to each other, and afterwards, my best friend, who also had a crush on her and who happened to be in the theater at the same time, ended up walking her home. This made me feel really dejected.*

However, it was not long before Fred developed a crush on another girl who never did learn about his feelings.

> *She was 17 years old and two years ahead of me in school. She had the prettiest platinum hair I'd ever seen outside of a movie. Whenever I masturbated, I'd imagine her seducing me and showing me how to have sex.*

After she graduated from school, Fred actually made contact with a new love.

> *We would talk on the phone sometimes for an hour or even more. Sometimes she'd say, "I got to go" and I'd try to get her to talk some more. She never once hung up on me or told me not to call. When I'd get off the phone my father would ask if she was going to go out with me and that he'd give me whatever money I needed for a date. This would be very embarrassing, his overhearing me on the phone with her, building myself up as a big time operator with all kinds of money, when he knew very well I was lying to her. It made me feel so little inside that it got to the point where I wouldn't call her from the house anymore. Instead, I'd go to a pay phone to make the call.*

It appears that Fred was much freer in his telephone contacts with his girlfriend than on other occasions when they met face to face:

> *Almost every morning I'd be standing with my buddies by the telephone pole near school smoking cigarettes before classes started. She would come walking by with her girlfriend, get all red in the face, and say, "Hi, Fred" and I'd say, "Good morning, Margaret." I felt sorry for her, having to approach me with all my buddies standing around. I wanted to leave them and walk her into school, but I didn't know how she'd react to that. I keep wondering if things would have turned out differently if I'd been more assertive with her. I didn't even give her a goodnight kiss after the prom. My sister had told me not to do it on the first date. You better believe that became the talk of the whole damn school.*

Not much later he learned that Margaret was getting married and that he would not be able to call her up anymore: *That's when I decided that I wasn't going to chase after any more girls, that if they wanted a relationship, they'd have to come after me!* The summer after Fred's senior year in high school he had sexual intercourse with a girl he hardly knew.

> *She was just somebody my buddy and I picked up in the car. While my friend was out of the car taking a leak we started making out. I'm grateful to her to this very day for how tolerant she was with me. I had no trouble getting an erection, although I was half drunk at the time, but I did have trouble finding the right spot. My buddy got in the back seat and told me later that it must have taken me an hour and a half before I finally ejaculated.*

The discomfort Fred reported having in his contacts with girls, the embarrassment he felt after learning that his father had overheard his telephone conversations, and the concern he had over being smaller than his friends, were feelings which extended to his classroom activities as well. Unable to make much headway in mathematics and with parents hardly in a position to tutor him, Fred recalled at age 35 a particularly painful event which occurred during the fourth grade: *Since I was so slow in math, my teacher wanted to make an example of me. She nicknamed me "doofus" and told everyone else in the class to call me that.* Later, in high school, he was asked to read a poem in front of his speech class.

> *When I came to the word "bust," I felt very self-conscious and deliberately said "boost" instead. Well, the whole class burst out laughing, and I was razzed for days. I was just ashamed to say that word in front of boys and girls. At home certain words were not allowed, like "douche," for instance. When I asked my mother what the word meant I thought she was going to order me out of the house!*

Career Exploration

During high school Fred continued to do poorly in mathematics, disliked science even more, did acceptably in history and general business, but particularly enjoyed English where he read two books for each one assigned -- his favorite book being a biography of *Will Rogers* (Yagoda, 1970). At age 43, Fred vividly recalled one of the few instances in school when he was made to feel proud of himself. It dealt with *The Ballad of the East and West* (Kipling, 1889), a verse about two teenage boys who were sons of warring leaders.

> *I was sitting in the back of the room reading The Ballad of the East and West when all of a sudden the English teacher came by to see what I was doing. When he noticed what I was reading, he never said a word, but when the class was over, he said, "Fred, I want to see you." I waited for everyone to leave and then I went up to his desk. He says to me, "Were you really reading that book there or did you just have the page open to that?" I said, "No. I read that poem about once a week. I really like it. It gives me goose bumps right up and down my back." Then he leaned over and said, "Have you ever thought about becoming an English teacher?" I said, "No. My math grades aren't good enough." Then he said "Well, anybody who can read The Ballad of the East and West and get goose pimples on their back must have something going for them in English!" I've never forgotten that. It really boosted my ego.*

Not enough, however, to inspire him to devote more time to study. The other teachers did not involve him in class discussions, they were distant and demanded too much. In the 12th grade, Fred described his high school years as *pretty hard*. As a senior, typing was his best subject because *the teacher is really friendly and she talks to us*. Throughout his high school years Fred seldom brought work home from school, rarely discussed his assignments or his course of study with his family, had no particular interest in the school's extracurricular activities, and figured that he could get at least passing grades without doing homework as long as he paid enough attention in class.

As a high school senior Fred reported having thought many times about quitting school and going to work:

> *Every once in a while I'll have a sudden urge to quit, but I've always backed down. If I keep going I'll be the first one in my family to ever graduate. Also, I have one girl cousin who is a high school graduate, and I don't like the idea of her graduating and not me.*

Thus, Fred continued to attend school with his classmates. On May 3 of Fred's senior year, the high school counselor sent home a letter saying that he must pass all of his courses to graduate but things were almost hopeless in Business Mathematics, worth a half credit. The counselor urged: *He needs encouragement to keep up the fight until the very end.* In the end, Fred failed his final examination in the course. He was disappointed, yet still thought he would graduate because a teacher had told him that he would.

One of the many reasons that Fred had done poorly in school was the amount of time he spent working at his uncle's produce stand at the city's central market: full-time during the summers beginning in the seventh grade, and part-time after school and on weekends during his last two years in high school. Prior to this employment he had spent most of his leisure *time riding with friends after school, stopping for a coke, playing the pinball machines, looking through the magazine racks, and then going home.* Although he earned very little money and worked excessively long hours, his mother was pleased that Fred had a regular job and discouraged him from seeking more pay elsewhere:

> *My mother always stressed the importance of getting a job and sticking to it regardless of the kind of money you made. From the time I was 13 years old she discouraged me from bettering myself. All she wanted for me was to be somewhere where I could work every day.*

Given his mother's wishes, Fred settled into a routine working for his uncle. His outdoor produce stand was one of about 20 adjacent stands which circled 30 indoor butcher shops. Each stand sold similar types of fruits and vegetables, the difference being that the stands were owned by individuals from various ethnic groups who spoke different languages. The outdoor working conditions were very cold in the winter and very hot in the summer. And of course Fred's long hours ruled out much time or energy for schoolwork and the usual social activities enjoyed by others his age.

> *It was a real grind, moving produce from storage bins to the stand, carrying stuff to the car for old people, and cleaning up the place. My uncle told me that the first day I went to work there he didn't think I'd make it through the day, much less seven years [ages 13 to 20].*

By the end of his senior year, Fred looked forward to buying his uncle's produce stand or owning a vegetable stand next to his uncle's produce stand. He calculated how much it would cost and thought that if he could save most of the money he expected to earn in the next few years, then he would be in a position to fulfill his dream of taking care of his family.

> *I would like to buy some property, large enough to put two houses on it, one for me and my parents and the other for my sister and her family. It would have to be out in the sticks because of zoning ordinances.*

Only later would Fred regret the amount of time he spent working at the produce stand.

> *I shouldn't have stayed there as long as I did. I blame my parents for that. All they cared about was that I was off the streets and not the fact that when I was only 13 years old I was working 36 hours a week at a dollar per hour.*

At age 35, he believed that two important turning points in his life involved his association with the market.

> *First was when I left my neighborhood gang and went to work at the market where I was isolated. If that hadn't happened, maybe I'd have had more of an opportunity to relate to girls in the neighborhood. Another turning point was when I quit the job. It was awfully hard work and it made me feel better about myself when I finally left it.*

After leaving high school Fred continued working for his mother's brother.

> *He treated me like he enjoyed my companionship -- not just tolerated me. He was a great story teller. He made the characters seem to live. He gave me physical contact that seemed to say "I love you." I can never remember my mother or father trying to reach out to me in this way.*

It was during work at the market that Fred met and soon married his first wife who worked at another stand: *It was my first real sexual affair, and I felt obligated to marry her.* Although at the time of their marriage she was only 16 years old, two years younger than he, she was more sexually experienced:

> *She was into all kinds of things that I had never done before, and when she asked me to perform anal intercourse, I refused. I made a big deal over it being dirty and kept putting her down for asking me to do it.*

Tensions between them mounted as she insisted on her freedom to go out every night and suggested that he become sexually involved with other females. When he finally did, with a stranger in the back seat of a friend's car, the marriage ended.

> *After we broke up I was really a mess. I got so depressed I didn't show up for work half the time. Everybody told me I was a fool to marry her in the first place. Her own mother told me I was too good for her.*

Eventually, Fred quit his job at the market because I wanted to forget it, to get away from the location where I might run into my wife. She was running around.

Career Establishment

At age 21, Fred was divorced, unemployed, drinking to excess, and supporting himself by doing odd jobs. This noxious interlude came to an end after about a year when one of his friends suggested that he apply for work at a local factory: *I had no idea of what the work required. In fact I figured I wouldn't be able to do it and that the employers would have me back on the street before I could turn around.* Much to his relief he discovered that his new job required more practice than skill and that before long it became more of a bore than a challenge. Although initially opposed to unions and forced to join the local unit against his will, Fred soon began to attend meetings and volunteered to serve on several committees. Due to his active participation, he was appointed to the executive board and eventually was elected vice-president of the union.

> *The whole thing was very gratifying to me. First, I gained the respect and admiration from the people I worked with. Second, the employers would go out of their way to say "good morning" to me instead of being so cold and just walking by as if I wasn't there. Third, at the meetings I would meet with a bunch of guys and women, and we'd talk over a lot of things, even our personal problems.*

It was during this relatively happy period that Fred met his second wife, four years older than he, married and the mother of two children at the beginning of their affair: *Actually I knew her for years. She lived right around the corner from me on the next block.* The affair began with a few beers downstairs on the back porch, soon involved her making sexual overtures to him and finally coital contact upstairs in his room *every afternoon as soon as I got home from work.* The two married soon after she obtained a divorce from her husband, and within ten months their first child, a son, was born, with Fred then 24 years old. With the births of two more children and having to support his wife's two children by her previous marriage, Fred also worked part-time as a security guard to make ends meet. Although Fred continued to enjoy his job at the factory, he learned that the substances with which he worked gave him ear infections. At age 29, after almost eight years at the plant, Fred resigned his position and took a job as a personal care attendant in an Alzheimer's unit at a private nursing home. A position which he still held at age 60. As an attendant Fred fed, showered, shaved, moved, walked, and diapered patients. Because he had to work nights, he exchanged his part-time evening job as a security guard for part-time work in the morning cleaning a movie theater.

Although he was away from home much of the day and five nights a week, Fred spent enough time with his wife to realize that their marriage was deteriorating: *I couldn't stand her nagging and bickering all the time. She was so different from the girls I worked with at the nursing home.* Catching him in the middle of a sexual escapade, his wife threw him out of the house. With nowhere to go except his mother's and so distressed that he seriously considered suicide, Fred committed himself to a state hospital where he remained for three weeks. He received psychiatric treatment for the next five years. Looking back on this experience at age 56, Fred said:

> *I wish some wise person had put me into therapy when I was twelve years old. I was all mixed up about sex way back then. It was always a no-no, something I took no responsibility for or knew very much about. That's why my fantasies always involved older women in the neighborhood seducing me. It was never the other way around, I never fantasized about girls my age. I could never relate to them.*

In addition to being overshadowed by sexual matters, Fred's life had also been darkened by another, not unrelated, issue -- his lack of self-assertion. As a high school freshmen he reported: *I don't think I have many enemies. I don't think I could be disliked by anyone because I don't talk very much.* As a high school senior he said: *I'm too shy to speak up about how things around here could be improved.* Whenever Fred encountered a new situation or clashed with a person in authority, he described himself as *tongue-tied*:

> *As a little kid I used to love to go down to the bank and watch people use a special machine that counted money for you. You'd just dump change into the tray, and it would work its way down these slots, and numbers would appear in the front as the money passed*

through. One day as I stood there watching the machine, a guard came over and told me to get out of there. He made me feel small, really bad about myself.

Fred happily recalled, at age 35, the one instance in high school when he refused to accommodate another's request:

The teacher in my retailing class told me I'd do better taking agriculture since I was working with produce. When I told him I didn't want to switch over, he said, "What do you expect to get out of retailing?" I answered, "I'll learn how to sell myself." He never questioned me again from that day on, and it really felt good. I had somehow boosted my own ego.

Later, during the time that he was the vice-president of his factory union, he reported: *Up until now I had always been shy. I never stuck up for my rights when it came to employers. I can handle this pretty well now.* Nevertheless, he rejected his employer's offer to make him a foreman: *I told them I was not a leader and that I didn't want that kind of responsibility.* There were other examples of how difficult it had been over the years for Fred to stand his ground, to be autonomous, or to take the risks associated with self-assertion. For instance, he attributed the breakdown of his second marriage partly to his lack of self-assertion: *I wasn't assertive enough with her. I've been told that the guy she's with now rules her with an iron hand.*

Fred admired his one close friend, his sister's husband, for his *self-control and the responsibility he has and the way he has accepted it*. To Fred, his brother-in-law was *more or less my ideal, almost the perfect man I'd say*. Unlike his brother-in-law, Fred had been held back by a *pessimistic attitude and inferiority complex*. Fred explained, at age 35, what he meant by this.

I have always taken a pessimistic attitude, looked out for the worst. And I am a very nervous person in crowds or talking to people or starting something new, afraid to be the first or second one to start, or even the twentieth. Ah...I think you call that an inferiority complex. Stick me in a new situation and I'm tongue-tied.

Although his work was where he felt most successful, he still articulated a negative vocational self-concept. For example, in his early 40s when his cousin suggested that he attend community college to become a licensed practical nurse, Fred responded:

> *Oh no, no way. I am just a plain ordinary ass wiper, I don't want to be a professional ass wiper. I'm satisfied just being the little guy ass wiper that I am.*

Despite his social inhibition and inferiority feelings, it seems that at age 40 Fred had finally begun to address the two major issues in his life: how to cope with his sexual and aggressive impulses. He could imagine a brighter future and had moved out of his mother's house into an apartment that he rented. He had become increasingly comfortable with his sexual feelings as well as his relationships with other people. His work in particular had come to be an important opportunity for him to experience a relatedness to others and to express an empathy he never had in his relationship with his father and which was especially apparent in the relationship he enjoyed with his own children. Having overcome a poor start, he hoped that he would find the hurdles less difficult than he had always found them to be.

Career Management

Unfortunately, at age 59 Fred found that his circumstances closely replicated all he knew as a youngster. His every step, his every gesture, whatever he sees and thinks and feels and wants, could be guessed by anyone whoever walked in his shoes. But who would have wanted to? Who would have wanted to know what it was like to have a father too despondent to do anything but endure a living death? Fred had never been able to shake that image of him nor an even sharper, more poignant one.

> *I'll never forget how I slammed the door of the car on his fingers. It was one of the most traumatic things in my life. Once when I related the story to this girl I worked with, she said, "That must have been horrible. I can see it in your eyes, the way you're feeling it, exactly what your father's fingers looked like in the door."*

It took little effort to observe in Fred the residues of sights, sounds, and feelings that surrounded his father's protracted suffering following a stroke:

> *In the final stages of his illness, he asked me to use a shotgun on him. He pointed to the closet. "It's right there, Fred. Nobody will feel bad." I don't think I said anything. I just stared down at him.*

Despite his father's eventual death, his imprint on Fred was as clear as the fossilized tread of a dinosaur. Fred reported that he always had *a hard job finding my father's grave* until one of his sons pointed it out to him in back of the church he had attended: *I knew it was on the corner, but I couldn't find it.*

Perhaps one reason he could not find his father's grave was the predicament he thought he would be in if he ever found it. Desperately wanting to enact his devotion to his father yet mindful of one of his father's last admonitions, he would have been stymied.

> *My dad asked me when he was alive never to put flowers on his grave. But this week I did. I planted a little flower. That's the very first time. I'd done it before to my mother's grave but not to his. I figured it was so long ago that he said it that maybe he'd forgive me for going ahead and doing it.*

Fred's mother was gone yet not forgotten as well, and his images of her always cast a shadow of pain.

> *My mother's buried alongside my stepfather, which I have no qualms about at all. They'd gone together before she married my father, and after he died they got back together again. They got along real well. I never saw my mom and dad hug or kiss each other, but my mother and my stepfather were huggin' and kissin' all the time. So when my sister asked me where I thought my mother should be buried, I said, "I think she oughta be buried alongside of Art!" They always seemed to be more comfortable together.*

Another legacy his mother left him was the knowledge of what it might be like for him to work taking care of patients with dementia. As it turned out, Fred did this work for more years than he could remember. His shift began at 3:15 p.m. and ended just before midnight. In the nursing home environment on a floor with 14 residents, all Fred's previous training at home with his father came to the fore. There was nothing there that he was unprepared to do, and he worked with a spirit that honored both himself and those he served.

> One of the ladies with Alzheimer's used to be a school teacher. I think the world of her. I didn't know her back then, but she must have had one hell of a personality! I feel very warmly toward her. She doesn't know her kids, but she'll talk about them like they are still youngsters. There is a male patient who keeps saying he is going home tomorrow. One woman will start crying as soon as she sees me. Even though it's the afternoon, she'll ask me, "Can I go to bed?" and I have to put her to bed. She's paralyzed from the waist down. You have to use a Hayes lift to get her up out of her chair.

There were male patients who had to be showered, others in need of a shave, most of them so out of it that they were unaware of Fred's ministrations. After spoon-feeding them and before putting them to bed, he changed their diapers because they all were incontinent: Hardly anybody ever asks for a bedpan. They just go in their pants. There was one male patient who stood out from the rest, and with good reason.

> I hadn't seen him in four years and didn't know he had returned to the unit. All of a sudden there he is, pointing at me: "That's Fred Montgomery. He used to take care of me!" This new aide I was breaking in couldn't believe it, his jaw dropped. "Holy Christ, these patients know you so good!" That was a real ego boost for me. A lot of the aides won't tell the patients what their names are so that they can't report on them if something goes wrong. I've never felt that way.

What better place, what better position, to enact the love he felt for the less fortunate, as much a part of him as his fingerprints. Clearly he was where he was by no accident, and he had stayed the course because of what, probably, he admired most about himself:

> *The patients see the compassion in me. If you've got something in your eye, and you're rubbing it, my eye will start to water for sympathy with you. That's been there all my life. And it can hurt sometimes.*

Reflecting further on his extraordinary capacity for empathy toward the less-fortunate, Fred recalled an incident involving his niece's husband, who worked as a prison guard:

> *They have a term, "being shit down," which refers to prisoners taking their own feces, putting it in a styrofoam cup, making a paste out of it and then when the guard comes close to their cell, throwing the contents into his face. Well, one day that happened to my niece's husband. I happened to be visiting at the time, and he came home all upset. He really felt bad. He said, "He got it all over my uniform, at least not on my face. They told me to go to the shower room and get a medical scrub." When he related this story to me and went to take another shower, I just sat at the kitchen table not knowing what to say. We ended up going downtown for a drink at a local bar. That's when I told him about an incident at work where this really foolish resident told one of the aides he had something to show him. Before he knew it the patient took this pair of underwear he'd been hiding with his own feces in it and pulled it down over the attendant's head. After I related this story to him, he said, "Uncle Fred, I don't think I had it quite that bad. I'm glad you were here to tell me somebody else had it worse than I did." He'd really been feeling put down by the whole thing!*

If Fred knew anything at all, he knew what it was like to feel put down. Feelings of humiliation had haunted him everywhere, including at work where his responsibilities far outweighed his authority and where his commitment to the welfare of his patients was sometimes questioned or even baselessly denigrated. One of the nurses who worked with him on the second shift was especially demeaning.

> *She tells me I don't do no fuckin' work! I'm the only male on that shift, and all the females seem to get a kick out of harassing me, but she's the worst. If she's in the right mood, she'll talk to me, otherwise it's like, "Don't talk to me today" or "Try to talk to me tomorrow." Sometimes she'll complain that I have to use a lift to move my patients in and out of bed. She'll say, "We did it and didn't spend all fuckin' day doing it with a Hayes lift either!" Another nurse usually doesn't even speak to me and when she does, she'll say, "When are you goin' to do some fuckin' work?" That's one of the reasons I try to get here early and get as much work done as possible before these nurses start their shifts. Once I nicked a patient when I was shaving him. It was just a nick, no big thing. But then this nurse hollers out, "Did you cut Louis when you shaved him tonight?" So I said, "Yes, I did, Mary, and I told him I wished it was you!" I feel that whatever trouble she could make for me, she'd do in a heartbeat.*

Fred was clearly not indifferent to female opinion. In fact, much of his waking life, at work or elsewhere, revolved around his interactions with women. He was consumed most of all by those toward whom he would draw close if only they would encourage him. Reporting on his life at age 56, Fred could not speak very long without recalling an incident involving a woman, usually one laced with feelings of fear and caution or frustration and regret, yet sometimes pleasure and dedication. What happened between himself and women was what mattered most to him; all else was background. It was with women that he found himself most engaged, dwelling on every nuance of their interaction. Thus it has been, it seems forever, from the time he felt crippled when one woman abandoned him; he remained determined to find successful ways of drawing close to a woman. This drama has been played out many times with the nurses whose criticisms he feared and resented and sometimes with female patients in circumstances that might elicit taboo feelings and impulses:

> *I never tried to explain this to my (female) supervisor, but I never liked to walk this particular patient because her boobs are so big. Here I am with my hands underneath her arms to hold her up, and her boobs are hanging on my arms. Give me anything else to do! What if she realizes that it's a man walking her and all of a sudden she feels my hairy arm? I don't need that nonsense.*

Fred was far more comfortable with women as comrades, and only occasionally would he venture forth into treacherous territory. It has been a long time since he tried to make a relationship with a woman into anything more than a friendship.

> *She was a nurse who took care of male patients. She told me she had a boyfriend and that they were talking about getting married. So I said, "Well, if you really want to do that, Chris, why don't you think of me?" She said, "Fred, I'd feel like I was marrying my grandfather!" She's only two years older than my oldest boy. I really liked her. I used to pick her up and carry her around. She is such a little thing. I just felt like protecting her, it was like fatherly feelings I had for her. I've only seen her two or three times since she left to work with a local doctor.*

> *Once, when she came back for a visit, I came on awful hard, even though she was already married. We sat in the office and just talked, but I came on so hard to her, I cried afterwards. It was like, why did I make such an ass of myself? I'll never forget the last night she worked with me. We went out for a couple of drinks. When she got into her pickup truck and drove off. I watched her go up over the hill. The next day, when I went to work,*

I went to put the key in the door to go into and all of a sudden I started crying. It hit me all of a sudden, like, "Chris ain't gonna be here anymore." All of a sudden, I don't know where she came from but my unit chief walked into the locker room and said, "Fred, I'll do all I can to get her back." She actually put her arms around me! When I said, "But she's only two years older than my oldest boy!" She says to me, "'Fred, love knows no age boundaries!" I'll never forget what she did for me. I've never felt so strongly toward a woman as I did Chris.

God, how many times have I hesitated! I've always kicked my butt for never coming across stronger than I did. If she were here right now, I'd apologize for never coming on to her strong enough for her to really believe me. She'd sit on my lap intentionally just to upset another girl who was interested in me. I should have said, "I don't want you to be doing this just for that reason. I want you to sit on my lap for the rest of my life!" The perfect woman for me would be someone like her. She brought something out in me, some kind of inner gift. I learned to express myself more with her than with anybody else in my life. I really felt like I opened up with her. I hope someday I'll meet somebody as good as her or better.

It never took much for Fred to see an assortment of imperfections in himself. He remains painfully aware of them, all adding up to the grand conclusion that he is not a bona-fide male and that when it comes to seducing women or even to relating to them as an adult, he was not playing on a level field.

Once I was reminiscing with my girlfriend, Ginny, about high school. Once in the shower room after gym class the guys started teasing me about the size of my penis. This one guy who was really hung yelled out, "There he goes, needle dick, the bug fucker!" I'd take it good naturedly but it was really embarrassing. When I

> told my girlfriend about this, she said, "Now I know I never want to go to bed with you!"

Fred's lack of self-confidence and low self-esteem were most apparent in his relationships with women, especially when he compared himself unfavorably to other males he thought were far bolder than he. It was then that pronounced fears of rejection immobilized him. Often he was painfully reminded of all he never dared to do.

> The other day I was reading the horoscope for those born under Aries. I call it the "horriblescope!" It predicted that this month I was gonna be like some sort of super salesman or something, a super confident guy. I thought to myself, "They must be talking about somebody else!" After all, I'm not the only one born under Aries. I only wish I would be that kind of guy. It's the kind of person I've always wanted to be.

Fred's reaction to the horoscope -- *They must be talking about somebody else* -- was not unlike his reaction to others' favorable appraisals of him. Because their assessments did not coincide with his own self-appraisals, he became bewildered and warded them off as decisively as a soccer goalie:

> One time at work, my boss and these two nurses, Sue and Carol, couldn't remember a certain kind of medication. All of a sudden it was like a book opened up in my mind, and I told them the kind of medication they were trying to think of and I described its effect. I stood there dumbfounded! Where the hell did that come from? Sue keeps telling me now what a wonderful memory I have, like, "Leave it to him; he can tell us!" Sue gives me credit for more intelligence than I feel I have.

There are other examples of how Fred refused to believe good things about himself, to agree with others' positive appraisals:

> *Once, when I was out with this woman who had the hots for me, she says to me, "You know, I think that, except for my father, I feel closer to you than any other man I've ever been with." I figured she'd had too much to drink!*

Fred's lack of confidence, his lack of assertiveness, and his fear of negative appraisals by others have made his interpersonal world a treacherous place. People were not to be trusted.

> *I am viewed as a soft touch, and people will try their best to take advantage of me. People are out to get what they want for themselves. They don't genuinely care for others, and especially not for me. Given half a chance, they will say things designed to put me to shame.*

They were not ever meant to be a source of comfort or nurturance.

> *As my father said, "All the help you'll ever need you'll find right at the end of your own arm." Beware of women, they're always looking for ways they can use you. Count me out of that game! Sooner or later you get dumped.*

There was, however, one occasion when Fred's deepest convictions were sorely tested. It involved the same woman who had once told him how close she felt to him and whose words of affection he had rejected out of hand *as the sauce talking*:

> *It was during my birthday week. She says to me, "If neither of us gets stuck for overtime tonight, I'm taking you down to The Tavern and buyin' you a drink for your birthday." I'm like, "Okay. Fine." Well, we both made it outta there that night and got down to The Tavern for a couple of drinks. At one point, she gets up and goes to the back room with this female bartender I knew. I thought they were probably smoking a joint. But all of a sudden she comes out with this sheet layer cake almost as big as the table with "Happy Birthday,*

> Fred!" on it. At that point 15 more people, almost everybody from the whole building, came in. Guys were shaken' hands with me. Girls were kissing my cheek. Everybody was wishing me a happy birthday. I couldn't believe it. I felt wonderful.

The celebration was almost more than he could take. Somehow his final memories had to be made to fit his more accustomed view of himself and of his value to others. These were, after all, what he had depended upon to make sense of his entire world all of his life. He could not make sense of a world in which people made a fuss over him, in which others held him in high esteem, where he was fully embraced. Thus, his final words about what really happened at his surprise party: *She ended up having to pay for the whole thing out of her own pocket. Everybody else was supposed to contribute, but nobody did.* This story exemplifies Fred's life-long conviction that those who should have contributed to his well-being never did.

PART II

The life portrait of Fred Montgomery tells a complex story shaped by multiple influences and forces. In the second half of this chapter, I view his portrait from two different vantage points, first from the perspective of self-construction processes and content and then from the perspective of career construction processes and content.

Self-Construction

Individuals such as Fred repeat without mastery, again and again, the search for solid ground in which to root themselves. It is clear from Fred's life portrait that his history had a way of repeating itself. It is as though he arranged the present as a vivid replica of what he had endured as a child. Fred typically misread the genuine warmth and approving smiles offered by others as the patronizing smirks of yesteryears. Generous praise puzzled or discomforted him because his long-ago days seldom included it. It would seem that to which he was accustomed as a child colored his perceptions as an adult. New experiences were interpreted using expectations and convictions absolutely mandated by his past but of little relevance to his present circumstances. Like fruit that never fall very far from the tree, human lives seem never to amount to much more than the seeds that originally shaped them.

Given these circumstances, how did Fred construct a self to survive when he always *looked out for the worst*? I address this question about self-construction -- or *how* he shaped who he was and what he became -- by examining the process and content of his self-making (Bruner, 2001). For our purposes herein, *self-constructing processes* broadly comprehended refer to *how* Fred shaped himself as a social actor, motivated agent, and autobiographical author. In comparison, *self-construction content* broadly comprehended refers to *who* Fred became, that is, the outcomes of self-construction in terms of in terms of enduring personal characteristics and motives. Before appraising Robert's personality and motives, let us first consider the processes that he used to constitute himself.

Self-Construction Processes

Three interwoven processes for self-construction are the social actor's self-organizing, the motivated agent's self-regulating, and the autobiographical author's self-conceiving. As a preview, Fred's fearful-disorganized attachment schema and introverted, norm-accepting disposition led to amotivation (Ryan & Deci, 2000) defended by a prevention-focus schema and reinforced by a diffused vocational identity strategy as a Drifter resulting from a fragmented reflexivity schema.

Social Actor. In Erikson's (1968) model of psychosocial development, each infant first encounters a crisis of trust versus mistrust. After establishing a relationship with a dependable caretaker, the toddler generalizes this trust to other people and invests hope in the future. Having learned to depend on reliable others, the toddler encounters the next epigenetic task -- developing autonomy and self-control. Unfortunately, some individuals such as Fred Montgomery fail to securely attach themselves to a dependable caretaker. Fred's early experiences of relationships were isolating and difficult. He never had a safe haven within which to deal with his pain. As a result, Fred spent his entire life seeking a dependable other, unable to even conceive of becoming autonomous similar to the brother-in-law whom Fred admired.

Fred's parents failed to provide safety and security in the form of a holding environment that would allow him to contain his emotional experiences (Bion, 1962) and express his inner potential (Winnicott, 1986). Holding, which precedes attachment, is the feeling that someone envelops and supports us so that we do not fall or fail (Josselson, 1996). Simply stated, Fred had difficulty feeling held by his mother, which is the most fundamental relationship an infant needs. Overwhelmed by circumstances and unable to offer nurturance, Fred's fragile mother found it difficult to attend to him. Instead, she moved away from him, avoiding contact or doing so with hesitation. Fred's efforts to obtain closeness and comfort only annoyed his mother, leaving Fred to suppress his need for protection and nurturance. Even when his father did engage Fred, he did little to open new vistas, encourage his intellectual interests, or prepare him for a world he hardly understood himself. Fred became afraid to venture forth into the outside world, hesitating everywhere, and only able to reduce his anxiety by seeking comfort, protection, and affirmation from mother-substitutes.

In terms of Bowlby's (1982) model, Fred's dispirited pattern of both high avoidance and high anxiety may be called a *fearful-disorganized attachment schema*, sometimes referred to as disoriented attachment. Not securely connecting with his parents was a catastrophe that trapped Fred in an aloneness with an accumulation of deep fears and difficult experiences. He suffered -- without repair -- regular and traumatic bouts of fear, helplessness, humiliation, shame, and abandonment. His mother's withdrawal was disorganizing because it left Fred without parental regulation of overwhelming affect. Detached from a mother who failed to contain his anxieties, Fred never learned how to contain himself, causing him at one point to confine himself in a psychiatric hospital. Unable to regulate his own emotions, Fred's sentiments were inaccessible, overwhelming, and confusing. Unable to swallow his grief, his grief swallowed him. In his bleak family environment, Fred was left to feel unrelenting fear and persistent uncertainty, making it difficult to function at all. In due course, all of these difficulties repeated themselves in his relationships with other people. Viewing both himself and others as negative in his dispirited working model of relationships, Fred felt unsure whether to move toward or away from people. On the one hand he wanted relationships yet on the other hand he was at a loss to know how to begin contact with others, what to say that might have made a difference, how to carry on a conversation, or how to invite others into his life. In the end, this confusion resulted in socially-avoidant behaviors, leaving him to live inside his own skin.

During childhood, Fred's fearful-disorganized attachment schema led him to develop a fragmented personality structure and reputational pattern. In Gough's (1990) cuboid model of personality dispositions, Fred resembles the Delta type in being introverted in interpersonal orientation and doubting social norms, values, and rules. He exemplifies the characterization of those Delta types who function at a low level of integration: withdrawn, shy, quiet, detached, preoccupied, self-defeating, and poorly organized. Similar to the Delta personality type, Fred seemed focused on deep inner conflicts and overly absorbed in his own daydreams. He appeared socially awkward, ineffective in coping with frustration, devoid of personal meaning, and prone to decompensation and fragmentation of the ego (Domino & Domino, 2006; Gough, 1987).

Motivated Agent. With neither familial support nor proper encouragement, a boy can find the world so dangerous that his every impulse becomes a "better not," his every thought a muddle, and his every gesture a study in caution. Fred's aspirations were never discussed in his household. He had no coach on the sidelines encouraging him to reach out to his male and female peers, no one there to help him process his exchanges, his thoughts, his feelings, his intentions. He did not know how to cope with even minor changes in circumstances, what efforts he could make to improve his lot in life, how to deal with trouble and stressful school experiences, nor what it takes to succeed at work. He could not identify risks that were at once feasible and salutary -- ones that could make him feel more pleased with himself. The family environment to which he had adjusted was a disorganized social matrix. When he moved to the larger world, he seemed unprepared to cope and just did what he had always done.

Lacking a secure base from which to explore the world, Fred could not form the attitudes, beliefs, and competencies required to author a life plan and actively construct a career. Attempts at self-regulation and impulse control in the present took precedence over preparing for the future. With a regulatory focus low in both promotion and prevention concerns (Higgins, 1997), Fred relinquished attempts at self-realization, instead he focused on avoiding mistakes and possible danger by safely pursuing goals with high security value.

Living in the moment, Fred never developed the adaptability resources of concern about the future, control to delay gratification, curiosity about affordances, nor confidence in implementing plans. Rather than look ahead and look around, Fred choose not to look at career possibilities, he just looked-out not to get hurt in the detritus of daily living. Fred's typical reactions to vocational development tasks, occupational transitions, and work troubles were rarely integrative coping that could have moved him to greater stability at a higher level of development by solving problems. Fearful and worried, he typically responded to baffling personal difficulties with superficial adjustive defending responses or maladaptive emotional reactions, repeatedly making the same mistakes. To quell his chronic nervousness and worry, Fred withdrew from or remained passive in social situations. On occasion, his amotivation left him with no interest in doing anything and his maladaptive fragmenting responses produced an extremely painful despondency.

Autobiographical Author. The formation of an identity is considered to be one of the most important developmental tasks (Erikson, 1968), and one that Fred neglected. To disregard identity-formation issues and protect his self-esteem. Fred used the cognitive strategy of self-handicapping, *just taking things as they come* in the belief that that things would work themselves out and circumstance would write his life story (Berzonsky, & Ferrari, 2009).

Fred's disorganized attachment schema and maladaptive responses to developmental tasks predisposed him to this *identity diffusion*. Even after Fred had made decisions, he had "no set occupational or ideological direction" (Marcia, 1980, p. 181). When forced to make a decision or take action, he reacted to the immediate external demands with adjustive defending or maladaptive fragmenting. Lacking a safe haven at home, Fred never reconciled himself with the necessity of growing up. He remained a frightened child, with his anxiety thwarting the formation of a vocational identify.

Individuals with diffused identities such as Fred's often emerge from developmental environments with a mother who induces feelings of abandonment and isolation along with a father who remains distant and detached (Marcia, 1980). If parents truly are the ultimate reference point for finding our way in the world, Fred was surely lost. Beginning in childhood, his parents did not provide a reliable based from which to explore the world nor reassure him that they would provide a safe haven if things went sideways. Stuck in the present with little sense of a future, Fred neither explored his values and interests nor shaped his purpose and goals.

Fred suffered all the classic characteristics of living with identity diffusion: lost, directionless, isolated, passive, emotionally unstable, feeling empty, meaninglessness, low self-acceptance, dissatisfaction with his place in the world, and weak commitments. Despite being beset by these issues, Fred eventually attained a superficial adjustment to life in his work as an attendant. His floor at the nursing home provided what Kroger and Marcia (2011) described as "a defining context to supply externally what is internally lacking" (p. 35).

Self-Construction Content

Fred was the passive recipient of deeply troubling circumstances during his formative years because his mother and father were ill-equipped for parenting. In important ways they abandoned Fred, leaving him exposed to the "accidents" of whatever happened to occur outside the home. Looking back, the family physician who diagnosed Fred as "homesick" offered a penetrating insight. As an aftermath of his homesickness, Fred avoided interpersonal relations and communication, leading to the withdrawal and isolation that would characterize his entire life. Fred even boasted once that he was the favorite child because he was quiet, refusing to speak until his parents asked him a question. Of course, they rarely did.

Two of Fred's psychiatrists over the years wondered if Fred should be diagnosed with a schizoid personality disorder. That disorder has overlapping criteria with avoidant personality disorder, making differential diagnosis complicated. From my perspective, I doubt that Fred experienced a schizoid personality disorder, yet the features of an avoidant personality disorder do seem to comprehend his experiences. While both personality disorders avoid close interpersonal relationships and distance themselves from other people, they differ in that avoidant individuals want these relationships but fear humiliation, rejection, and embarrassment, whereas schizoid patients feel little need or desire for close interpersonal relationships (American Psychiatric Association, 2013). Fred wanted to connect with others but was thwarted by a sense of personal inadequacy and intense fear of social rejection.

Fred's life portrait displays the pervasive pattern of social inhibition and feelings of inadequacy that characterize an avoidant personality. Fred ruminated about closeness to and rejection from other people and, unfortunately, this apprehension perpetuated his social awkwardness and inappropriate behavior. For example at age 35, he stated

> *I am usually reticent in the presence of females. I feel more relaxed in male company. I have this feeling that I may offend a female by saying damn or hell.*

In the interpersonal domain, Fred wanted to have relationships, which distinguishes his approach from schizoid personality disorders, yet the intensity of his fearful anxiety about being embarrassed, criticized, and rejected led him to avoid social interaction. The discomfort caused by this fearfulness and anxiety, which he called nervousness, provoked painful feelings of inferiority, unfulfilled dependency needs, and pervasive social inhibition.

Inferiority feelings. Fred's description of himself as having an inferiority complex is probably accurate. In making the diagnosis of avoidant personality disorder, the most striking clinical feature is anxiety in talking with another human being (Kaplan, Sadock, & Grebb, 1994). Consider the field notes from the first interview with Fred:

Fred was late for the interview, saying that he had forgotten about it. Fred kept an almost expressionless look on his face throughout the interview. He held his chin down and looked up with his eyes. His face was pale, and he seemed to be physically uncomfortable. The interview seemed to embarrass him somewhat. Although he was quite cooperative, he did not seem to enjoy what was going on.

These notes, along with the interview data and test results, suggest that Fred experienced the inferiority feelings which characterize an avoidant personality. He shared his parents' lack of sophistication and remained embarrassed by the many deficiencies of his home. He knew that his family differed from his peers' families with respect to socioeconomic status, and only later did he realize that the difference went far beyond the matter of income. His feelings of inadequacy at school and work made him worried, fearful, and high-strung. He was afraid to compete for fear of failing. Maybe because he felt inferior to others, Fred developed the dependency needs, social inhibition, and depression that also characterize avoidant personalities.

Dependency Needs. During Fred's childhood, an older sister who was responsive to his need for emotional security provided a surrogate attachment. I call it a surrogate attachment rather than a secondary attachment because Fred's insecure relationship with his parents prevented a primary attachment to them. Fred was deeply involved with his sister, came to share her feminine interests and activities, and then never recovered from her abandonment. Her marriage, which involved her leaving the household, spelled the end of his attachment to a nurturing figure upon whom he could rely as well as the beginning of his search for a replacement among his teachers and his female peers. This search for a secure base became the superobjective in his leitmotif, as revealed in his early recollections. When asked for his earliest memory, Fred at first said *I really can't say*. When asked to try, he talked about his grandfather: *I can remember running across the kitchen floor when he would hold out his arm. He would say here comes my little man and hold out his arms*. When asked what this memory meant to him, Fred said *I guess I was wanting affection*. In his second early recollection he told how he went to his mother for protection after he ignored his father's admonition to

> *Stop picking up a glass with his teeth and drinking out of it that way. I ignored him and the glass broke in my mouth. I can remember getting under the kitchen table and hugging my mother's legs because he was after me with belt.*

Fred's early *crush* on a teacher and his constant lookout for a girl to comfort him were part and parcel of an effort to be assured of a mother he never had and to be reassured that his sister was not so far away after all. The importance of that quest was suggested by the Om scale score on the *Dynamic Personality Inventory* (Grygier & Grygier, 1976), taken at age 40, which indicated Fred's need for emotional involvement with another and, as he said, his *desire for connection*. It was suggested further by the extent of his suicidal despair following the breakdown of his two marriages.

Except for his brother-in-law, whom he admired for his autonomy and appreciated for his tutelage, there were never any other male in his life whom he sought as eagerly as he did a veritable succession of females. Fred's father could never display a guiding line in that he was a *slave* at work, despondent at home, and pitied by his wife. Never having achieved a stable sense of interpersonal trust or hope for the future, Fred's life became a quest for someone on whom he could count. He could not skip this developmental task and just count on himself as could the brother-in-law whom he admired. Thus, Fred spent his life looking for acceptance and direction from others. This explains why he remained so dependent on the opinions of other people, usually females who were less threatening because they were older or younger than he.

Social Inhibition. Because of his pervasive social inhibition, Fred found it difficult to fulfill his strong needs for attention and support. Fred's shyness and social isolation repeatedly stymied his search for connection. In many important respects, Fred remained immobilized throughout much of his life because of his preoccupation with being criticized or rejected in social situations. We know from Fred's life portrait that he was reticent and self-conscious, especially in groups, and that he avoided social situations that required him to meet new people. Adding to the problem was his tendency, because of his sensitiveness and suspiciousness, to misinterpret the motivation of others. Having been rewarded by his parents for being quiet, he found it difficult to talk, even in fairly familiar situations. He avoided expressing his opinions or letting people know very much about him, remaining quiet and inhibited in new interpersonal situations because of his feelings of inadequacy.

Fred was particularly conflicted when his social inhibition clashed with his desire for connection with females who might provide him the attention and support for which he so desperately yearned. His fear of being shamed or ridiculed, as he was when at age ten the little girl dumbfounded him and the older boy laughed at him, restrained his efforts to establish intimate relationships. Feeling socially inept, personally unappealing, and inferior to others, Fred remained reluctant to risk engaging in new relationships that might prove to be embarrassing. His unusual dependency on prospective female partners together with the urgency of his need for their acceptance made it difficult for him to feel comfortable about his overtures. Fred desired the warmth and security of human companionship yet his timidity paralyzed him when he tried to reach out to others. Part of his awkwardness and inferiority feelings can be accounted for by the shame surrounding sexual impulses and contact. The "facts of life"-- how one deals with sexual impulses and troublesome urges and what it takes to fall in love -- were never discussed in his household. His own inhibitions in this important area of his life were evident in much of what he had to report. Moreover, his responses to the *Thematic Apperception Test* (*TAT*; Morgan & Murray, 1943) at age 35 suggest that the idea of sexual contact was not entirely pleasant to him. He perceived sex as dangerous, illicit under any circumstances, and potentially ruinous. His responses to the *Minnesota Multiphasic Personality Inventory* (*MMPI-2*; Butcher, Graham, Tellegen, & Kaemmer, 1989) taken at age 40 suggest that he was riddled with conflicts about sexuality and dependency as well as concerned about masculine adequacy. Thus, his emotional needs for a mother/sister substitute were frustrated by equally strong fears of sexual contact, making it impossible to find comfort in his relationship with any female. It also exacerbated his need for supportive relationships of any kind. His score on the Dependence Scale of the *Dynamic Personality Inventory* (*DPI*; Grygier & Grygier, 1976) indicated a dependency upon parental substitutes, need for guidance, and a clinging attitude.

Depression. Obviously, Fred's painful feelings of inferiority, unfulfilled dependency needs, and pervasive social inhibition made it difficult for him to successfully adapt to the life tasks of work, friendship, and intimacy. His scores on the *DPI* indicated rigidity, a lack of drive and self-confidence, and a tendency to give-in under stress. His *MMPI*, taken at age 40, showed elevations greater than a T-score of 75 on four different scales. Fred's "2547" code reflected his depression, passivity, resentment, and timidity. The *MMPI* narrative reported the following personality features: feelings of inadequacy, sexual conflict, rigidity, and a lack of self-confidence. Fred was also described as unduly sensitive, self-conscious, lonely, and shy. Only among the members of his family and the patients on his floor was Fred able to move with much certainty. In these two settings he created a special refuge for himself and for those who surrounded him. And as long as he is able to maintain such circumstances he need never face a world within and without which could demand far more of him. Like the young man he saw at age 35 in Card #14 of the *TAT*, he can *lull himself to sleep* with dreams that are not at all disquieting. But each day as he awakes, he feels unhappy and discouraged because life has not worked out well for him. Filled with regrets and guilt about the past, feeling ineffectual in present, and with little hope for the future, Fred faces each day doing the best he can. As the Greek dramatist Menander (342-290 BC) wrote, "We live, not as we wish to, but as we can" (Allinson, 1921, p. 317).

Career Construction

To examine how Fred manifested his character in the world of work, I focus first on the processes by which he constructed his career and then on the content of that career. In considering process, I concentrate on how Fred's character, with its disorganized and insecure attachment schema prevented him from forming vocational goals and planning his career, all the time concentrating his interest in work only on the extrinsic rewards of money and security. Then, I discuss how Fred eventually found himself in a fitting occupational position and turned it into a safe haven for himself, almost a home away from home where every day he could give to others the nurturance that as a child he had sought for himself.

Career Construction Process

Fred's vocational immaturity as an adolescent and his career stagnation as an adult both illustrate the importance of a future time perspective. Career adaptability in adolescence and young adulthood rests on a future orientation that fosters exploratory behavior and sustains a readiness to make fitting educational and vocational decisions. Fred never developed the planning attitudes and self-determination competencies needed to design his career because he was mired in the present, worrying about getting through the day unscathed. Planning his future at work, or anywhere else for that matter, was not a salient issue. When he did think about the future, Fred just assumed that the future would repeat the present that he endured and the past that his family had suffered. Rather than plan a career, Fred expected that his work-life would consist of the demoralizing labor that crushed his father and monopolized his mother. Accordingly, he expected little from work, viewing it as a means of survival and as a place to meet females. Work did not promise him an identity or personal meaning -- or even much economic return. Although he participated in the work role, he never committed himself to his job or employer.

Fred's low work motivation and lack of career planning can be easily traced across each of his interviews. During high school, Fred dared no ambition. When asked what he would like to get out of life and what are some reasons for living Fred responded, *I can't think of none.* When asked what sort of things he would like his job to give him, he again said, *I don't know.* His parents also lacked a vision for their son's future. During the parent interview, his mother when asked about her hopes and ambitions for her son replied, *Well, I don't know.* His father's only ambition for Fred was that he finish high school, which Fred almost did. However, even in the ninth grade Fred was already thinking of quitting school. He had given no thought to the type of curriculum he would follow the next three years and reported that he was *just taking things as they come.* He did not see much practical application for the subjects he studied in school. He estimated that the chances of him graduating at *half and half*. He thought that if he quit school he would join the Air Force yet he knew no one in the service and had no idea what it involved.

> *I don't know whether I would like it or not, but there's no choice. I don't have any ambition now. Maybe I'll stay in the Air Force a few years, save all my money and buy a produce stand.*

The idea of career exploration never occurred to him because he lacked a secure base from which to venture out into the world.

Obviously, Fred rarely looked ahead to consider what the future might bring. Even worse, he rarely looked at himself, so Fred possessed only minimal self-knowledge. In the ninth grade, when asked to describe himself, all he could come up with was *I don't know what kind of guy I am*. When pressed to describe his strengths, Fred said, *I don't know what my strong points are*. The one thing he admitted liking about himself was that *I don't have very many enemies*.

When at age 25 he was asked about future plans, he said something similar to what he had said in the ninth grade: *I'm playing it by ear. Well I think I will start planning more in the future, in about six months. Maybe I'll buy a produce stand*. When asked if he thought planning his life would be useful, Fred replied: *Well, I don't have much of a skilled trade or anything, I mean, I'm just not qualified in any type of skilled work that I could plan. So, it's either get a skill or take it as it comes*. Thus, at age 25, Fred was still *taking it as it comes*. This remained true at age 35 when Fred reported that his career goals were never clear to him and even at that time he did not have a long-term career objective. When asked how certain he was that he would be in the same job ten years from now, he replied, *very uncertain --* and he was correct.

Career Construction Content

Fred's role model was Will Rogers, a warm and friendly man who never met a person he did not like, and surely one who would not abandon a baby on railroad tracks. It seems that Will Rogers served as both a goal and example for Fred in his quest for acceptance from other people. The same can be hypothesized for Fred's favorite poem because it tells the tale of enemies who eventually accept each other. In the poem entitled *The Ballad of the East and West* Rudyard Kipling (1889) described how two boys, one a Colonel's son who rode the mare and the other a thief's boy who rode the dun, forged a bond. Despite their different stations in life, they became blood brothers after they *looked each other between the eyes, and there they found not fault*. Fred's interest in Will Rogers and blood brothers suggests that he might, if he felt secure, be attracted to work where he could connect to people and then win them over. However, as noted earlier, Fred expressed few vocational interests. During his first interview in the ninth grade, he reported no vocational interests. In the spring of the ninth grade, he said he would like an outdoor job. In March of the tenth grade, and again in October of the eleventh grade, he was not sure of any vocational interests yet thought he would join the Air Force after high school. In January of his senior year, he said that he might work at the produce market. Although Fred did not express crystallized vocational preferences, his measured interests were surprisingly well-defined.

Measured interests and abilities. Fred responded to the *Work Values Inventory* (*WVI*; Super, 1970) three times: once in the ninth grade, then again in the twelfth grade, and yet again at age 35. What he considered important in work remained quite stable across these three occasions. Each time he placed a premium on good pay, a friendly supervisor, and being accepted by other people. In high school, he valued independence yet as he grew older his focus on independence was replaced by an increasing desire for security and routine. He never valued work that involved creativity, variety, intellectual stimulation, or mastering challenges.

As a ninth grader, Fred's *Kuder Preference Schedule - Vocational Form CH* (Kuder, 1956) profile indicated strong interest in Literary (86th percentile) and Persuasive (78th percentile) activities, along with some interest in Social Service (59th percentile), Artistic (57th percentile) and Outdoor (56th percentile) activities. He eschewed (below the 33rd percentile) Clerical, Scientific, Mechanical, and Computational activities. Converting this profile to a RIASEC code results in a vocational personality type of Enterprising-Social-Artistic (ESA). Combined with his level of academic aptitude and achievement, this code and its variations seem to fit with Enterprising-Social-Realistic jobs such as housekeeper, waiter, barber; Social-Enterprising-Artistic jobs such as day-care center director, recreation supervisor, attendant at a children's institution; and Social-Enterprising-Realistic jobs such as nurse's aide, home health aide, day care worker, and attendant at a lodging institution. These jobs resemble the one he has held as a nursing home attendant for more than 29 years. Fred's persuasive interests probably illustrate the view that vocational interests can express solutions to problems in growing up, in his case a mother who would not listen to him when he talked as well as the problems of being *nervous in crowds or talking to people* and being *tongue-tied in new situations*. Fred's ability to overcome to some degree his social anxiety is indicated by success as a union vice-president and by his supervisor's recruiting him as a foreman.

Fred's two highest occupational interests on the *Strong Vocational Interest Blank-Revised* (Strong, Campbell, Berdie, & Clark, 1966) coincided with his interest in Persuasive and Literary activities. He scored A both on real estate sales and on author-journalist. His next highest scores were B+ for artist, physician, and farmer. Of course, some of these occupations might be unrealistic for Fred because of his general academic aptitude and achievement. He scored at the 15th percentile on the *Otis-Lennon Mental Ability Test* (Otis & Lennon, 1967), the 24th percentile on the *Nelson-Denny Reading Test* (Nelson & Denny, & Brown, 1960), the 10th percentile on the *Differential Aptitude Test* (*DAT*; Bennett, Seashore, & Wesman, 1966) for *Numerical Ability*, and the 10th percentile on the *Test of Mechanical Comprehension* (Bennett, 1940). However, on the *DAT* for *Verbal Reasoning* he scored at the 33rd percentile and his score on the *DAT* for *Abstract Reasoning* was even higher, falling at the 50th percentile. On the whole, Fred's measured abilities suggest that he could have achieved more in school, if he had only felt safer there. The highest grade on his high school transcript was 73 in ninth-grade and in tenth-grade social studies and in eleventh-grade English. His only other grades above 70 were in the eleventh-grade for retail selling and for typing.

Occupations. When counselors think of Super's (1963) classic dictum that choosing an occupation implements a self-concept, they almost always think of positive self-concepts. For example, nurturant and dominant people frequently implement their self-concepts in occupations such as teacher, counselor, nurse, or minister. Super's dictum, however, holds as well for negative self-concepts. Individuals who evaluate themselves negatively may convert this self-appraisal into destructive occupations such as thieves or drug pushers. Fred was able to avoid such a ruinous outcome because of his courage and social interest. Fred worked in a constructive occupation, one that manifested his negative self-concept as *just a plain ordinary ass wiper* yet still allowed him to make a social contribution by taking care of *infirmed patients*.

Fred's vocational behavior as a nursing home attendant closely resembles that predicted for individuals with avoidant personality disorders (Kaplan, Sadock, & Gregg, 1994). Fred's *MMPI* narrative report accurately described his narrow range of interests and likelihood of participating in housekeeping activities. Acting shy and eager to please, Fred remained on the sidelines engaged in tasks that implement the nurturant aspects of his personality -- walking patients and changing their diapers as well as feeding, showering, shaving, and moving them. His patients appreciated his ministration, and he was justifiably proud of his skill at working with and pleasing them. Of course, this did not mean that he liked himself or his occupation. Fred wished that he could obtain a better job at the nursing home. At age 35, Fred stated that he disliked his job because of the duties, lack of variety, and physical working conditions. Moreover, he disliked his supervisor, the benefits, and the workload. Occasionally over the next 20 years, Fred applied for other jobs in the nursing home, *but someone else always beat me out*. He attributed his lack of career progress to insufficient training and knowledge. Of course, I think that his parents had a role in his vocational stagnation (cf., Super, Kowalski, & Gotkin, 1967), including his mother's admonition about *getting a job and sticking to it regardless of the kind of money you made* and her discouraging him from bettering himself: *All she wanted for me was to be somewhere where I could work every day*. Clearly, Fred's three-decade tenure as a nursing home attendant has more than fulfilled his mother's ambition for him.

Nevertheless, Fred frequently ruminated sullenly about his lack of career progress and felt aggrieved by his station in life. Beneath Fred's brooding and resentment over what the fates had offered him was the dream of a far different world in which he would become a champion for his family and an advocate for hapless individuals. His ideal self-concept appears to be that of a savior. Early on he had thought in terms of finding a place of refuge for his family where his parents could end their days and where his sister and her husband could enjoy the privileges of a special community. While that particular dream was never realized, it still remains. His world was sustained by the hope for a miracle such as the one he described at age 35 for *TAT* Card 8BM in which a divine figure intervenes on behalf of a person who has accidentally shot himself. A similar refrain appeared in his response to *TAT* Card 13MF. The hero's life is dedicated to the service and salvation of a young girl who has been sick all her life and whose survival depends upon whatever acumen the physician has gained through years of medical education. In a profound way, Fred over the years was able to actualize at least part of this ideal self-concept because, in no small measure, he did become a savior of sorts to the patients on his floor.

Clearly, Fred's occupation implemented his self-concept, yet it did even more for him. Fred's job enabled him to become more whole, more complete, as he actively mastered what he had passively suffered as a child. His job allowed him to heal some of the pain he felt by giving to his infirmed patients the nurturance that he had craved as a child. Fred's occupational role in a defining context enabled him to repeat and improve on his role in the family drama of his childhood and youth (Chusid & Cochran, 1988). In restaging this drama, he underscored themes of attachment and belongingness -- the very essence of family. Fred used, implicitly and unconsciously, the scenario of his family drama and his childhood position in this drama to make sense of and interpret the occupational drama that he lived, with its super-objective of finding a maternal figure to care for him. His occupational duties repeated, with slightly different content and new characters, the earlier drama he had lived in his family. In this sense, work made up for what he had missed in childhood by allowing him to enact a more fulfilling dramatic role. The role was more fulfilling, not in being radically different, but in turning passivity into activity by doing for others what had not been done for him. In this way his tension became intention and his preoccupation became occupation, explaining in part why each day he reported early to work.

Throughout his work life, Fred did his best, usually with moderate success, to create for himself a surrogate family. His extensive involvement at the produce market provided him with such an opportunity. His union activities could be viewed in a similar fashion, as could Fred's attempt to become involved in a caring community. He was gratified by the respect and admiration he earned from employers who were warmer than his parents and from the co-workers who discussed personal problems with him as his sister had years earlier. Rather than replicating his detached family-of-origin at work, Fred was able to experience a warmer and more caring "work family."

His present work as a nursing home attendant is probably the best example of how Fred has managed to *make do* with respect to his unrelenting quest for a nurturant milieu. Among the patients on his floor, Fred is able to move with much certainty. He has created a special refuge for himself and for those who surround him. In this setting he feels at home as he attends, to an extraordinary degree, to the patients' needs. Moreover, the patients appreciate the attention and love that he gives them. He has found himself in those for whom he cares, and in nurturing them he has become the caring figure he could never find for himself. What also makes his position so attractive to him is that it does not involve the risk of rejection. Unlike the dejected male suitor he described at age 35 in *TAT* Card 6BM whose need to possess a female becomes his undoing, Fred can always be sure of his patients' welcome because they rely on him for protection and servicing. He acts as the mentor he never had, as the understanding teacher he never found in school, and as the spokesperson for the oppressed individual he so often felt himself to be.

Fred's active mastery of what he had once passively suffered turns his torment into his element. In his early years a despondent father and an unapproachable mother failed to bond with him and nurture his development. Now, Fred bonds with elderly patients and gives them the both the nurturance that as a child he craved for himself and provides the guidance and reassurance that as an adolescent he never received. He has become for others the nurturing person who he could not find for himself. In so doing, Fred transformed his negative self-concept as an *ass wiper* into meaningful work as a caregiver. His work allows him to relate to others and to express an empathy he had never received from his parents. In the nursing home, all his previous training at home with his father has come to the fore. He is prepared to meet his patients' every need, and he does so with a dignity that ennobles both himself and those he serves. He has created an environment, and a position in it, wherein he can enact the love he feels for the less fortunate. Clearly he is where he is by no accident, and he has stayed the course because his work expresses his empathy for the abandoned and allows him to act as their savior in many small ways. At age 59, Fred understood deeply what his role model Will Rogers meant when he said, *What you get makes a living but what you give makes a life.*

CHAPTER SEVEN
A Collective Perspective on the Case Studies

The case studies reported in this book were presented for expository and didactic purposes, not to validate propositions in Career Construction Theory (CCT). The density of details in the participants' career stories was used to illustrate, explain, and demonstrate propositions in CCT. The present chapter reviews and compares the life portraits as a group to understand something more general about how well CCT comprehends careers. This collective perspective on the multiple cases brought forth themes as they relate to theorems in CCT. Connecting the particulars of the four case studies to CCT concepts and propositions helped to explore and interrogate the theory. The following discussion considers ways in which personality and work interact to scrutinize how character is formed in families, expressed in vocational interests, implemented in occupations, and maintained in careers. I describe how each of the four participants organized his life around a problem that preoccupied him and solutions that occupied him. I also consider the effectiveness of a technique for articulating career themes, namely drawing a career construction line from childhood memories through adolescent role models to adult occupations. In this way, I trace the trajectory of how each participant brought his inner world into relation with the outer world -- first in play, then through hobbies, and finally at work.

Meta-Theory

CCT's meta-theory connects conceptual models and important constructs usually studied in isolation. It provides a broad yet theoretically-integrated perspective on how the self-constructing functions of organizing, regulating, and conceiving operate together in making the social actor, motivated agent, and autobiographical author. The meta-concepts of agency and communion provide a large-scale model for integrating pre-existing concepts and well-established mid-range theories. Viewing the life portraits from the perspective of the meta-theory reveals how the fundamental modes of agency and communion condition psychological schemas concerning attachment, motivation, and reflexivity and their related psychosocial strategies of disposition, adaptability, and identity. The prospective design of the case studies allowed observation of how the pairs of psychological schema and psychosocial strategy related to each other within their respective dimensions of actor, agent, and author. The resulting observations suggest that attachment schemas lead to dispositions; motivation schemas regulate adaptability strategies; and, reflexivity schemas shape identity strategies. In addition to relations between the pairs of schema and strategy within each of the three dimensions, the prospective design enabled observation of relations among dimensions that revealed how early patterns of schemas and strategies prefigured later patterns and forecast long-term developmental outcomes. For just one example, consider the relation between the most basic schema of attachment and the most advanced strategy of identity performance. In considering how attachment schemas condition identity strategies, CCT proposes that secure-autonomous attachment associates with making identity commitments following exploration; anxious-ambivalent attachment associates with making commitments without exploration; dismissive-avoidant attachment associates with continual exploration without making commitments; and fearful-disorganized attachment associates with neither exploration nor commitment.

The Self-Organizing Social Actor

CCT Premise A: Individuals co-construct a psychological self as a social actor within their families by organizing an attachment schema and dispositional strategy.

The cases in this study showed that where you end up depends a great deal on where you begin. In the words of T. S. Eliot (1943, Part I, Line 1), "In my beginning is my end." For CCT, an individual's career story begins at home because what happens in childhood foreshadows the future. The participants in this study became who they were by interacting with the people in their families; and their family's messages remained in their heads forever. Attachments to their parents had a profound influence on their lives by conditioning how they made sense of experiences and prompting strategies for living that they carried forward into adulthood. During times of transition and trauma, without fully realizing it, they brought their attachment schemas to bear on judging current situations and then reacted with well-practiced patterns of behavior.

Each of the four prototypical attachment schemas were reflected clearly in the lives of the four participants. Their life portraits showed how individuals methodically and unknowingly recreate the world of their childhood in their adult lives. Steadied by the embrace of his family, Robert became careful and competitive. Shaped by loyalty to family messages, William became bored and busy. Ignored and invalidated by a detached father, Paul became angry and adventurous. Trapped in aloneness and fearfulness by his family, Fred became wary and weary.

From what can be seen in the case studies, relationships with parents had a strong determinative effect on career construction and vocational development behavior. However, relationships with mother and father operated differently in the lives of the four participants. The participants' interactions with their mothers profoundly affected their experience of themselves and the world around them, particularly evident in their interpersonal relationships.

Robert had a warm and loving relationship with his mother. However, when his brother's children joined the household, his mother had little time for Robert, forcing him to seek important satisfactions outside the home. There his mother's encouragement and hopes that he would achieve in ways that she never had were less evident and became less influential in his motivation. William's mother was indulgent of him and perhaps overprotective. At the same time her son felt her prodding, was made aware of her expectations of him, and came to enjoy pleasure in his accomplishments. Although he might have bridled under restrictions and sometimes felt misunderstood, he could be confident of her good will toward him and shared perhaps the value she placed on achievement. Paul enjoyed an unusually close relationship with his mother, but her premature death when he was nine-years old subjected him to a trauma from which he barely recovered. He experienced a maternal abandonment that aggravated his experience of adolescence. Similarly, Fred felt abandoned by a mother whose work outside the home and responsibilities in the household left her with little time or energy for him. Each participant's relationship with his mother, his first companion, had a considerable, if not exclusive, impact upon his impressions of how rewarding interpersonal relationships were likely to be.

While the mother-son relationship may have shaped much of each participant's internal working model of interpersonal relations, the participant's relationship with his father may have been even more influential in the son's career construction and vocational behavior. For each participant, the father's expectations and insistence that his son behave in accordance with family rules was important in his son's socialization, preparing the son for survival outside the family. Out of this experience came the son's attitude toward persons in authority and the confidence (or lack of it) that he could meet others' demands without forfeiting his personal integrity.

The amount and quality of each participant's contact with his father seemed to determine the extent to which the father served as a guiding line with whom the participant identified. A detached, absent, or hostile father is in no position to serve as a positive guiding line for his son. Only William and Robert were confident about their father's acceptance of them, although both fathers demanded obedience and expected much of their sons. Robert had what could be described as a warm and lovingly relationship with his father. Yet Robert's father told him to not be like him, and with the support of family members Robert acted on this admonition. William did spend a good deal of time with his father yet the relationship centered more on William's respect for his father and strong identification with his occupation than on casual, loving, affectionate encounters. For Paul and Fred the absence of loving contact made it well-nigh impossible for them to truly incorporate their fathers' expectations and follow their guiding lines. Paul hardly got to know his usually-absent father. He viewed his father as a stranger who experienced life as a struggle and felt enslaved by work. At his earliest opportunity Paul looked elsewhere for norms to guide his behavior, rejecting his father's reproofs and attempts to regulate his son's conduct from afar. When dealing with authority figures outside the home such as teachers and employers Paul, at best, superficially acknowledged them and grudgingly followed their rules. Fred reported an increasing lack of closeness to his father and often felt guilty about his treatment of a father in a pitiable predicament. Similar to Robert, Fred was told by his father not to be like him, yet Fred had neither the encouragement nor confidence to act on this admonition. Fred never did overcome the immobilizing feelings of guilt which his paternal relationship elicited in him. In sum, the participants' paternal relationships -- constructive for Robert and William and destructive for Paul and Fred -- determined much of what they would make of their careers.

Notably, the careers that the participants made suggest a relationship between the four attachment schema and the four career patterns described by Super (1957). Secure-autonomous attachment schemas lead to comfort with intimacy and autonomy that may make for a *stable career* pattern in which one enters a congruent occupation and stabilizes rather quickly, as Robert did in the field of accounting. An anxious-ambivalent attachment schema characterized by a preoccupation with relationships may lead to a *conventional career* path such as the one followed by William. A dismissive-avoidant attachment schema seems likely to produce a *multiple trial career* pattern marked by a disconnected work history of frequent job changes without stabilization, such as experienced by Paul. And finally, a fearful-disorganized attachment schema characterized by socially-avoidant behaviors may make for an *unstable* career pattern. Viewing the self and others negatively certainly can produce repeated frustration and cause individuals such as Fred to drift in different directions without finding much success.

Role Models

CCT proposes that to address problems, troubles, and conflicts with parents, children incorporate and rehearse characteristics of role models who demonstrate a way to resolve the issues. The life portraits illustrated how the participants as social actors modeled their further self-making and life roles on strategies displayed by their heroes, who had provided them with cultural sources of the self. In many important ways, the participants became similar to who they admired. Consider Robert. As a young boy reflecting on the lives of his father and brother, Robert may have concluded that men do not achieve their dreams. Instead, they must take whatever jobs are available and then temporarily or even permanently lose these jobs due to circumstances beyond their control. The male guiding line drawn by his father and walked by his brother probably felt like destiny to Robert. To avoid a similar fate, Robert identified at least one role model who portrayed a solution, namely, an uncle who was exact, set goals, finished high school, learned a profession in night school, worked his way up the ladder, and earned good pay in a secure job. In other words, Robert's uncle did what his brother and father had not done. Similar to his uncle. Robert finished his education in night school and trudged steadily to succeed in an occupation that rewarded his planning and conscientiousness. As a role model, Robert's uncle showed him how to actively master what his father and brother continued to suffer.

As a guiding line, the main role played by William's father seems to have been to connect William to work at the family mill. From his father, William learned to deny his own ambitions -- maybe for music or journalism -- because *a father's need requires a son's deed*. William found his solution to the problems propounded by his guiding line when he read *The Adventures of Tom Sawyer* (Twain, 1884), a story about a young man who devised many schemes and entrepreneurial projects. Similar to Tom Sawyer, William became a venturesome young man whose exploits culminated in insouciant flight from the dreary respectability of his village. Ultimately Tom's conscience prompted him to return home. In similar fashion, William "escaped" to the city for a time, yet he returned to the mill where he played the role of a wheeler and dealer, much like Tom Sawyer.

As a teenager, Paul dis-identified with an uptight father who provided a guiding line for how to travel through life by avoiding risks and settling for barren survival. At first immobilized by his father's detached domination, Paul prioritized freedom to move -- the opposite of his father who steadfastly remained in place. In the ninth grade Paul named John Wayne as a role model who he viewed as *an adventurer*. Paul also greatly admired his aunt, a *free thinker* who *had been all over the country, traveling and working until she got tired of it and she would just move on.* She modeled an approach to work that could meet Paul's needs for autonomy, activity, and adventure. Paul followed the lead of his role models, enjoying adventures as an independent consultant who solved practical problems and managed crises. As Paul explained, he became an *adventure type boy* who enjoyed being on the move.

Parallel to Paul's experience, Fred never found the father he had needed. The guiding line provided by Fred's father plotted a trajectory of dissatisfaction at work and despondence at home. To attempt to rid himself of the rack and ruin, Fred chose as his role model Will Rogers, a warm and friendly man who never met a person he did not like, and surely a man who would not abandon a baby on railroad tracks. It seems that Will Rogers served as both an example and goal for Fred in his quest for acceptance from other people.

If one is willing to consider a correspondence in some functions between a supervisor and an authoritative parent, then attachment theory suggests ideas about providing guiding lines at work. In the socialization of new employees, managers may foster organizational commitment and work adjustment by offering relational support in the form of connections to veteran employees and supervisors. To foster position performance, supervisors may offer more than instrumental support. They could try to provide employees with safe havens when they are anxious about their performance, secure bases to encourage them when they take on challenging assignments, and cooperative partnerships when they encounter interpersonal conflict.

Dispositional Strategies

Following from their attachment schemas, the participants formed dispositions toward acting in social contexts. The attachment schemas constructed by the four participants certainly seemed to serve as the foundation of their vocational personality dispositions. Based on their attachment schema, they rehearsed behaviors and habits that would, in due course, shape their personal characteristics and establish their dispositions. They seemed to give to other people that which they were given by their families.

CCT views four personality dispositions (Gough, 1987) as flowing from the fountainhead of attachment schema: extroverted and accepting Alphas from the wellspring of secure-autonomous attachment, introverted and accepting Betas from anxious-ambivalent attachment, extroverted and questioning Gammas from dismissing-avoidant attachment, and introverted and questioning Deltas from a fearful-disorganized attachment. The life portraits showed the tight fit between attachment schemas and dispositional strategies. Robert's secure-autonomous attachment schema enabled him to develop an Alpha (extroverted, accepting) disposition characterized by a healthy personality and rewarding interpersonal relationships. William's anxious-ambivalent attachment schema led to a Beta (introverted, accepting) disposition of conformity in which he lacked assertiveness and put the needs of others before his own. Paul's dismissive-avoidant attachment schema produced a Gamma (extroverted, questioning) disposition of counter-dependency through which he eschewed interpersonal closeness and strove compulsively for self-reliance. Fred's fearful-disorganized attachment schema led to a Delta (introverted, questioning) disposition that made him a prisoner of his past, trapping him in a dangerous world that provoked deep fears and produced difficult experiences.

The Self-Regulating Motivated Agent

CCT Premise B: Late in childhood, individuals become motivated agents who direct their own lives toward congruent positions in society through self-regulation, that is, the process by which individuals adapt their perceptions, feelings, and actions in the pursuit of a goal.

Motivational Focus

In due course, social actors become agents who focus their motivation with a persistent, self-regulation strategy concentrated on promotion or prevention goals. The two foci differ because, in simple terms, promotion focuses on what one wants to do whereas prevention focuses on what one ought to do. For the participants in the present study, attachment schemas conditioned the formation of motivational schemas. The participants' attachment schemas and dispositional strategies led them to construct motivational orientations consistent with the social roles they had prepared to enact.

Given his secure attachment and industrious disposition, Robert's self-regulation strategy balanced promotion and prevention goals that set a path forward. He was competitive yet careful in combining what he wanted to do with what he ought to do. Given his preoccupied attachment to pleasing his parents and conventional disposition, William focused on motives and goals that allowed him to avoid threat and failure. He was both bored and busy as he played it safe. Of course Paul never played it safe. With a detachment from his father and a derring-do personality, Paul relentlessly pursued promotion goals and remained angry and adventurous. With a fearful approach to life engendered by his parents and a disquieted personality, Fred remained wary and weary. Rather than focusing on promotion or prevention goals, he lacked motivation in all areas of his life, preferring to remain apathetic and avoid catastrophes.

Adaptability

The results of the present study suggest that individuals' motivational foci influence the development and use of adaptability resources. For example, the balance of promotion wants and prevention oughts shown in Robert's motivational focus led to well-developed adaptability resources. Recall that he said, *I like to plan*. His adaptability strategy included concern about the future, control to delay gratification, curiosity about options, and confidence in implementing plans. When faced with educational and vocational decisions, Robert's willingness to look ahead and look around prepared him to make fitting choices and then implement those choices in stable and satisfying work.

William's prevention focus on what he ought to do restricted his development of adaptability resources to concern about his future and curiosity for in-depth exploration of parental goals, thus limiting his adapting responses to looking ahead not around. Paul's promotion focus on playing to win led him to develop strong resources of control and confidence but not concern and curiosity. Paul did not look ahead to the future, he just looked around to deal with problems as they arose. Fred lived in the present, and with little sense of a future he did not develop the adaptability resources. Rather than look ahead and look around for fitting occupations, Fred choose not to look; instead, he just remained on the look-out not to get hurt, *taking it as it comes*.

Work Roles and Interests

As agents directing their own lives through motivational schemas and adaptability strategies, individuals implement their self-concepts by developing interests and selecting work roles in which to pursue their career goals. Vocational interests and work-role preferences emerge through the interaction of inherited aptitudes, physical make-up, opportunities to observe and play various roles, and evaluations of the extent to which the results of role playing satisfy needs and meet with the approval of peers and supervisors. Role playing by children and adolescents typically occurs in avocational activities and school functions, both curricular and extra-curricular.

Avocational activities. Children's interests are shaped first by biological endowments, parent reinforcement, and affordances offered by objects in the household and around the neighborhood. Then, their motivational goals and adaptability resources direct them to prefer some activities and avoid others. As children grow, they test the potential of different activities to meet their needs. Based on these practical tests of interest and ability, they usually form preferences for avocations. Super (1940) suggested that

> *avocations are chosen according to the present needs of an individual in a given situation, and on the basis of the possible ways in which that individual can meet those needs in that situation (p. 114, italics in original).*

By engaging in avocational activities, children and adolescents manifest interests, learn skills, and develop competencies that serve as rehearsal for particular occupations. To conceptualize the relation between an individual's major avocations and eventual vocation Super (1940) proposed an "individualized theory" that distinguished between avocations that either support or balance a vocation.

A support avocation resembles the vocation in terms of required interests and skills. For example, Robert's adolescent avocations of stamp collecting, playing cards and board games as well as his participation in sports teams supported his adult vocation because these activities helped him to develop the conscientiousness and competitiveness he displayed as a C.P.A. Both his avocations and vocation reflect his RIASEC vocational personality type of Conventional-Realistic-Enterprising. Paul's adolescent and adult avocations also supported his vocation. Pauls' adolescent avocations of competing in soap box derbies, operating a railroad set, and building model airplanes and race cars were early manifestations of his interest in adventure. As an adult, he continued to seek adventure in physical activities that involved trying new things, taking risks, and competing with others -- especially when he could move from place to place in cars, trucks, motorcycles, snowmobiles, trucks, boats, and travel trailers. In short, Paul's enduring interest in adventure kept him moving in both his vocation in the trucking industry and his avocation in recreational vehicles. Paul's RIASEC vocational personality type of Realistic-Enterprising-Investigative represents both his avocations and his vocation as an independent consultant who solved practical problems and managed crises.

While a support avocation resembles the vocation, a balancing avocation differs from the vocation in terms of required interests and skills. Super (1940) concluded that individuals choose balancing avocations because they work in vocations that they would not choose if given freedom of choice. Viewed from this perspective, a balancing avocation provides catharsis in exercising skills and interests that cannot be expressed in the vocation. The case of William illustrates how an avocation may supplant a vocation. William's gemstone business was a compensatory avocation that was so much more satisfying than his vocation, and often threatened to usurp it. When engaged in trading gemstones, William felt intrinsically satisfied and free from claims by intrusive people. In due course, he turned his aesthetic (Artistic) collection (Conventional) into an entrepreneurial (Enterprising) business that fully implemented his RIASEC vocational personality type of Artistic-Conventional-Enterprising (ACE).

Fred's amotivation and insufficient adaptability resources left him detached from the work world, as he had been detached from his parents during childhood. With regard to avocational and vocational interests, Fred was mainly unconcerned, bored, and disengaged. He expressed few vocational interests beyond maybe working outdoors or at a produce market. In terms of avocational interests, as a child Fred and his sister played with dolls and cut-out magazine pictures of things they wanted. Beginning in the seventh grade, he worked excessive hours -- full-time during the summers and part-time after school and on weekends. He spent his little free time hanging out with friends, drinking cokes at a drugstore, playing pinball machines, and looking through the magazine racks. As an adult, Fred's vocational opportunities were at the unskilled level, forcing him to take a job that was available and then express his social interests in that occupational context. As a nursing home attendant, he continued his lifelong search for rewarding relationships by befriending coworkers and patients. His interest inventory results indicated his RIASEC vocational personality type as Enterprising-Social-Artistic. His job let him express his relationship interests (Social) yet his attempts over three decades to earn a promotion (Enterprising) were stymied.

Holland's (1997) RIASEC typology of personality types provides a coherent classification of both avocational and vocational activities. When adolescents leave home, they prefer vocations that make use of the characteristic capabilities and interests that they have rehearsed in their avocations and with their peers. A job that suits them will enable them to reenact at work, to some degree, their major avocational preferences. In short, many individuals' leisure activities during childhood and adolescence provide important rehearsal for adult occupations. For others, leisure can correct cases of mistaken identity.

School experiences. In addition to avocational pursuits, school activities provide another source for career construction. While avocational activities relate more to job satisfaction and frustration, school activities relate more to job success and failure. Children's earliest experiences at school generally reflect the degree to which their even earlier experiences at home have prepared them for the outside world. They also prompt lasting impressions of that world and how one can cope with its sometimes arbitrary requirements. In large measure, school experiences can powerfully determine a young person's sense of herself or himself as a success or failure and set the tone for many future experiences. Furthermore, the school they attend can also determine how and with whom they spend free time.

At school, Robert and William found success but not satisfaction. Robert initially had a relatively easy and enjoyable time in elementary school. These circumstances changed once he entered the less-structured milieu of high school. There, and afterwards at college, he became far more engrossed in sports and social activities than in academic pursuits. His career in accounting returned him to a structured environment where he flourished. William was bored by the new academic surroundings that failed to challenge him. Eventually William was able to lose himself in extracurricular activities and function academically at a superior level. William graduated from college and earned an advanced degree, yet his educational experiences tended to be more a matter of endurance than of delight.

Paul and Fred found neither success nor satisfaction at school. Paul viewed school as a milieu indifferent to his needs for personal attention, acceptance, and even affection. For a time, he had an elementary school teacher who related warmly to him and a high school teacher who became something of a father-surrogate, yet by his senior year he was totally alienated from academic milieu, believing that school was irrelevant and no longer entertaining notions of continuing his education. Fred's parents did not go far occupationally nor educationally. Their limited perspectives and socioeconomic situation led Fred to conclude that school matters had no particular relevance and that academic efforts would have no future payoff. Fred was unable to defy his demographic destiny.

Attachment and interests. The results of the present study certainly support the call made by Brown, Lum, and Voyle (1997) for a reappraisal of Anne Roe's (1956) theory of occupational choice. Researchers who have been attracted to Roe's theory have found it difficult to test because it requires long-term studies that relate parental caregiving to adult behavior. The four life portraits herein provide this longitudinal perspective and support Roe's conceptualization that parenting styles determine the development of psychological needs which in turn shape occupational interests.

Roe identified the three parenting styles called accepting, protecting, and avoiding, which CCT aligns with resulting attachment schemas. Accepting parents share love and satisfy needs so their children learn to become capable of satisfying their own needs, as seen in the case of Robert whose occupational preferences according to Roe's prediction would be in the clusters of service, business, and organization -- which include his work as a C.P.A. and company president. The anxiety produced by emotional concentration on the child by over-protecting parents imposes conditions of conformity to parental values and achievement expectations in return for love, as seen in the case of William who's occupational preference according to Roe's prediction would be in the clusters of general culture, arts, and entertainment which include editors, performers, museum curators, art critics, and advertising executives -- all of which fit William's gemstone business but not managing the mill. The avoidance style of parenting has two categories. With the rejecting style of avoidance parents may be insensitive to the emotional needs of their children by being cold, critical, and demanding, as seen in the case of Paul whose occupational preference according to Roe's prediction would be in the clusters of outdoor and science which include consulting specialists, engineers, inventors, contractors, county agents, and ship captains -- which encompass all of Paul's many jobs. The neglecting style of avoidance can lead to emotional deprivation, as seen in the case of Fred whose occupational preference according to Roe's prediction would be in the service cluster at the unskilled level that includes attending to the personal needs of other people -- which fit Fred's occupation as a nursing home attendant. Consistent with Roe's conceptualization, each of these four different parenting styles represented in the present study produced distinct psychological needs and dispositions that led to different occupational orientations.

The Self-Conceiving Autobiographical Author

Premise C: After first constructing a psychological self as a social actor and then pursuing goals as a motivated agent, individuals compose a vocational identity and author a career story to impose continuity and coherence on their actions over time.

Reflexivity

Reflexive deliberations enable individuals to mediate the effects of social systems and cultural structures on their personal agency and courses of action. This autobiographical reasoning provides the means by which individuals compose a vocational identity and author a career story with which to (a) understand the self in relation to social contexts, (b) recognize patterns in self-defining narratives, (c) determine and plan projects taking into consideration objective social circumstances, and (d) guide action by conditioning responses to particular social situations. These self-conceiving internal dialogues are shaped by an individual's reflexive schema (Archer, 2003).

The reflexive schemas of the participants in the present study coincided with their attachment schemas. It appears that reflexive schema evolve from working models of family relationships and then mediate between earlier attachment schema and later identity strategies. In the present study, secure attachment appears to be a necessary precursor of the capacity for autonomous reflexive thinking about life-stories and emotional functioning (Main, 1991). Robert, who constructed a secure-autonomous attachment schema, used autonomous reflexivity in purposeful, self-contained, and instrumental deliberations. He set his own goals and independently directed his actions without the need for validation by other individuals.

Attachment insecurity caused by anxiety or avoidance may lead to communicative, meta-, or fractured reflexivity. For example, with an anxious-ambivalent attachment schema William used communicative reflexivity in which his internal dialogues led to action only after being completed and confirmed by his parents. His deliberations focused on replicating the family way of life and reproducing the status quo. Paul used meta-reflexive deliberations to criticize and disengage from parental values. Rather than commit to something, he kept thinking and searching. And finally, Fred's fractured reflexivity produced internal dialogues that did not properly address his social circumstances nor design purposeful courses of action. His internal deliberations left him disoriented and confused.

Identity

CCT asserts that reflexive self-authorship produces identity. It proposes that reflexive thinking about the self in social roles enables one to dig deep into the past, the soil from which identity grows. Viewing the four distinct modes of reflexivity in relation to psychosocial strategies for dealing with career concerns leads directly to analogous types of vocational identity formation and functioning. The four modes of reflexive self-authorship identified by Archer (2012) related directly to four types of vocational identity narratives. CCT proposes that autonomous reflexivity schema support identity achievement and sustain functioning as a Pathmaker. For example, Robert used autonomous reflexivity to narrate the story of a Pathmaker who traveled a self-determined life course and achieved his identity through exploration and commitment to self-chosen goals. Robert displayed autonomous reflexivity to "think and act" (Archer, 2003, p.7). He did not attempt to replicate his parents' way of life. Instead, he set his own goals.

Communicative reflexivity schema form identity foreclosure and sustain functioning as a Guardian. The case of William illustrates the use of communicative reflexivity to narrate a story of a Guardian who made choices to preserve the collective good of his family. William displayed communicative reflexivity in "thinking and talking" (Archer, 2003, p. 7) as he replicated his parents' way of life and maintained the status quo. Guided by family tradition, he set clear priorities within the confines of his family's expectations.

Meta-reflexivity schema form identity moratorium and sustain functioning as a Searcher. For example, Paul used meta-reflexivity to narrate the story of a Searcher who avoided commitments and demanded the freedom to keep exploring. Paul routinely engaged in meta-reflexivity to criticize and disengage from his father's values. As an adolescent and emerging adult, Paul experimented with different lifestyles; as an adult he kept "thinking and thinking" (Archer, 2003, p. 7) in his search for new adventures and different jobs.

Fractured reflexivity schema form identity diffusion and sustain functioning as a Drifter. For example, Fred used fractured reflexivity to narrate the story of a Drifter who, beset by feelings of emptiness and meaninglessness, was lost and directionless. With no set ideological commitments nor occupational direction, he just would "think and talk to himself" (Archer, 2003). His goal was just to get bye and take things as they come. Fortunately, the nursing home in which Fred worked provided a defining context that supplied externally what he lacked internally in terms of a reflexively authored story. At work, he enacted the occupational role of a health-care aide following its script to narrate his vocational identity and guide his behavior. Each of the four cases in the present study traveled a different reflexive path to identity formation and functioning.

Attachment and identity. A meta-analysis by Arseth, Kroger, Martinussen, and Marcia (2009) reported weak to moderate links between attachment schema and identity strategies. Based on cross-sectional studies, they concluded that attachment experiences and internal working models of relationships have links to identity development. For example, individuals with a secure base provided by their families will likely feel safe enough to explore the work world and crystallize a self-chosen identity (Marcia, 1989).

Based on the longitudinal case studies reported herein, I concluded that attachment and identity are linked in that they are mutually determined by an individual's modes of agency and communion, and furthermore that reflexive schema is the consequential link that mediates the connection between attachment schemas and identity-formation strategies. Attachment security links to an autonomous reflexivity that more fully produces coherence and continuity in a narrative identity with which to interpret the past, explain the present, and imagine the future (Mikulincer & Shaver, 2013). Identity narratives rooted deeply in secure attachment schemas unite separate scenes to discern general insights, enhance self-understanding, and create a sense of meaning in life. In comparison, identity narratives rooted loosely in insecure attachment schemas tend to link separate scenes that portray a specific lesson without uniting them into a general insight.

Authoring a Career Story

Narratives provide a way to script an identity. Through reflexive selection and organization of experience, narratives substantiate an identity. For CCT, narrative identity is a story that individuals construct to explain and direct their lives. Furthermore, a career is a story that individuals tell about their work lives. These stories make sense of experiences by imposing order and stating superordinate goals. CCT pays particular attention to stories about childhood experiences, viewing them as acts of identity in which people reveal both their personal identities and social role preferences. Early recollections offer concrete examples of abstract claims about a life that inform what one wants and needs in occupational landscapes. CCT advises listening to early recollections for the preoccupation that is repeatedly interwoven throughout the macro-narrative, recurring like an echoing theme in a grand fugue.

For each of the four cases in the present study, the earliest recollection may be viewed as a controlling image that is emblematic of the participant's life theme. Robert's earliest recollection of building a snowman with his older brother revealed his desire to build something with the support of mentors. William's earliest recollection described him accepting the responsibility when parental figures transmit their agenda to him. Paul's earliest recollection announced this career theme of riding through life, without always knowing where he was going. Fred's earliest memory had him seeking affection. For each participant, the earliest recollection showed a fundamental perspective for life positioning (Martin, 2013), suggesting that where they had come from had much to do with where they had gone.

Through-Lines Link Narratives

The stories told by the participants in the present study included vignettes that support elements in the model for the practice of career construction counseling. Informed by CCT, the counseling discourse concentrates on first understanding clients' narratives about themselves as social actors, motivated agents, and autobiographical authors. To understand a client, practitioners ask story-crafting questions to prompt vignettes about early recollections, role models, manifest interests, and favorite stories. Client and counselor then unite the micro-narrative scenes into a comprehensible macro-narrative story and articulate its theme by tracing a through-line of development from early recollections to adolescent role models and then to adult occupations. In the next step, client and counselor use the new perspective and insights provided by the theme to reconstruct a vocational identity with deeper meaning and a longer through-line. Finally, clients use that portrayal of vocational identity as a guide as they make career choices and take actions to lead a more satisfying life, which is the superordinate goal of career construction counseling (Savickas, 2015, 2019).

The life portraits in the present study contain numerous examples of short micro-narrative scenes that can be united into a long macro-narrative story with a theme. The first link in the through-line is between earliest memories and role models. Robert building a snowman with a mentor connects to an uncle who set goals and worked toward them to become an engineer, modeling for Robert how to construct his own career and cooperate with his Board of Directors. In leisure time, Robert manifested interest in Conventional activities that included stamp collecting, and playing cards and board games -- which may be viewed as rehearsal for an accounting career. He went on to build a C.P.A. firm. William being thrown the ball of obligation by his family turned to Tom Sawyer as a role model who showed him how to negotiate. William's major avocational activity was gemstone dealing -- which may be viewed as rehearsal for his career as an entrepreneur in the gem trade. Paul at first immobilized by the death of his mother turned to adventurers as role models, including John Wayne, an aunt who was a free thinker, and an uncle who had his own business in the field of mechanics. His leisure activities included driving recreational vehicles and staying in motion -- certainly a prelude to his career in dispatching trucks and repairing boats. And Fred with a recollection seeking nurturance and relationship admired Will Rogers -- a "common man" who liked other people. Fred's manifest interest centered on relationships, including playing dolls with his sister and hanging with friends. In conceptualizing a through-line, CCC advises practitioners to concentrate on verbs. In the four life portraits herein the critical verbs were build, negotiate, venture, and care. In the end, Robert built an accounting firm, William negotiated deals in the gemstone trade, Paul ventured forth in the "moving" industry of trucking, and Fred cared for other people. Although nothing in the case studies concentrated on counseling interventions, the cases do contain vignettes that support the discourse about story-crafting questions in career construction counseling.

Active Mastery

In articulating a career theme, CCT uses the narrative paradigm to articulate how an individual has moved from passive suffering to active mastery. The through-lines for the individuals in the four life portraits herein personify the hypothesis that the self-authoring of an identity involves turning preoccupation into occupation. Each of the four participants organized his life around a problem that preoccupied him beginning in the family-of-origin and solutions that eventually occupied him in the world-of-work. As the psychoanalyst William Stekel (1920) noted, "To be psychically healthy means to overcome one's past" (p. 16). In making and implementing career choices, each participant strove to actively master what he had previously passively suffered. The problem that they wished to resolve above all others became their chief preoccupation and the base of the arc in their career themes. Repeating the thematic material with increasing mastery fueled career construction and vocational development, as can easily be recognized in each life portrait.

Robert moved from chaos to order. His training and work in accounting was a way for him to organize his world. He was able to move from chaos during adolescence and young adulthood through conscientiousness and competiveness. His preference for planning and conventional values helped him to avoid chaos as well as served those who employed his accounting services. Robert's path to mastery fits well with what McAdams (2008) named the redemptive pattern. McAdams (2008) explained that many highly productive and caring individuals, such as Robert, portray their lives as a story of redemption. McAdam's (2008) precis of a redemptive story fully comprehends Robert's life. In the beginning Robert was blessed with a caring family who instilled in him core values to guide his life. However, during adolescence several bad things happened, including chaos in his home and disappointment at school. Fortunately, Robert was able to achieve good outcomes by using conscientiousness to turn this chaos into goals and plans. His redemption from negative experiences came in the form of social mobility and actualization of inner goodness. As his adult life unfolded, he continued to grow and progress.

William moved from obligation to negotiation. William's foreclosed vocational identity drew the lines between which he constructed his conferred career. He adapted to the obligation imposed by his parents by becoming interested in activities that allowed them to actively deal with what he had passively experienced in his family. He went from being pulled to pulling the strings. His interest in negotiating enabled him to turn tension into intention and private preoccupation into public occupation. Yes, he accepted his parents' occupational choice, yet he shaped it to suit himself. As a mill owner, William emphasized his role as negotiator with major customers. On the side, he negotiated real estate deals. He structured his occupational activities to maximize his autonomy, working alone as much as he could. In the process, he transformed what he passively experienced in his family into a strength. He could not negotiate with parents, so he learned to be a negotiator with the customers. In his avocation or second occupation, we see even more clearly the manifestation of William's self-concept as a negotiator. In his highly successful gemstone business he enjoyed selling, yet as he himself stated, *Actually, I enjoy buying and negotiating; I don't enjoy the physical act of selling and buying. It's the negotiating.*

Paul went from staying put to peripatetic. Rather than getting stuck in any job, he moved on. Paul mastered the suffering and immobilization he experienced with the loss of permanence and place when his mother died by relishing change and adventure. He learned to move from being lonely to comfort in being alone. He never moved from outsider to insider, rather he remained outside as an adventurer. He dealt with impermanence and unpredictability by becoming resilient and flexible. As he said, he had to run away from things (suffering) to do what he wanted (mastery).

Fred moved from needing care to affording care and from getting little to giving much. He made his workplace almost a home away from home where every day he could give to others the nurturance for which, as a neglected child, he had yearned. Clearly, Fred's occupation implemented his self-concept, yet it did even more for him. Fred's job enabled him to become more whole, more complete, as he actively mastered what he had passively suffered as a child by proffering to his infirmed patients the nurturance that as a child he had wanted. Fred's occupational role in a defining context enabled him to repeat and improve on his role in the family drama of his childhood and youth. The occupational role was more fulfilling, not in being radically different, but in turning passivity into activity by doing for others what had not been done for him. In this way his tension became intention, explaining in part why each day he reported early to work to become a champion for hapless individuals. In restaging his childhood drama, Fred repeated and repaired, with slightly different content and new characters, the earlier drama he had lived in his family. In this sense, work made up for what he had missed in childhood by allowing him to enact a more fulfilling dramatic role. He found himself in those for whom he cares, and in nurturing them he became the caring figure he could never find for himself.

Concluding Comments

The life portraits and case study materials herein were viewed from the perspective of CCT. The density of details provided much more than could be discussed, both from the perspective of CCT and other career theories. I encourage readers who prefer a different lens on careers to analyze the portraits from the perspective of disparate theorems and concepts. Considering the life portraits from multiple perspectives can lead to better understanding of various career theories and their inter-relationships. Furthermore, academics may demonstrate for graduate students a variety of career theories by using the life portraits as teaching cases, either through didactic lecturing or discovery learning. And finally, researchers may find it intriguing to examine further the CCT propositions with quantitative studies that investigate, for example, relationships among attachment, adaptability, and identity. I end by offering my deep gratitude to the four participants in this study who bravely shared their life stories to advance our understanding of careers and how people construct them.

REFERENCES

Adler, A. (1956). *The individual psychology of Alfred Adler*. New York: Basic Books.

Ainsworth, M. D. S., & Bowlby, J. (1991). An ethological approach to personality development. *American Psychologist, 46*, 331-341.

Allinson, F. G. (1921). *Menander: The principal fragments*. New York: G. P. Putnam Sons.

Allport, G. W. (1937). The functional autonomy of motives. *American Journal of Psychology, 50*, 141-156.

Allport, G. W. (1961). *Pattern and growth in personality*. New York: Holt, Rinehart, & Winston.

American Psychiatric Association (1994). *Diagnostic and statistical manual of mental disorders* (4th ed.). Washington, DC: APA.

Angyal, A. (1965). *Neurosis and treatment: A holistic theory*. New York: John Wiley & Sons.

Archer, M. S. (2003). *Structure, agency and internal conversation*. Cambridge: Cambridge University Press.

Archer, M. S. (2012). *The reflexive imperative in late modernity*. Cambridge: Cambridge University Press.

Arseth, A. K., Kroger, J., Martinussen, & Marcia, J. E. (2009). Meta-analytic studies of identity status and the relational issues of attachment and intimacy. *Identity: An International Journal of Theory and Research, 9*, 1-32.

Bakan, D. (1966). *The duality of human existence: Isolation and communion in Western man*. Boston: Beacon Press.

Bartholomew, K. (1990). Avoidance of intimacy: An attachment perspective. *Journal of Social and Personal Relationships, 7*, 147-178.

Bartlett, F. C. (1932). *Remembering*. Cambridge: Cambridge University Press,

Beall, L., & Bordin, E. S. (1964). The development and personality of engineers. *Personality and Guidance Journal*, 48, 23-32.

Bell, A. P. (1969). Role modeling of fathers in adolescence and young adulthood. *Journal of Counseling Psychology 16*, 30–35.

Bell, A. P. (1970). Role models in young adulthood: Their relationship to occupational behaviors. *Vocational Guidance Quarterly, 18,* 280-284.

Bell, A. P., et al. (1978). *Sexual preference: Its development in men and women.* Bloomington, IN: Indiana University Press.

Bennet, G. K. (1940). *Test of Mechanical Comprehension-Form AA.* New York: The Psychological Corporation.

Bennett, G. K., Seashore, H. G., & Wesman, A.G. (1966). *Differential Aptitude Test fourth edition manual.* New York: Psychological Association.

Berdie, R. F. (1943). Factors associated with vocational interests. *Journal of Educational Psychology, 34,* 257-277.

Berzonsky, M. B. (1985). Diffusion within Marcia's identity status paradigm: Does it foreshadow academic problems. *Journal of Youth and Adolescence, 14,* 527-538.

Berzonsky, M. B. (1989). Identity style: Conceptualization and measurement. *Journal of Adolescent Research, 4,* 267-281.

Berzonsky, M. D. (2004). Identity style, parental authority, and identity commitment. *Journal of Youth and Adolescence, 33,* 213–220.

Berzonsky, M. D., & Ferrari, J. R. (2009): A diffuse-avoidant identity processing style: Strategic avoidance or self-confusion? *Identity: An International Journal of Theory and Research, 9,* 145-158.

Bion, W. R. (1962). *Learning from experience.* London: Heinemann.

Blatt, S. J., & Levy, K. N. (2003). Attachment theory, psychoanalysis, personality development, and psychopathology. *Psychoanalytic Inquiry, 23,* 102–150.

Bordin, E. S. (1990). Psychodynamic model of career choice and satisfaction. In D. Brown & L. Brooks (Eds.), *Career choice and development: Applying contemporary theories to practice* (pp.102-144). San Francisco: Jossey-Bass.

Bordin, E. S., Nachmann, B., & Segal, S. J. (1963). An articulated framework for vocational development. *Journal of Counseling Psychology, 10,* 107-116.

Bowlby, J. (1969). *Attachment and loss: Vol. 1. Attachment.* New York: Basic Books.

Bowlby, J. (1973). *Attachment and loss, Vol. 2: Separation.* New York: Basic Books.

Bowlby, J. (1982). Attachment and loss: Retrospect and prospect. *American Journal of Orthopsychiatry, 52,* 664-678.

Bowlby, J. (1988). *A secure base.* New York: Basic Books.

Bradley, L., Prokop, C. K., Margolis, R., & Gentry, W. D. (1978). Multivariate analysis of the MMPI profiles of low back pain patients. *Journal of Behavioral Medicine, 1,* 253.

Bradley, R. W., & Mims, G. A. (1992). Using family systems and birth order dynamics as the basis for a college career decision-making course. *Journal of Counseling & Development, 70,* 445-448.

Brehm, J. W. (1966). *A theory of psychological reactance.* New York: Academic Press.

Brisbin, L. A., & Savickas, M. L. (1994). Career indecision scales do not measure foreclosure. *Journal of Career Assessment, 2,* 352-363.

Brockner, J., & Higgins, E. T. (2001). Regulatory focus theory: Implications for the study of emotions at work. *Organizational Behavior and Human Decision Processes, 86,* 35–66.

Brown, M. T., Lum, J. L., & Voyle, K. (1997). Roe revisited: A call for the reappraisal of the theory of personality development and career choice. *Journal of Vocational Behavior, 51,* 283-294.

Butcher, J. N., Graham, J. R., Tellegen, A., & Kaemmer, B. (1989). *Manual for the restandardized Minnesota Multiphasic Personality Inventory: MMPI-2.* Minneapolis: University of Minnesota Press.

Campbell, D. P., Hyne, S.A., & Nilsen, D. L. (1992). *Manual for the Campbell Interest and Skill Inventory.* Minneapolis, MN: National Computer Systems.

Carver, C. S., & Scheier, M. F. (1998). *On the self-regulation of behavior.* New York: Cambridge University Press.

Chusid, H., & Cochran, L. (1988). Meaning of career change from the perspective of family roles and dramas. *Journal of Counseling Psychology, 36,* 34-41.

Claudy, J. G. (1984). The only child as a young adult: Results from Project Talent. In T. Falbo (Ed.) *The single child family* (pp. 211-254). New York: Guilford Press.

Crites, J. O. (1969). *Vocational psychology*. New York: McGraw-Hill.

Crites, J. O. (1971). *The maturity of vocational attitudes in adolescence*. Washington, DC: American Personnel and Guidance Association.

Crites, J. O. (1978). *Career Maturity Inventory theory and research handbook*. Monterey, CA: CTB/McGraw-Hill.

Csikszentmihalyi, M., & Beattie, O. V. (1979). Life themes: A theoretical and empirical exploration of their origin and effects. *Journal of Humanistic Psychology, 19*, 45-63.

Domecka, M., & Mrozowicki, A. (2013). Linking structural and agential powers: A realist approach to biographies, careers and reflexivity. In J. D. Turk & A. Mrozowicki (Eds.) *Realist Biography and European Policy* (pp. 191-214). Leuven, Belgium: Leuven University Press.

Domino, G., & Domino, M. (2006). *Psychological testing: An introduction* (2nd ed.). Cambridge: Cambridge University Press.

Dysinger, W. S. (1950). Maturation and vocational guidance. *Occupations, 29*, 198-201.

Eliot, T. S. (1943). *The Four Quartets: No. 2 East Coker*. New York: Harcourt, Brace and Co.

Erikson, E. H. (1963). *Childhood and society* (2nd ed). New York: Norton.

Erikson, E. H. (1968). *Identity: youth and crisis*. New York: Norton.

Eryigit, S., & Kerpelman, J. L. (2011). Cross-cultural investigation of the link between identity processing styles and the actual work of identity in the career domain. *Child & Youth Care Forum, 40*, 43–64.

Fadiman, C., & Bernard, A. (2000). *Barlett's book of anecdotes*. New York: Little, Brown and Company.

Fandakova, Y., Selmeczy, D., Leckey, S., Grimm, K. J., Wendelken, C., Bunge, S. A. & Ghetti, S. (2017). Changes in ventromedial prefrontal and insular cortex support the development of metamemory from childhood into adolescence. *Proceedings of the National Academy of Science, 114*, 7582-7587.

Florack, A., Keller, J., & Palcu, J. (2013). Regulatory focus in economic contexts. *Journal of Economic Psychology, 38*, 127-137.

Flugel, J. C. (1929). *The psychoanalytic study of the family*. London: Hogarth Press.

Ford, D. H. (1987). *Humans as self-constructing living systems: A developmental perspective on behavior and personality.* Hillsdale, NJ: Lawrence Erlbaum Associates.

Ford, D. H., & Lerner, R. M. (1992). *Developmental systems theory: An integrative approach.* Newbury Park, CA: Sage Publications.

Ford, M. E. (1992). *Motivating humans: Goals, emotions, and personal agency beliefs.* Newbury Park, CA: Sage Publications.

Ford, M. E., & Ford, D. H. (Eds.). (1987). *Humans as self-constructing living systems: Putting the framework to work.* Hillsdale, NJ: Lawrence Erlbaum Associates.

Fosha, D. (2003). Dyadic regulation and experiential work with emotion and relatedness in trauma and disordered attachment. In M. F. Solomon & D. J. Siegel (Eds.). *Healing trauma: Attachment, trauma, the brain and the mind* (221-281). New York: Norton.

Fraley, R. C., Davis, K. E., Shaver, P. R. (1998). Dismissing-avoidance and the defensive organization of emotions, cognition, and behavior. In J. A. Simpson & W. S. Rholes (Eds.) *Attachment theory and close relationships* (pp.249-279). New York: Guildford Press.

Fraser, J. S., & Solovey, A. D. (2007). *Second-order change in psychotherapy.* Washington, DC: American Psychological Association Press.

Freud S. (1920). Beyond the pleasure principle. In J. Strachey (Translator & Editor) *Complete Psychological Works* (Standard Edition Vol. 3). London, Hogarth Press, 1954.

Freud, S. (1930). Civilization and its discontents. In J. Strachey (Translator & Editor) *Complete Psychological Works* (Standard Edition Vol. 21). London, Hogarth Press, 1961.

Friedman, M., & Rosenman, R. (1974). *Type A behavior and your heart.* New York: Knopf.

Ginzberg, E., Ginsburg, S. W., Axelrad, S., & Herma, J. L. (1951). *Occupational choice: An approach to a general theory.* New York: Columbia University Press.

Glass, D. (1977). *Behavior patterns, stress, and coronary disease.* Hillsdale, NJ: Erlbaum.

Glasser, W. (1965) *Reality therapy.* New York: Harper & Row.

Gottfredson, G. D., & Holland, J. L. (1996). *Dictionary of Holland occupational codes* (3rd ed.). Odessa, FL: Psychological Assessment Resources.

Gough, H. G. (1987). *CPI administrator's guide*. Palo Alto, CA: Consulting Psychologists Press.

Gough, H. G. (1990). The *California Psychological Inventory*. In C. E. Watkins & V. L. Campbell (Eds.), *Testing in counseling practice* (pp.37-72). Mahwah, NY: Lawrence Erlbaum Associates.

Grant, H., & Higgins, E.T. (2013). To you play to win – or to not lose? *Harvard Business Review, 91*(3).

Griffith, J., & Powers, R. L. (1984). *An Adlerian lexicon*. Chicago: Americas Institute of Adlerian Studies.

Grotevant, H. D. (1992). Assigned and chosen identity components: A process perspective on their integration. In G. R. Adams, R. Montemayor, & T. Gulotta (Eds.), *Advances in adolescent development* (Vol. 4, pp. 73-90). Newbury Park, CA: Sage.

Grygier, T. G., & Grygier, P. (1976). *Dynamic Personality Inventory*. Montreal, Quebec, Canada: Institute of Psychological Research.

Haan, N. (1977). *Coping and defending: Processes of self-environment organization*. San Diego, CA: Academic Press.

Hardy, G. E., & Barham, M. (1994). The relationship between interpersonal attachment styles and work difficulties. *Human Relations, 47*, 263-281.

Harling-Stalker, L. L. (2009). A tale of two narratives: Ontological and epistemological narratives. *Narrative Inquiry, 19*, 219-232.

Harren V. A. (1979). A model of career decision making for college students. *Journal of Vocational Behavior, 14*, 119-133.

Hartman, B. W., Fuqua, D. R., & Hartman, P. T. (1983). The predictive potential of the *Career Decision Scale* in identifying chronic career indecision. *Vocational Guidance Quarterly, 32*, 103-108.

Hazan, C., & Shaver, P. (1990). Love and work: An attachment-theoretical perspective. *Journal of Personality and Social Psychology, 59*, 270-280.

Higgins, E. T. (1997). Beyond pleasure and pain. *American Psychologist, 52*, 1280-1300.

Higgins, E. T. (1998). Development of regulatory focus: Promotion and prevention as ways of living. In J. Heckhausen and C. S. Sweck (Eds.) *Motivation and self-regulation across the life-span* (pp. 78-113). Cambridge: Cambridge University Press.

Higgins, E. T., Roney, C., Crowe, E., & Hymes, C. (1994). Ideal versus ought predilections for approach and avoidance: Distinct self-regulatory systems. *Journal of Personality and Social Psychology, 66,* 276-286.

Hillel. (1897). *Pirke avot* (Sayings of the Jewish fathers). Translated by Charles Taylor. Cambridge: Cambridge University Press.

Hogan, R. (1983). A socioanalytic theory of personality. In M. M. Page (Ed.), *1982 Nebraska symposium on motivation* (pp. 55–89). Lincoln: University of Nebraska Press.

Holland, J. L. (1966). *The psychology of vocational choice.* Waltham, MA: Blaisdell.

Holland, J. L. (1985). *Making vocational choices: A theory of vocational personalities and work environments.* (2nd ed). Englewood Cliffs, NJ: Prentice-Hall.

Holland, J. L. (1994). *The occupations finder-Form R (4th ed.).* Odessa, FL: Psychological Assessment Resources.

Holland, J. L. (1997). *Making vocational choices: A theory of vocational personalities and work environments* (3rd ed). Odessa, FL: Psychological Assessment Resources.

Hollway, W., & Jefferson, T. (2000). *Doing qualitative research differently.* London, UK: Sage.

Ibarra, H., & Barbulescu, R. (2010). Identity as narrative: Prevalence, effectiveness, and consequences of narrative identity work in macro work role transitions. *Academy of Management Review, 35,* 135-154.

James, W. (1892). *Psychology.* New York: Henry Holt and Company.

Johnson, R.R., & Chang, C-H. (2010). Commitment and motivation at work: The relevance of employee identity and regulatory focus. *Academy of Management Review, 35,* 226-245.

Josselson, R. (1996). *Revising herself: The story of women's identity from college to midlife.* New York: Oxford University Press.

Josselson, R. (2017). *Paths to fulfillment: Women's search for meaning and identity.* Oxford, United Kingdom: Oxford University Press.

Kaplan, H. I., & Sadock, B. J. (1991). *Synopsis of psychiatry* (6th ed.). Baltimore: Williams & Wilkins.

Kaplan, H. I., Sadock, B. J., & Grebb, J. A. (1994). *Synopsis of psychiatry* (7th ed.). Baltimore: Williams & Wilkins.

Kegan, R. (1994). *In over our heads: The mental demands of modern life.* Cambridge, MA: Harvard University Press.

Kelly, G. A. (1955). *The psychology of personal constructs.* New York: Norton.

Kernberg, O. F. (1978). The diagnosis of borderline conditions in adolescence. *Adolescent Psychiatry, 6,* 298-319.

Kipling, R. (1889). *The ballad of the East and West.* New York: Alex Grosset & Company.

Klonen, E. C., & Bera, S. (1998). Behavioral and experiential patterns of avoidantly and securely attached women across adulthood: A 31-year longitudinal perspective. *Journal of Personality and Social Psychology, 74,* 211-223.

Kroger, J. (1995). The differentiation of "firm" and "developmental" foreclosure identity statuses: A longitudinal study. *Journal of Research on Adolescence, 10,* 317—337.

Kroger, J., & Marcia, J. E. (2011). The identity statues: Origins, meanings and interpretations. In S. Schwartz, K. Luyckx & V. Vignoles (Eds.), *Handbook of Identity Theory and Research* (pp. 31-53). Springer Science+Business Media.

Krout, M. H., & Krout-Tabin, J. (1951). *Personal Preference Scales.* Chicago, IL: Chicago Psychological Institute.

Kuder, F. G. (1956). *Kuder Preference Record, Vocational Form CH - Examiner's manual* (6th ed.). Chicago IL: Science Research Associates.

Kurman, J., & Hui, C. (2011). Promotion, prevention or both: Regulatory focus and culture revisited. *Online Readings in Psychology and Culture, 5*(3).

Kurman, J., Hui, C. M., & Dan, O. (2012). Changing the world through changing the self: Understanding a new control strategy through self-reported coping plans in two cultures. *Journal of Cross-Cultural Psychology, 43*, 15-22.

Lamiell, J. T. (2003). *Beyond individual and group differences: Human individuality, scientific psychology and William Stern's critical personalism.* Thousand Oaks, CA: Sage.

Lawrence-Lightfoot, S. (2005). Reflections on portraiture: A dialogue between art and science. *Qualitative Inquiry. 11*, 3-15.

Leary, M. R., & Tangney, J. P. (2003). The self as an organizing construct in the behavioral and social sciences. In M. Leary & J. Tangeney (Eds). *Handbook of self and identity* (pp. 3-14). New York: The Guilford Press.

Levin, I., & Levin, I. (1992). *Working on the play and the role: The Stanislavsky method for analyzing the characters in a drama.* Chicago: Ivan R. Dee.

Locke, E. A. (2007). The case for inductive theory building. *Journal of Management, 33*, 867-890.

Lofquist, L. H., & Dawis, R. V. (1991). *Essentials of person-environment correspondence counseling.* Minneapolis: University of Minnesota Press.

Lopez, F. G. (1995). Contemporary attachment theory: An introduction with implications for counseling psychology. *The Counseling Psychologist, 23*, 395-415.

Luszczynska, A., Diehl, M., Gutiérrez-Doña, B., Kuusinen, P., & Schwarzer, R. (2004). Measuring one component of dispositional self-regulation: Attention control in goal pursuit. *Personality and Individual Differences, 37*, 555-566.

MacGregor, A., & Cochran, L. (1988). Work as enactment of family drama. *Career Development Quarterly, 37*, 138-148.

Main, M. (1991). Metacognitive knowledge, metacognitive monitoring, and singular (coherent) vs. multiple (incoherent) model of attachment: Findings and directions for future research. In C. M. Parkes, J. Stevenson-Hinde, & P. Marris (Eds.). *Attachment across the life cycle* (pp. 127-159). New York: Routledge.

Marcia, J. E. (1980). Identity in adolescence. In J. Adelson (Ed.) *Handbook of adolescent psychology* (pp. 159-187). New York: Wiley.

Marcia, J. E. (1989). Identity diffusion differentiated. In M. A. Luszez & T. Nettelbeck, (Eds.). *Psychological development: Perspectives across the life-span* (pp. 289–294). Amsterdam; North-Holland: Elsevier Science.

Marcia, J. E. (2002). Identity and psychosocial development in adulthood. *Identity: An International Journal of Theory and Research, 2*, 7–28.

Marquard, O. (2001). Zukunft braucht herkunft: Philosophische betrachtungen über modernität und menschlichkeit [The future needs origins: Philosophical considerations about modernity and humanity]. In *Philosophie des Stattdessen [Philosophy of the Instead]*. Stuttgart, Germany: Reclam Philipp Jun.

Martin, J. (2013). Life positioning: An analytic framework for the study of lives and life narratives. *Journal of Theoretical and Philosophical Psychology, 33*, 1-17.

Matthews, K. A., & Siegel, J. M. (1982). The Type A behavior pattern in children and adolescents: Assessment, development, and associated coronary-risk. In A. R. Baum & J. E. Singer (Eds.), *Handbook of health and medical psychology* (Vol. 2, pp. 99-116). Hillsdale, NJ: Erlbaum.

Mayseless, O., Daniels, R., & Sharabany, R. (1996). Adults' attachment patterns: Coping with separation. *Journal of Youth and Adolescence, 25*, 667-690.

McAdams, D. P. (1995). What do we know when we know a person? *Journal of Personality, 63*, 365-396.

McAdams, D. P. (1999). Personal narratives and the life story. In L. Pervin & O. John (Eds.) *Handbook of personality and research* (2nd ed.; pp. 478-500). New York: Guilford Press.

McAdams, D. P. (2008). American identity: The redemptive self. *The General Psychologist, 43*, 20-27.

McAdams, D. P. (2013). The psychological self as actor, agent, and author. *Perspectives on Psychological Science, 8*, 272-295.

Menkel-Meadow, C. (2000). Telling stories in school: Using case studies and stories to teach legal ethics. *Fordham Law Review, 69*, 787-816.

Mikulincer, M., & Shaver, P. (2013). Attachment orientations and meaning in life. In J. A. Hicks & C. Routledge (Eds.) *The experience of meaning in life: Classical perspectives, emerging themes, and controversies* (pp. 287-304). New York: Springer Science+Business Media Dordrecht.

Miller, D. C., & Form, W. H. (1951) *Industrial sociology*. New York: Harper & Bros.

Minuchin, S. Montalvo, B., Guerney, B. G. Jr., Rosman, B. L., & Schumer, F. (1967). *Families of the slums: An exploration of their structure and treatment*. New York: Basic Books.

Molden, D. C., Lee, A. Y., & Higgins, E. T. (2007). Motivations for promotion and prevention. In J. Shah & W. Gardner (Eds.). *Handbook of Motivation Science*. New York: Guilford Press.

Morgan, C. D, & Murray, H. A. (1943). *Thematic Apperception Test*. Cambridge, MA: Harvard University Press.

Mosak, H. H. (1977). *On purpose*. Chicago: Alfred Adler Institute.

Mrozowicki, A. (2010). The agency of the weak: Ethos, reflexivity and life strategies of Polish workers after the end of State Socialism. In M. S. Archer (Ed.) *Conversations about reflexivity*. London: Routledge, pp. 167–86.

Murray, H. A. (1938). *Explorations in personality*. New York: Oxford University Press.

Murray, H. A. (1943). *Manual for the Thematic Apperception Test*. Cambridge, MA: Harvard   University Press.

Nauta, M. M., & Kahn, J. H. (2007). Identity status, consistency and differentiation of interests, and career decision self-efficacy. *Journal of Career Assessment, 15*, 55–65.

Nelson, M.J., & Denny, E, C., & Brown, J. I. (1960). *Nelson-Denny Reading Test: Forms A and B*. Boston: Houghton-Mifflin.

Overton, W. F., & Muller, U. (2012). Meta-theories, theories, and concepts in the study of development. In I. B. Weiner (Series Ed.) & R. M. Lerner, M. A. Eastbrooks, & J. Mistry (Vol. Eds.), *Handbook of psychology: Vol. 6. Developmental psychology* (pp. 19-58). New York: Wiley.

Otis, A. S., & Lennon, R. T. (1967). *Otis-Lennon Mental Ability Test technical handbook*. New York: Harcourt, Brace, & World.

Oyserman, D., & Markus, H. R. (1990). Possible selves and delinquency.

Journal of Personality and Social Psychology, 59, 112-125.

Parsons, R. (1909/1967). *Choosing a vocation.* New York: Agathon Press.

Peeler, G. H. (1996). *Selling in the quality era.* Cambridge, MA: Blackwell Publishers.

Piper, W. (1930). *The little engine that could.* New York: Platt & Munk.

Roe, A. (1956). *The psychology of occupations.* New York: Wiley.

Rotter, J. B., & Rafferty, J. E. (1950). *Manual* for the *Rotter Incomplete Sentences Blank.* New York: Psychological Corporation.

Ryan, R. M., & Deci, E. I. (2000). Intrinsic and extrinsic motivations: Classic definitions and new direction. *Contemporary Educational Psychology, 25,* 54-57.

Savickas, M. L. (1995). Examining the personal meaning of inventoried interests during career counseling. *Journal of Career Assessment, 3,* 188-201.

Savickas, M. L. (1995). Constructivist counseling for career indecision. *Career Development Quarterly, 43,* 363-373.

Savickas, M. L. (2002). Career construction: A developmental theory of vocational behavior. In D. Brown (Ed.) *Career choice and development* (4th ed; pp. 149-205). San Francisco: Jossey-Bass.

Savickas, M. L. (2005). The theory and practice of career construction. In R. W. Lent & S. D. Brown (Eds.). *Career development and counseling: Putting theory and research to work* (pp. 42-70). Hoboken, New Jersey: John Wiley & Sons.

Savickas, M. L. (2012). Life design: A paradigm for career intervention in the 21st century. *Journal of Counseling and Development, 90,* 13-19.

Savickas, M. L. (2013). Career construction theory and practice. In R. W. Lent & S. D. Brown (Eds.). *Career development and counseling: Putting theory and research to work* (2nd ed., pp. 147-183). Hoboken, New Jersey: John Wiley & Sons.

Savickas, M. L. (2014). Work values: A career construction elaboration. In. M. Pope, L. Flores, & P. Rottinghaus (Eds.).*Values in vocational psychology* (pp. 3-19). Charlotte, NC: Information Age Publishing.

Savickas, M. L. (2015). *Life-design counseling manual*. www.Vocopher.com [Free].

Savickas, M. L. (2019). *Career counseling* (2nd ed.). Washington, DC: American Psychological Association Press.

Savickas, M.L., & Porfeli, E. J. (2012). *Career Adapt-Abilities Scale*: Construction, reliability, and measurement equivalence across 13 countries. *Journal of Vocational Behavior, 80*, 661-673.

Shafer, L. F. (1936). *The psychology of adjustment: An objective approach to mental hygiene*. Boston: Houghton-Mifflin.

Shapiro, D. (1965). *Neurotic styles*. New York: Basic Books.

Shaver, P. R. & Mikulincer, M. (2002), Dialogue on adult attachment: Diversity and integration. *Attachment & Human Development, 4*, 243-257.

Scheslinger, V. J. (1963). *Anal personality traits and occupational choice: A study of accountants, chemical engineers, and educational psychologists*. Unpublished doctoral dissertation. University of Michigan.

Segal, S. J., & Szabo, R. (1964). Identification in two vocations: Accountants and creative writers. *Personnel and Guidance Journal, 43*. 252-255.

Sperry, L. Hartshorne, T. S. & Watts, R. E. (2010). Ethical considerations and options in publishing clinical case material. *Journal of Individual Psychology, 66*, 135-143.

Stanislavsky, C. (1924). *My life in art*. New York: Little, Brown and Company.

Stake, Robert E. (1994). Case studies. In Norman K. Denzin (Ed.) *Handbook of qualitative research* (pp. 236-247). Thousand Oaks, CA: Sage.

Stedmon, J., & Dallos, R. (2009). *Reflective practice in psychotherapy and counselling*. London, UK: McGraw-Hill Education.

Stekel, W. (1920). A contribution to the psychology of exhibitionism. *Psyche and Eros: An International Bimonthly Journal of Psychoanalysis, 1*, 1-17.

Stern, W. (1911). *Methodological foundations of differential psychology*. Leipzig, Germany: Verlag von Johann Ambrosius Barth.

Strong, E. K. Jr., Campbell, D. P., Berdie, R. F., & Clark, K. E. (1966). *Strong Vocational Interest Blank for Men* (Form T399). Stanford, CA: Stanford University Press.

Strutton, D., Pelton, L. E., & Lumpkin, J. R. (1995). Personality characteristics and salespeople's choice of coping strategies. *Journal of the Academy of Marketing Science, 23*, 132-140.

Super, D. E. (1940). *Avocational interest patterns: A study in the psychology of avocations.* Palo Alto, CA: Stanford University Press.

Super, D. E. (1954). Career patterns as a basis for vocational counseling. *Journal of Counseling Psychology, 1*, 12-20.

Super, D. E. (1957). *The psychology of careers.* New York: Harper.

Super, D. E. (1963). Self-concepts in vocational development. In D. Super, R. Starishevsky, Matlin, & J. Jordaan. *Career development: Self-concept theory* (pp. 17-32). New York: College Entrance Examination Board.

Super, D. E. (1970). *Work Values Inventory.* Boston, MA: Houghton-Mifflin.

Super, D. E. (1990). A life-span, life-space to career development. In D. Brown, L. Brooks, & Associates, *Career choice and development* (2nd ed.; pp.197-261). San Francisco: Jossey-Bass.

Super, D. E., & Bohn, M. J. (1970). *Occupational psychology.* Wadsworth Publishing Company.

Super, D. E., Kowalski, R. S., & Gotkin, E. H. (1967). *Floundering and trial after high school: Career pattern study monograph IV.* New York: Teachers College.

Super, D. E., & Overstreet, P. L. (1960). *The vocational maturity of ninth grade boys.* New York: Teachers College Press.

Super, D. E., Savickas, M. L., & Super, C. M. (1996). The life-span, life-space approach to careers. In D. Brown & L. Brooks (Eds.) *Career choice and development* (3rd ed, pp.121-178). San Francisco: Jossey-Bass.

Taylor, C. (1989). *Sources of the self: The making of the modern identity.* Cambridge, MA: Harvard University Press.

Tiedeman, D. V., & Field, F. L. (1961). Guidance: The science of purposeful action applied through education. *Harvard Educational Review, 32*, 483-501.

Tiedeman, D. V., & O'Hara, R. P. (1963). *Career development: Choice and adjustment*. New York: College Entrance Examination Board.

Toman, W. (1970). Birth order rules all. *Psychology Today*, December, pp. 45-49, 68-69.

Trapnell, P. D., & Paulhus. D. L. (2011). Agentic and communal values: Their scope and measurement. *Journal of Personality Assessment, 94*, 39-52.

Twain, M. (1884). *The adventures of Tom Sawyer*. Hartford, CT: The American Publishing Company.

Tyler, L. E. (1961). *The work of the counselor* (2nd ed.). New York: Appleton-Century-Crofts.

Underwood, B. J. (1957). *Psychological research*. New York: Appleton-Century-Crofts.

Van Matre, G., & Cooper, S. (1984). Concurrent evaluation of career indecision and indecisiveness. *Personnel and Guidance Journal*, 637-639.

Vondracek, F. W., Ford, D. H., & Porfeli, E. J. (2014). *A living systems theory of vocational behavior and development*. Amsterdam: Sense Publishers.

Vondracek, F.W., & Ford, D. H. (2019a). The living systems theory of vocational behaviour and development. In N. Arthur, R. Neault, & M. McMahon (Eds.), *Career theory and models at work: Ideas for practice* (pp. 433-441). Canadian Education and Research Institute for Counselling (CERIC).

Vondracek, F. W., & Ford, D. H. (2019b). Living systems theory of vocational behavior and development. In N. Arthur & M. McMahon (Eds.), *Contemporary theories of career development: International perspectives* (pp. 121-134). New York: Routledge.

Vondracek, F. W., Porfeli, E. J., & Ford, D. H. (2019). Living systems theory: Using a person-in-context behavior episode unit of analysis in career guidance research and practice. In J.A. Athanasou & H. Perera (Eds.), *International handbook of career guidance* (2nd). New York: Springer Publishing.

Vygotsky, L. S. (1978). *Mind in society: The development of higher psychological processes*. Cambridge, MA: Harvard University Press.

White, J. C. (1963). Cleanliness and successful bank clerical personnel - A brief. *Journal of Counseling Psychology*, 10, 192.

Welty, E. (1998). *One writer's beginnings*. Cambridge, MA: Harvard University Press.

Williams, C., & Savickas, M. L. (1990). Developmental tasks of career maintenance. *Journal of Vocational Behavior, 36*, 166-175.

Winnicott, D. w. (1986). *Holding and interpretation: Fragments of an analysis*. London: Hogarth Press.

Wordsworth, W. (1807). My heart leaps up. *Poems in Two Volumes*. London: Longman, Hurst, Rees, and Orms.

Yagoda, B. (1970). *Will Rogers: A biography*. Norman, OK: University of Oklahoma Press.

Appendix A
Career Construction Theory Premises and Propositions

The Self-Organizing Social Actor

Premise A: *Individuals co-construct a psychological self as a social actor within their families by organizing an attachment schema and dispositional strategy.*

Propositions

1. The opportunities to perform work roles that individuals perceive are co-constructed by social forces in the family and conditioned by societal institutions in the community as well as the momentum propelled by earlier choices and actions.
2. Beginning in infancy, individuals learn to perform as social actors in the family drama by introjecting parental influences and coordinating their emotions and intentions with their parents, who serve as *guiding lines* for moving in the social world.
3. By rehearsing their generally consistent attachment schema, individuals establish mental representations that organize a prime way of thinking about the social world as well as a script for interpersonal interaction in social roles and need fulfillment in work roles.
4. Throughout life, individuals use their attachment schema as heuristic templates to guide interpersonal relationships, direct attention, interpret events, and generate expectations.
5. Following from their attachment schema, individuals form dispositional strategies for performing social roles, including the work role.
6. Together, attachment schemas and dispositional strategies condition how individuals seek to meet their basic emotional, social, and career needs.

7. As part of self-construction in early childhood, individuals select models who display characteristics and behaviors that would be useful in solving their own problems in growing up and for fulfilling their psychological needs
8. Identification as a core process of self-construction occurs as an individual imitates behaviors and incorporates personal characteristics of role models as a rather permanent part of the self.
9. Choice of role models is the first career choice because imitating a model in fantasy and play, in due course, mobilizes interests and activities that through repetition and rehearsal develop vocational skills and preferences.
10. Each individual leaves early childhood with an attachment schema for viewing interpersonal relationships, dispositional strategies for performing social roles, and role models that both cause and address unresolved issues and preoccupations.

The Self-Regulating Motivated Agent

Premise B: Late in childhood, individuals begin to function more often as motivated agents who direct their own lives toward congruent positions in society through self-regulation, that is, the processes by which individuals adapt their perceptions, feelings, and actions in the pursuit of a goal.

Propositions

11. The self-regulating agent's pursuit of goals around the neighborhood, in school, and at work can be understood as efforts by the social actor to move purposefully from a present position to envisioned future positions.
12. The key motivational constructs in assessing the suitability of possible positions are *needs* or why, *values* or what, and *interests* or how to realize values that satisfy needs.
13. With regard to forming and pursuing goals, the self as agent

adopts a persistent, self-regulation schema that focuses motivation and shapes adaptation strategies.
14. Children learn to self-regulate their actions and feelings based on reward contingencies in the social regulation provided by parents, especially in response to a child's needs for nurturance and security.
15. Self-regulation schema, whether focused on promotion or prevention, direct how people adapt to the vocational developmental tasks, occupational transitions, and work troubles involved in choosing and pursuing their career goals.
16. Vocational maturity indicates an individual's degree of development relative to social expectations about preparing for and participating in jobs, operationally defined by comparing the developmental tasks being encountered to those expected based on chronological age.
17. A need to adapt to vocational developmental tasks, occupational transitions, and work troubles activates self-regulation, that is, the capacity to alter one's responses so as to change oneself or the situation in order to implement a plan or reach a goal.
18. Self-regulated career adaptation strategies sequence the personality characteristics of adaptive readiness, the psychosocial capabilities of adaptability resources, the behaviors of adapting responses, and the outcomes of adaptation results.
19. As agents directing their own lives through motivational schemas and adaptation strategies, individuals implement their self-concepts by constructing activity preferences and selecting work roles in which to pursue their career goals.
20. Work-role preferences develop through the interaction of inherited aptitudes, physical make-up, opportunities to observe and play various roles, and evaluations of the extent to which the results of role playing meet with the approval of peers and supervisors.
21. Occupations provide a core role and a way of life for most people, although for some individuals this focus is peripheral, incidental, or even nonexistent. Then other life roles such as student, parent, homemaker, leisurite, or citizen may be at the

core (Super, 1990).
22. Because social actors differ in vocational characteristics and self-concepts, they enter different occupational environments, which Holland (1997) denoted as RIASEC environments. Each occupation requires a different pattern of vocational characteristics, with tolerances wide enough to allow a considerable variety of individuals in each occupation.
23. People are qualified for a variety of occupations based on the match of their vocational abilities and interests to occupational requirements and rewards. Personal preferences for life roles and occupations, however, are deeply grounded in the social practices that engage individuals and locate them in unequal social positions.
24. Role selection and entry involves a synthesis and compromise between individual and social factors.
25. Occupational success depends on the extent to which an individual's abilities and actions meet the requirements of work roles.
26. Job satisfaction depends on establishment in an occupation, a work situation, and a way of life in which one can play the type of roles that growth and exploratory experiences have led one to consider suitable for meeting needs, fulfilling values, and expressing interests.
27. An individual's career pattern -- that is, the occupational level attained and the sequence, frequency, and duration of jobs -- is determined by the parents' socioeconomic level and the person's education, abilities, preferences, self-concepts, and career adaptability in transaction with the opportunities presented by society.

The Self-Conceiving Autobiographical Author

Premise C: Social actors who pursue goals can deliberate as an autobiographical author to conceive a vocational identity and compose a career story that imposes continuity and coherence on their actions over time.

Propositions

28. During late adolescence and emerging adulthood, the subjective "I" deliberates on the objective "Me" to author a career story about the self as a social actor and motivated agent.
29. In the self-conceiving process of composing a career story, individuals form a *vocational identity* that declares an argument justifying occupational choices by relating their private inner world to the public outer world.
30. Career positioning, whether in aspiration or actuality, locates a vocational identity in a particular occupation, that is, self-in-a-work-role.
31. Autobiographical reasoning concentrated on the interchange between subjective personal dispositions and objective social positions enables individuals to deliberate about life strategies and career plans in a two-stage process of retrospective reflection and prospective reflexivity referred to as biographicity.
32. *Biographicity* is a means by which individuals may mediate the effect of societal systems and cultural structures on personal agency and courses of action, specifically in regard to interpersonal relations and the occupations that they seek, keep, or quit.
33. Autobiographical authors differ in their reflexive schemas for deliberating about life design and career construction.
34. Four distinct reflexive schemas produce four different strategies for forming a vocational identity and dealing with career concerns
35. Beginning late in adolescence, individuals make sense of their work lives by conceiving a vocational identity and composing a career story with an occupational plot and career theme.
36. A career story may be as simple as a resumé reporting a timeline of positions occupied.
37. More elaborate career stories add an occupational plot to the storyline to form a meaningful whole by connecting the positions and events in terms of cause and effect.
38. Thematic patterning of the occupational plot fully realizes a career story by adding a dominant motif to explain why things

happened, specify the means for meeting needs, highlight recurrent patterns of vocational behavior, and script future scenes.
39. A person's career themes may by recognized as an individual instance of the *narrative paradigm*, that is, a general pattern of moving from passive to active.
40. Although vocational identities become increasingly stable and career stories become more coherent from late adolescence forward, providing some continuity in choice and adjustment, occupational plots and career themes do evolve and may change with time and experience as the situations in which people live and work become different.
41. In responding to changes prompted by developmental tasks, occupational transitions, and work troubles, autobiographical authors re-conceptualize occupational plots and extend or amend career themes to redirect or revise their career stories in ways that reintegrate self, revitalize vocational identity, and rebuild work roles.
42. An elaborated or revised story meant to direct transition to a new scene, episode, or chapter in a career is both *constructed by* the person and *constructive of* future behavior.
43. Re-storied narratives empower individuals as motivated agents to make choices and adapt to changing career contexts and occupational situations.
44. In marked contrast to vocational guidance and career education, career construction dialogues focus on individual uniqueness to prompt autobiographical authors to reflexively transform career themes and extend their occupational plots by identifying fitting settings, possible scripts, and future scenarios.
45. Career construction counseling discourse proposes that vocational guidance and career education foster *reflection* within one's current perspective that can lead to small first-order change; whereas career constructing dialogues foster *reflexivity* from new perspectives that can lead to transformative second-order change.

APPENDIX B
Inventories, Tests, and Techniques Used in the Study

Differential Aptitude Tests

Bennett, G. K., Seashore, H. G., & Wesman, A. (1966). *Differential Aptitude Tests fourth edition manual.* New York: The Psychological Corporation.

Battery of tests designed to measure eight different abilities among students in grades eight through twelve. The three tests used in this study measured abstract reasoning, numerical reasoning, and verbal reasoning. *Abstract Reasoning Form A* consists of 50 series of changing geometric forms that measure reasoning without the use of words by having subjects identify the principle underlying each series of forms. *Numerical Ability Form A* consists of 40 arithmetic computations that measure understanding of numerical relationships and facility in handling numerical concepts. *Verbal Reasoning Form A* consists of 50 verbal analogies that measure the ability to think in words and to form generalizations.

Dynamic Personality Inventory

Grygier, T. G. (1976). Dynamic Personality Inventory. London, England: National Foundation for Educational Research.

Measures personality organization in developmental terms, following the psychoanalytic framework devised by Karl Abraham and elaborated by M. H. Krout and J. Tabin at the Chicago Psychological Institute. Originally called the Krout-Tabinn Personal Preference Scale (1951), it was revised by Grygier in 1956 and again in 1976. Designed for use with apprentices and employee applicants ages 15 and over, it consists of 325 items that include objects, concepts, and activities to which the individual responds "like" or "dislike." Items are scored on 33 scales that measure defense mechanisms, ego-strength, interests, and sublimations.

Kuder Preference Record Vocational

Kuder, F. (1956). *Kuder Preference Record Vocational Form CH – Sixth Edition*. Chicago, IL: Science Research Associates

Measures preferences for vocational activities in ten broad areas: outdoor, mechanical, computational, scientific, persuasive, artistic, literary, musical, social service, and clerical. Consists of 168 items, each containing a group of three activities. From each triad of activities, individuals select the one activity they most like to do and the one activity they least like to do. Scores for the ten scales are ipsative.

Minnesota Multiphasic Personality Inventory - 2

Butcher, J. N., Dahlstrom, W. G., Graham, J. R., Tellegen, A.M., & Kraemmer, B. (1989). The Minnesota Multiphasic Personality Inventory-2 (MMPI-2) manual for administration and scoring. Minneapolis, MN: University of Minnesota Press.

Consists of 567 true/false items that measure a person's psychological state. The items may be scored for numerous clinical scales that assess mental health problems, personality characteristics, and general personality traits. Narrative reports for each participant were prepared by The Roche Psychiatric Service Institute.

Nelson-Denny Reading Test

Nelson, M. J., & Denny, E. C., & Brown, J. I. (1960). *The Nelson-Denny Reading Test Form A and B*. Boston: Houghton Mifflin Company.

Designed to aid in the diagnosis of students difficulties in reading. It consists of two parts: a 100-word vocabulary test and a test of ability to read and understand 9 paragraphs of approximately 200 words.

Otis-Lennon Mental Ability Test - Fourth Edition

Otis, A. S., & Lennon, R. T. (1967). *Otis-Lennon Mental Ability Test technical handbook*. New York: Harcourt, Brace, & World.

Measures high school students' mental ability using multiple choice questions about varied content.

Rotter Incomplete Sentences Blank

Rotter, J. B., & Rafferty, J. E. (1950). The Rotter Incomplete Sentences Blank. New York: The Psychological Corporation.

A semi-structured projective technique that asks respondents to finish 40 sentences for which the first word or words are supplied. The Rotter has 40 stems. This study added 17 items designed to obtain work-oriented responses. The additional stems are: my greatest ambition, my family, a person's life, my standards, my friends, earning a living, people think of me as, my career, work, I admire, success, employers, the main thing in life, choosing a job, teachers, money, and I always wanted to be.

Strong Vocational Interest Blank - Revised

Strong, E. K., Jr. *Campbell*, D. P., *Berdie*, R. F., & *Clark*, K. E. (1966). *Strong Vocational Interest Blank for Men* (Form T399). Stanford, CA: Stanford University Press.

Uses 399 items to measures similarity to men employed in a 130 diverse occupations.

Test of Mechanical Comprehension

Bennet, G. K. (1940). *Test of Mechanical Comprehension - Form AA*. New York: The Psychological Corporation.

Measures recognition and understanding of physical forces and mechanical elements in practical situations. It consists of 60 items, presented with no time limit. The total score is interpreted as how much mechanical aptitude a person has for a wide variety of jobs as well as for courses in engineering at colleges and trade schools.

Thematic Apperception Test

Morgan, C. D, & Murray, H. A. (1943). Thematic Apperception Test. Cambridge, MA: Harvard University Press.

A projective technique for studying personality dynamics manifested in interpersonal relations. It consists of 31 pictures that each present a semi-structured scene, sufficiently ambiguous and with poorly defined action so that it requires respondents to project themselves into the situation and shape it according to their own needs and fears. The T.A.T. is designed to bring out the needs, strivings, and environmental pressures felt by an individual. In the ninth grade, the participants responded to 16 cards: 1, 2, 3BM, 4, 5, 6BM, 7BM, 8BM, 9BM, 10, 12BG, 13B, 14, 16, 20, 17BM. In the twelfth-grade, the participants responded to five cards: 2, 6BM, 7BM, 14, and 17BM. At age 38, the participants responded to 10 cards 1, 3BM, 4, 6BM, 7BM, 8BM, 9BM, 13B, 14, and 17BM.

Work Values Inventory

Super, D. E. (1970). *Work Values Inventory*. Boston: Houghton-Mifflin.

Measures the strength of 15 values which affect the motivation to work. The 15 scales are grouped into three categories. The five values intrinsic to work are creativity, esthetics, intellectual stimulation, management, and variety. The five values conceptualized as outcomes of work are achievement, altruism, economic return, prestige, and security. The five values viewed as concomitants of work are associations, independence, supervisory relations, surroundings, and way of life.

Glossary of Key Terms

AUTOBIOGRAPHY Life history that assigns present meaning to past experiences.

BIOGRAPHICITY Self-referential process by which individuals organize and integrate new and sometimes puzzling experiences into their autobiographies.

CAREER CONSTRUCTION Career counseling intervention that uses autobiographical narratives to script the next episode in a career. Compare to *career education* and *vocational guidance*.

CAREER EDUCATION Career counseling intervention that uses educational methods to teach and coach individuals on how to cope with imminent tasks of vocational development. Compare to *career counseling* and *vocational guidance*.

CHRONICLE Sequence of events arranged by time that merely terminates, without narrative closure. Compare to *plot*.

COUNSELING Dialogue between an individual and professional helper to empower that individual to function more effectively and achieve goals.

EMPLOTMENT Arrangement of diverse incidents and different episodes into a whole that imposes meaning on the parts.

IDENTIFICATION Form of internalization in which characteristics of role models are taken on and incorporated as part of personality. Compare to *influences*.

IDENTITY A story that an individual tells about one's self in some social role or context.

INFLUENCES Form of internalization in which parental guides are taken in whole and introjected into personality. Compare to *identification*.

INTEREST Psychosocial tensional state between an individual's needs and social opportunities to attain goals that satisfy those needs.

LIFE PORTRAIT Macro-narrative that organizes a client's perspective, self-concepts, preferred settings, script, and advice to self into a portrayal of the occupational plot, career theme, and character arc.

MACRO-NARRATIVE Narrative identity that integrates several small stories into a large story that consolidates self-understanding, goals, and performance in social roles.

MICRO-NARRATIVE Small story about an important incident, significant figure, self-defining moment, or life-changing experience.

NARRATIVE IDENTITY An autobiography that provides life with meaning and purpose.

PLOT Explanations and ending that structure a sequence of events into a coherent whole with a beginning, middle, and end. The end or conclusion brings the narrative closure lacking in a chronicle.

REFLECTION Thinking about the past and focusing serious consideration on memories, experiences and cognitions. It is retrospective and brings the past into the present. Compare to *reflexivity*.

REFLEXIVITY A second-order cognitive process of strong evaluation, that is, self-conscious evaluation of conscious knowing to determine alternate ways of acting in the future. It is prospective and connects the present to the future.by reflecting on reflections. Compare to *reflection*.

STORY Organization of events into a sequence.

THEME Pattern woven by a recurring, central idea that provides the primary unit of meaning used to understand the facts of a plot.

VOCATIONAL GUIDANCE Career counseling intervention that uses inventories and information to match individuals with fitting positions. Compare to *career education* and *career construction*.